T0382706

ROUTLEDGE LIBRARY EDITIONS: AGRIBUSINESS AND LAND USE

Volume 22

COPING WITH HUNGER

COPING WITH HUNGER

Hazard and Experiment in an African Rice-Farming System

PAUL RICHARDS

Routledge
Taylor & Francis Group

LONDON AND NEW YORK

First published in 1986 by Allen & Unwin (Publishers) Ltd

This edition first published in 2024
by Routledge
4 Park Square, Milton Park, Abingdon, Oxon OX14 4RN

and by Routledge
605 Third Avenue, New York, NY 10158

Routledge is an imprint of the Taylor & Francis Group, an informa business

© 1986 Paul Richards

British Library Cataloguing in Publication Data
A catalogue record for this book is available from the British Library

ISBN: 978-1-032-48321-4 (Set)
ISBN: 978-1-032-46913-3 (Volume 22) (hbk)
ISBN: 978-1-032-46925-6 (Volume 22) (pbk)
ISBN: 978-1-003-38382-6 (Volume 22) (ebk)

DOI: 10.4324/9781003383826

Publisher's Note
The publisher has gone to great lengths to ensure the quality of this reprint but points out that some imperfections in the original copies may be apparent.

Disclaimer
The publisher has made every effort to trace copyright holders and would welcome correspondence from those they have been unable to trace.

COPING WITH HUNGER

Hazard and experiment in an African rice-farming system

Paul Richards
Department of Anthropology, University College London

London
ALLEN & UNWIN
Boston   Sydney

Allen & Unwin (Publishers) Ltd,
40 Museum Street, London WC1A 1LU, UK

Allen & Unwin (Publishers) Ltd,
Park Lane, Hemel Hempstead, Herts HP2 4TE, UK

Allen & Unwin, Inc.,
8 Winchester Place, Winchester, Mass. 01890, USA

Allen & Unwin (Australia) Ltd,
8 Napier Street, North Sydney, NSW 2060, Australia

First published in 1986

British Library Cataloguing in Publication Data

Richards, Paul, 1945–
    Coping with hunger: hazard and experiment in an African rice
farming system. – (The London research series in geography,
ISSN 0261-0485; no. 11)
1. Farms, Small – Sierra Leone 2. Farm mechanization – Sierra Leone
I. Title   II. Series
338.6'42   HD1476.S5
ISBN 0-04-333025-8

Library of Congress Cataloging-in-Publication Data

Richards, Paul, 1945–
    Coping with hunger.
(London research series in geography; 11)
Bibliography: p.
Includes index.
1. Rice – Sierra Leone. 2. Rice farmers – Sierra Leone.
3. Agriculture – Sierra Leone – Technology transfer. 4. Food supply –
Sierra Leone. I. Title. II. Series
SB191.R5R536 1986   338.1'6   86-8059
ISBN 0-04-333025-8

Set in 10 on 11 point Bembo by
Computape (Pickering) Ltd, North Yorkshire
and printed in Great Britain by
Anchor Brendan Ltd, Tiptree, Essex

Acknowledgements

In acknowledging the debts I have incurred in writing this book pride of place should go to the Mogbuama community. I was their guest for a year while with skill, generosity and good humour they taught me about farming. Particular thanks are due to the following: Madam Boteh Sovula (Paramount Chief of Kamajei Chiefdom), Major J. G. Amara, Section Chief Pa Adu Kongla, Pa Haruna Tarawali (my landlord) and Mamawa and Mariama Tarawali for their hospitality, Ansumana Karimu and Daniel Sesay for field assistance, and last but not least, my friend Pa Lamin Kobai for his conversation, historical insights, 'cold water' and skill with a gun.

The research was funded by a grant from the Economic and Social Committee for Overseas Research (ESCOR) of the United Kingdom Overseas Development Administration, to whom grateful acknowledgement is due. (I have to add the usual caveat that responsibility for the conclusions reached in the study is mine alone.) Thanks are also due to colleagues and students at Njala, where I was a visiting lecturer for the session 1982–3 – in particular to Professor John Kamara, the Principal, and his administrative staff, and Professor Harry Turay, Head of the Department of Environmental Studies and Geography, who invited me to Njala in the first place, and then, in looking after my academic interests, proved a most genial patron. I would also like to thank my colleagues Philip Burnham, John Landers, Murray Last and Barrie Sharpe both for the stimulus of their ideas and, on a more practical level, for making it possible for me to spend a year in Sierra Leone at short notice by agreeing to take over my teaching and tutorial duties while I was away.

Anyone who attempts interdisciplinary studies (in my case combining perspectives from geography, anthropology and ecology) is heavily dependent on the advice of expert colleagues. It gives me great pleasure to acknowledge the help and comments I have received from F. C. Deighton, Georg Elwert, John Hargreaves, Michael Johnny, John Karimu, Serrie Kamara, Bob Kandeh, Agnes Lappia, Joe Lappia, Michael Lipton, Akin Mabogunje, Volker Metz, Andy Millington, Friedrich Muehlenberg, Stuart Phethean, Steve Riley, Joko Sengova, George Tengbeh, B. M. S. Turay, Peter White and Roger Wright. I am particularly conscious of the debt I owe to Kathy Baker, Caroline Bledsoe, Jane Guyer, Dick Hodder, David McMaster, Tony O'Connor and Adam Pain who each read the manuscript in its entirety, helped me see the wood for the trees, provided encouragement when it was most needed, and saved me from many errors and misjudgements (though, of course, those that remain are entirely my responsibility). I am also grateful for timely editorial encouragement from David Lowenthal.

At Njala Dr Abu Sesay kindly entrusted me with some of his planting materials for a number of groundnut trials in Mogbuama. Soil analysis was carried out under licence PHF 417A/28 issued under the Import and Export (Plant Health) (Great Britain) Order 1980 by the Ministry of Agriculture, Fisheries and Food) and with guidance (and timely intervention!) from Dr Stuart Phethean at University College London. For maps and diagrams I am once more mainly indebted to E. A. Okine of the Department of Environmental Studies and Geography, Njala University College. Other maps were drawn at short notice by Alick Newman in the Geography Department at University College London. Chris Cromarty (of the same department) was generous with his time in helping me prepare my photographs for publication, and is himself responsible for the photograph appearing as Figure 8.1. Professor Gordon Innes of the School of Oriental & African Studies, University of London, introduced me to the study of Mende and my research assistant Ellis Peter John took me further. My project depended a great deal on Ellis, not least for duties he can never have imagined he was in for when he took on the job (my ability to move back and forth between Mogbuama and Njala to give lectures often depended on his entrepreneurial skill in locating sources of fuel!).

Since Sue and Steve (with some justification) consider this book as much theirs as mine I am not sure whether they want to be thanked formally. I paid off some of the debt to Sue by carrying bags of cement for the school she decided to rebuild (as a break from teaching in one). Stephen managed to persuade himself that he actually enjoyed being up to his elbows in swamps or balanced on top of termite heaps in the broiling sun holding ranging poles. This seemed to me to be beyond the normal call of filial duty. Anyhow, thanks all the same.

Paul Richards
University College London

Contents

Acknowledgements   *page* vii

List of tables   xi

Notes on terminology, conventions and units of measurement   xiii

Introduction   1

1   *Food crises and technology transfer: Sierra Leone 1919–1949*   4

    The rice crisis of 1918–19   5
    The Asian option   6
    Strengthening the research base   9
    The indigenous alternative   10
    The return of technology transfer: the polder irrigation scheme   12

2   *Bringing the Green Revolution to Sierra Leone*   15

    The Green Revolution   16
    Green Revolution in Sierra Leone   18
    Limitations to the Green Revolution swamp package   22
    An alternative to technology transfer   25
    Conclusion   27

3   *Mogbuama: landscape and society*   28

    A general introduction to the case study   28
    The landscape   29
    Administration and politics   45
    Settlement pattern and population characteristics   49
    Social organisation   52
    Summary   57

4   *Land and labour*   58

    Types of farm   58
    Who can farm?   60
    Land types and land tenure   60
    Land availability and fallow periods   63
    The farm household   65
    Household work – the roles of men, women and children   68
    Non-household labour   69
    Summary   74

5   *The farming year*   76

    Choosing and brushing a farm site   76
    The burn   79
    Clearing   85
    Rice planting   86

Weeding, pest control and bird scaring   92
Harvesting   97
Conclusion   98

6   *The harvest*   102

Data sources   102
Mogbuama agricultural output   104
Agricultural savings in Mogbuama   107
Rice farm yields   108
Failure and success   111
Conclusion   114

7   *The hungry season*   115

The anatomy of pre-harvest hunger in Mogbuama   116
Coping with hunger in Mogbuama   118
Patronage and entitlement   128
Conclusion   129

8   *Rice varieties and farmer experiments*   131

Rice classification in Mogbuama   134
Development of indigenous rice varieties: selection and experiment 138
Adoption and abandonment of rice varieties   143
Conclusion   144

9   *Rice R&D in Sierra Leone: a farmer-first-and-last scenario* 147

Lessons of the case study   147
Early rice   148
Upland farms   152
Swamp rice   153
Conclusion   155

Conclusion   156
Postscript   157

References   158

Glossary   165

Index   169

List of tables

2.1 Planned crop targets for Sierra Leone IADPs   *page* 20
3.1 Analytical data for ten soil samples from Mogbuama farms   40
3.2 Sample data for Soil Series represented in the Senehun
    boliland (van Vuure *et al.* 1972)   44
5.1 Broadcasting and 'ploughing' rates on different soil types   87
5.2 'Ploughing' work rates (m²/person/hour) with and without the
    assistance of drumming   95
5.3 'Ploughing' work rates (m²/person/hour) on different soil
    types, group and casual hired labour compared   95
5.4 Impact of pre-planting weed emergence on 'ploughing' work rates   100
5.5 Main weeds on 30 Mogbuama rice farms   100
5.6 Farmer rankings of weed problems on Mogbuama rice farms
    between clearing and planting and after planting   101
8.1 Rices planted by Mogbuama farmers in 1983   131
8.2 Planting to flowering intervals for eight Mogbuama rice varieties   134

TITLES OF RELATED INTEREST

African environments and resources
L. A. Lewis and L. Berry

Development guide
Overseas Development Institute

Development planning
W. Arthur Lewis

Development economics and policy
I. Livingstone (ed.)

Egypt: politics and society 1945–1981
D. Hopwood

Environment and development
P. Bartelmus

Faces of hunger
O. O'Neill

Female and male in West Africa
C. Oppong (ed.)

The Green Revolution revisited
B. Glaeser (ed.)

Integration, development and equity
P. Robson

Interpretations of calamity
K. Hewitt (ed.)

An introduction to the politics of tropical Africa
R. Hodder-Williams

Learning from China?
B. Glaeser (ed.)

Life before the drought
E. Scott (ed.)

Rich and poor countries
H. Singer and J. Ansari

Southern Africa in the 1980s
O. Aluko and T. M. Shaw (eds)

Technology and rural women
L. Ahmed (ed.)

The theory and experience of economic development
M. Gersovitz et al. (eds)

A Third World proletariat
P. Lloyd

Towards an alternative for Central America and the Caribbean
G. Irvin and X. Gorostiaga

Tropical development 1880-1913
W. Arthur Lewis (ed.)

Underdevelopment and development in Brazil
N. H. Leff

Notes on terminology, conventions and units of measurement

(a) Mende words cited in the text are, with one or two exceptions, given in the indefinite singular form and follow as far as possible the orthographic conventions of Innes' *Mende–English dictionary* (1969). Apart from (rare) cases of ambiguity, tones are not marked in the text but are given in a glossary. High tones are marked with an acute accent and low tones with a grave accent (it is unusual in written Mende to mark low tones, but I have chosen to do so explicitly, to avoid confusion with words for which I have not yet been able to ascertain tones). Tables 5.5 and 8.1 are listings of the main weeds and rice varieties found in Mogbuama farms, and it seemed appropriate to mark tones here also.

(b) The process of hoeing in rice after broadcasting is generally known in Sierra Leone English as 'ploughing', a usage to which I have adhered in the following pages. Similarly, when referring to plants and animals I have used the common names most familiar to readers in Sierra Leone, thus 'bush cow' not 'buffalo' and 'beniseed' not 'sesame'. A list of common and scientific names for crops is to be found in the glossary.

(c) The unit of currency in Sierra Leone is the Leone. At the time of fieldwork the official exchange rate was approximately Le 3.70 to £1.00 Sterling.

(d) Farm input–output data have been cited in the volumetric units farmers themselves use to measure their crops and assess agricultural productivity. The four main units are the bushel, the four-gallon (kerosine) can, the threepence pan and the butter cup. There are (approximately) 2 cans, 24 threepence pans and 132 butter cups in one bushel. A bushel contains about 27.5 kg of husk rice and 38.0 kg of clean rice. Some farmers use a bushel box (**kɔwu**) 20–25% larger (not smaller, as given by Innes 1969) than the standard. There is also in use a threepence pan, known as the One Party Pan, some 8–10% larger than its standard equivalent.

(e) Rice farmers in Sierra Leone reckon input-output relationships in terms of bushels of rice planted and harvested. The question of the relationship between bushels of seed broadcast and area is complex, varying with soil type, rice variety and planting date. The convention widely adopted in Sierra Leone is to treat one bushel of seed broadcast on an upland farm as equivalent to one acre (0.4 ha). In cases for which I have direct measurements actual seed rates are somewhat lower (averaging 0.70 bu/acre). These figures make no allowance, however, for land taken by intercrops, tree stumps, termite heaps, rock outcrops, pathways and farm structures. In the following pages I have assumed that if such allowances were to be made the adjusted net average would be close to the conventional equivalence of one bushel/one acre.

(f) All direct measurements of area are based on compass traverses in which distances have been estimated by pacing, and are subject to a margin of error of perhaps plus or minus 10%.

Introduction

Recent events have focused international attention on the state of African agriculture. Many commentators see the prevalence of 'primitive' cultivation practices as a major factor in present food production difficulties. Permanent solutions to the famine problem, it is supposed, will depend on closing the 'gap' between science and a 'backward' peasantry, hence the stress placed on 'top-down' agricultural extension systems for the efficient delivery of 'modern' inputs to small-scale farmers. According to this viewpoint, the key to an agricultural revolution in Africa is technology transfer.

This book challenges the assumptions of this approach. It argues that technology transfer is part of the problem not the solution. There is indeed a major gap between science and the peasantry, but this gap is conceptual not historical. Tropical agricultural science is out of touch with its clientele. The problem is not how to bridge the centuries and reach 'backward' farmers with 'modern' inputs and advice, but that these inputs and advice are in many cases totally inappropriate to African food-crop producers because they have been designed without reference to the problems, priorities, and interests of those who are supposed to use them.

Disillusion with technology transfer is a marked feature of recent debates about Third World agricultural development. A new consensus is emerging in which stress is laid on the ecological and regional specificity of agricultural development problems, and the need to mobilise local initiatives in solving these problems (Byerlee & Collinson 1980, Biggs & Clay 1981, Byerlee, Harrington & Winkelmann 1982, Rhoades & Booth, 1982, Biggs & Clay 1983, Biggs 1984, Heinemann & Biggs 1985). Chambers and Ghildyal (1984) argue that 'the normal "transfer of technology" model for agricultural research has built-in biases which favour resource-rich farmers whose conditions resemble those of research stations' and instead call for the application of what they term 'farmer-first-and-last' research to meet the needs of resource-poor farmers. Farmer-first-and-last research 'starts and ends with the farm family and the farming system'. 'Holistic and interdisciplinary appraisal of farm families' resources, needs and problems' leads to a programme of on-farm experiments and trials in which 'scientists, experiment stations and laboratories' operate 'in a consultancy and referral role' with farmers themselves heavily involved in defining research agenda, evaluating trials and even designing experiments. The present study is conceived in the spirit of 'farmer-first-and-last' research.

I begin by assessing the extent to which the course taken by food-crop research policies in one country (Sierra Leone) has been set by 'dead reckoning' – navigation according to some grand evolutionary design of what ought to be appropriate to farmers' needs at this or that 'stage' in the country's development – rather than by reference to real-life problems. On three separate occasions – the famine of 1919, the wartime food emergency of 1940 and the diamond boom at the time of Independence – food shortages forced policy makers to pay detailed attention to the condition of peasant agriculture. In all three cases it was concluded that the slow rate of change from 'primitive' to more 'modern' cultivation practices was at the root of the problem, and that the answer was to facilitate certain historically 'inevitable' transitions (e.g. the replacement of upland rice cultivation by wetland production methods) through vigorous programmes of technology transfer drawing on Asian experience.

The failure of these technology transfer initiatives gives pause for thought. One of the fascinations of the Sierra Leone case is the durability of peasant practices. Cultivation of upland rice by 'slash and burn' methods – according to the colonial Department of Agriculture a 'primitive' technology deeply implicated in the 1919 famine – is still commonplace today. Either the Sierra Leonian peasantry is singularly obdurate, and determinedly effective in resisting historically inevitable changes, or the self-evidently 'superior' techniques introduced under the technology transfer rubric are not so superior as was at first thought. The evidence favours the latter interpretation. At the same time I shall show by means of a case study of rice farming systems in central Sierra Leone that if we know what to look for there is abundant evidence of small-scale food producers' interest in and commitment to technological change. Indeed, many recent improvements in food production in Sierra Leone are largely the result of innovation and experiment in the peasant sector.

West African humid tropical environments are different from those in South and South-East Asia where many practices recommended under technology transfer programmes originate. When Sierra Leone rice farmers do things differently from peasants in Asia it is not because they are lagging behind Asian producers on an evolutionary timescale but because there are good ecological reasons for approaching the problem differently. The gap between science and the peasantry is that the experts have asked the wrong questions. Convinced that African agricultural practices were largely a hang-over from an earlier epoch, experts have failed to find out what worked and why. In effect, they have neglected the option of building on the best of local initiatives and supporting changes already taking place within the peasant farming community.

This book, then, is an attempt to change direction. It proposes that R&D strategies for the food-crop sector in Africa should be planned on the basis of listening to the farmer, and by paying careful attention to the internal dynamic of change among small-scale farmers. It is a case study in how this might be done through the systematic application of participant observation to farming systems research. I make no apology for the detailed case-study approach. Indeed, I shall argue that it is only by taking such an approach – attempting to understand African farming systems on their own terms – that real progress will be made. In my view, present inadequate understanding of the food production dilemmas of contemporary Africa is exacerbated by academic commentary that insists on seeing African agricultural problems through the refracting lenses of 'mainstream' debates in European social philosophy (cf. Hart 1982) or comparative historiography (cf. Goody 1971).

The book is organised as follows. Chapter 1 considers the history of the rice 'problem' in Sierra Leone and discusses the fate of various Asia-to-Africa technology transfer policy initiatives during the colonial period. Chapter 2 examines a more recent case – techniques, modelled on Asian Green Revolution precedents, for double-cropping high-yielding quick-maturing rices with the aid of water control and fertiliser. For a variety of socio-economic and ecological reasons, the double-cropping water-controlled cultivation 'package' is often ill-suited to the needs of small-scale cultivators. The farming system case study in Chapters 3–8 shows why. Peasant farmers are not averse to the idea of using swamp land for rice cultivation. Their principal objection to Green Revolution technology transfer in Sierra Leone centres on the assumption (on the part of development agencies) that 'improved' wet-rice cultivation practices should replace, rather than complement, indigenous rice cultivation practices based around the intercropped upland rice farm. In their own practices farmers in central Sierra Leone (the setting for the case study) place particular emphasis on integration of upland and wetland cultivation. Drawing on participant observation data relating to the 1983 farming season in Mogbuama, a village in Kamajei chiefdom, I show that this concern to integrate upland and wetland is a response to farm management crises triggered by the combined effect of rainfall irregularities and seasonal labour shortages. Local farming techniques are designed to minimise the extent and impact of such crises by subtle exploitation of variations in soil type and topography. By contrast the Green Revolution technology-transfer option makes difficulties of this kind worse.

What are the alternatives to technology transfer approaches to the development of rice farming systems in Sierra Leone? The case study illustrates the argument that the starting point for rice research in Sierra Leone should be a thorough analysis of the trajectory of indigenous agricultural change. In effect the material presented in this study maps out the current boundaries of peasant innovation and experimental initiative in the case-study area. Careful analysis of peasant innovation and experiment, I argue, provides clues as to the nature of local priorities and the scope and trajectory of endogenous agricultural change. Rather than concentrate on technology transfer, formal-sector R&D should lock on to local initiatives. Scientific research should be carried out within design parameters set by the farming community.

How can these design parameters be assessed? The field data show both the limits of existing practices and the extent to which farmers are testing these limits. Some local technological initiatives are already a success, and there is little need for duplication by expensive formal-sector scientific research. It would be better in these cases to concentrate on wider dissemination of the best local practices ('sideways extension'). In other cases, however, farmer experiments are less successful. A major theme of the case study is to assess the scope, direction and limitations of farmer experimentation. The significance of studying peasant experimentation in such cases is that it serves to identify the points at which formal-sector research initiative will prove essential and where scarce research resources might be deployed most cost-effectively. Research agenda for development of rice farming systems in Sierra Leone, arising from the case study materials and stressing the significance of integrated management of upland and wetland environments, are outlined in Chapter 9. A short general conclusion argues that agricultural development in a famine-afflicted continent needs new conceptual horizons. Agricultural researchers must learn to inhabit, by participant observation and imaginative effort, the landscapes for which their new technologies are intended.

1 Food crises and technology transfer: Sierra Leone 1919–49

One of the two cultivated species of rice (*Oryza glaberrima*) is indigenous to West Africa. Asian rice (*O. sativa*) may have been first introduced to West Africa by the Portuguese, or alternatively came via overland trade routes through the Middle East and across the Sahara (Carpenter 1978). Rice cultivation is widely, if patchily, distributed throughout the region, from the coast as far north as the great river valleys of the Sahel. Within a roughly triangular region stretching from the Bandama River in central Côte d'Ivoire along the coast as far as the Senegal River and inland as far as the Inland Delta of the Niger in Mali rice is a major and sometimes the dominant staple. This region is sometimes termed the West African Rice Zone (Fig. 1.1).

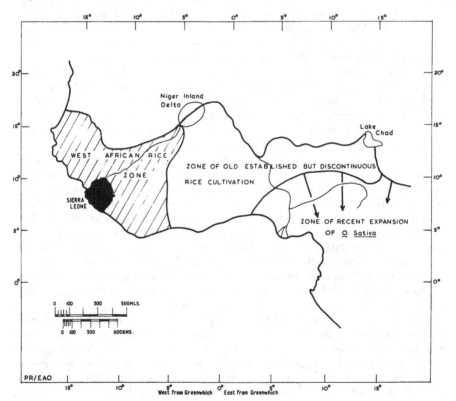

Figure 1.1   Sierra Leone and the West African Rice Zone.

In southern forested portions of the West African Rice Zone planting often follows the valley cross-sectional profile, thus permitting the farmer to exploit the full range of possibilities in the soil catena ('a sequence of somewhat different but related soils occurring from hilltop to valley bottom', Ahn 1970, p. 13). In farms of this sort upper slope rices are watered directly by rainfall, rices planted on colluvial footslopes derive their moisture from a combination of rainfall, run-off, and the rising water table, and rices planted in valley bottoms are watered either by riverine flooding or seasonal inundation of valley swamps. The difference between 'upland' and 'swamp' cultivation is more a question of land use than of botany. Some cultivars, by virtue of their rooting systems or ability to withstand flooding, are better adapted than others to upland or swamp conditions, but others can be grown equally well in either setting (Buddenhagen 1978, Moorman & Veldkamp 1978).

In more northerly savanna districts, rice cultivation is confined to river valleys, farmers most often making use of natural flooding. In a number of cases, however, earthworks and polders are sometimes constructed to control both estuarine floods and rainwater runoff. Such practices are especially common and long-established along the river estuaries of the Upper Guinea coast. In 1793 Samuel Gamble described a farming system of this type as practised by the Baga people of Guinea-Conakry (Littlefield 1981). Pelissier (1966) believes that the techniques involved were indigenous and not as some have supposed innovations first introduced by the Portuguese. Littlefield (1981) considers that Baga techniques in the 18th century were representative 'of the most advanced practice of rice cultivation in traditional agriculture' (p. 95). Later I shall argue that such judgements should not be taken to imply that there is anything especially primitive about upland cultivation in the forest zone. The catenary farming systems described in detail in later chapters are in their own way equally 'advanced' in their effective use of available resources, while being incontestably indigenous in origin.

Per capita output of rice is higher in Sierra Leone than in any other country in the West African Rice Zone (Pearson *et al.* 1981). Any difficulty over the rice harvest is a crisis of national importance. Colonial administrators first became sensitive to rice as a food security issue after a major harvest failure in 1918. This crisis prompted the idea that food security might be facilitated by the adoption of Asian wet-rice cultivation techniques. The present chapter traces the fate of this proposal, and of subsequent rice development policies in colonial Sierra Leone, as a prelude to an examination (in Ch. 2) of recent initiatives inspired by the Green Revolution in Asia.

The rice crisis of 1918–19

Unexpectedly early rainfall in 1918 (three times the average for March) made it difficult for shifting cultivators throughout Sierra Leone to burn the cleared forest on their upland rice farms. Without the ash from a successful burn upland farms are weedy and the harvest poor. In the event, yields in 1918 were even worse than expected because in the crucial weeks before harvest, when normally every able-bodied person is needed on the farm to scare birds from the ripening crop, the country was visited by influenza. The influenza pandemic of 1918-19, known in Europe as the Plague of the Spanish Lady (Collier 1974) was perhaps the single greatest epidemic disaster to befall Africa in modern times. Estimates of mortality, continent-wide, have been placed as high as 2 million (Patterson 1981). In rural Sierra Leone the epidemic was at its height in September. Spitzer (1975) estimates that in Freetown and the provinces up to 70 per cent of the population caught the disease. Although the great majority of victims subsequently recovered, pre-harvest labour supplies were badly affected and much of the rice crop was lost to the birds. In the Njala area of south-central Sierra Leone it was estimated that the 1918 rice harvest was 50-60 per cent below normal (Scotland 1918).

The consequences of this disaster were painfully apparent in the exceptionally severe pre-harvest hungry season of 1919. In the capital, Freetown, the government tried to maintain strict price controls on rice. This only made shortages worse, since traders had little incentive to bring rice into the city. Lebanese merchants, dominant in the rice trade, were widely accused of hoarding existing stocks and of returning supplies up-country out of the reach of government price controls. During July, when the shortages were at their most severe, the Governor, Wilkinson, was on leave. His deputy, apparently not realising the seriousness of the situation, failed to follow up the authorisation of the Executive Council to import rice on the government account to ease the difficulty. On the evening of 18 July the tensions caused by food shortages and high prices boiled over into serious rioting directed against the Lebanese community (Spitzer 1975).

The Asian option

Once public order had been re-established, the colonial administration began to address the agricultural questions raised by the riot and the incipient famine at its root. Why was the rice harvest of 1918 so poor? What might the Department of Agriculture do to prevent a recurrence?

Upland shifting cultivation of rice had long been seen in a poor light by the colonial administration because it was 'yearly carried on at the cost of forest land we are trying to reserve' for commercial timber exploitation (Dawe 1924, Millington 1985a). In 1912 the headquarters of the Department of Agriculture had been moved up-country to Njala, better to facilitate experimental work and farm trials. Douglas Scotland, the director, focused much of his attention in the period between 1912 and 1918 on experiments designed to replace shifting cultivation with a stable crop-rotation system. This work was still only at an exploratory stage. Furthermore, it failed to address the main issue raised by the events of July 1919, namely how to secure a more adequate supply of the country's principal staple. Rotation, however desirable on agronomic grounds, provided little or no scope for rice to be planted more frequently than under a bush-fallowing regime. Diverting labour to other crops in a rotational sequence might actually diminish rice supplies.

Governor Wilkinson decided that the gravity of the situation justified taking agricultural matters into his own hands. In a despatch to Viscount Milner,

Secretary of State for the Colonies, dated 21 January 1920, he advances the opinion that agricultural policy in Sierra Leone must shift its emphasis from uplands to river basin irrigation. His argument draws equally on a cultural evolutionist perspective and his own experience of agriculture in the rice-growing lands of South-East Asia.

> Dry rice requires less expert knowledge but it yields (usually) a smaller crop and is exhausting to the soil. So serious is this latter evil that I have known the cultivation of dry rice prohibited altogether in Malaya. Here in Sierra Leone it cannot be prohibited, but its exhausting character is the main source of our agricultural difficulties. Wet rice represents on the other hand a quasi-permanent form of cultivation. I have known land in the East that has been cultivated year after year for generations ... The dense and settled populations that irrigation (whether natural or artificial) supports lends itself to progress and power ... In my opinion it is largely due to this fact that all the great Empires of antiquity developed their civilizations in the basins of great rivers. (Wilkinson 1920)

He then goes on to suggest that Sierra Leone 'represents a curious and interesting transition stage' in which within the last generation or so some farmers had begun to move from uplands and to plant rice in seasonally inundated land in river valleys. 'Sierra Leone is therefore at the stage – very rare in the world – where wet rice is grown without the use of artificial irrigation.' He predicts that in time 'the native will learn to assist nature by regulating the overflow from the river by means of dams, channels, watergates and other simple contrivances'. The policy implications of this process were clear. 'I have consulted the members of the Executive Council, who agree with me that it is expedient to obtain from an expert in irrigation a report on the possibilities of the Protectorate in the growth of irrigated rice.'

In effect Wilkinson aimed to speed up an 'inevitable' evolutionary transition from dry-rice to wet-rice cultivation. The departments of agriculture and forestry were brought together into a single new Department of Lands and Forests, under the energetic direction of M. T. Dawe, with the new wet-rice policy emphasis apparently one of the considerations in mind. It was recognised that Njala was not well placed in relation to swamp rice cultivation, the bulk of which was to be found in northwestern Sierra Leone. Scotland remained in charge of the Njala station, but its research emphasis was re-directed towards upland export crops such as cotton and oil palm. Dawe subsequently mooted the idea of a rice research station in the Scarcies estuary where wet-rice cultivation was already well established, and from where Freetown obtained the bulk of its rice supplies. On Wilkinson's specific suggestion that the government examine the potential for irrigation in Sierra Leone, Milner took advice from Colonel W. N. Ellis, late chief engineer, Madras, and from Mr D. Chadwick. late director of agriculture, Madras. Neither thought the time ripe for a full-scale irrigation project (due to the paucity of basic topographic and hydrological data) but agreed with Wilkinson's suggestion that 'native agricultural instructors might be brought from India ... to train Protectorate natives in the technical details of cultivation of rice by simple methods of irrigation' (Wilkinson 1920).

Accordingly, A. C. Pillai of the Madras Department of Agriculture was appointed a senior agricultural instructor and posted to the Scarcies region to investigate and report on ways of improving local wet-rice cultivation practices. Another Madras rice cultivator, a Mr Naik, was appointed to offer practical assistance. Pillai submitted a report based on observation and trials in the Scarcies region during 1921. In it he describes methods for cultivating the mangrove swamps using the natural rainy-season flood worked out by local enterprise during the latter part of the 19th century. Failing to realise, perhaps, that indigenous methods were a skilful adaptation to the problems of labour shortage, Pillai thought that local farmers were 'negligent' in their approach. Nevertheless, he readily conceded that the results were better than those achieved by experienced rice farmers on the good deltaic lands of Madras. He describes the results of his investigations as 'startling':

> If it is made known to the rice growing public that the Africans are getting up to 4000 lb in an acre of swamp without tilth, without manure, without weeding, and without artificial irrigation, and lastly, by continual cropping for over thirty years, some will doubt the truth of the statement. But I submit as myself [sic] they did the work and saw the crop from planting to harvest. (Pillai 1921)

Pillai suggested that existing methods would be difficult to better without some years of scientific trials. For the present, he concluded, the best approach would be to extend indigenous methods to parts of Sierra Leone where they were not so familiar. Local expert farmers should be recruited for this purpose. The fate of Wilkinson's initial proposal that agrarian evolution in Sierra Leone might be speeded up by an injection of Asian technology was soon settled, therefore. By April 1922, the new Colonial Secretary, Winston Churchill, had decided that 'the native system of cultivation is a very good one and that all that is required to increase indefinitely the production of rice is that the natives should be induced to cultivate the undeveloped areas of swamp, and to this end be given security of tenure and freedom from unfair exactions' (Churchill 1922).

For the time being, then, the authorities were persuaded that 'there is little we can teach the denizens of the Sierra Leone swamps in the matter of rice cultivation' (Furley 1924). Departmental policy was still firmly directed towards encouraging wet-rice cultivation at the expense of upland rice, but efforts were concentrated on Pillai's recommendation to draw on local expertise to disseminate the best indigenous practices. The Annual Report of the Lands and Forests Department for 1927 records that 'a large number of experienced rice planters were selected from the Scarcies rice areas and were appointed as instructors with a view to teach the inland tribes the proper transplantation method for the purpose of utilizing the many inland swamps for growing rice.' The next year it was reported that 'swamp rice farms planted in the Timne method' were made in Moyamba District for the first time. By 1929 the method had been demonstrated in all districts of the Central Province. In some areas these demonstrations achieved rapid results. In Luawa chiefdom (Pendembu District) farmers made 3100 swamp rice farms on their own initiative in 1929.

Strengthening the research base

During the second half of the 1920s and early 1930s it became increasingly clear that future agricultural development initiatives would require more solid research foundations than hitherto. Four research officers appointed during the mid-1920s (F. C. Deighton, E. C. Doyne, E. Hargreaves, and F. J. Martin) began to place the study of Sierra Leonian soils, insect pests and plant diseases on a sound footing.

It was also realised that there was a need for an equally thorough understanding of the socio-economic context within which local agricultural practices operated. One of the earliest of these attempts to come to terms with the specific character of agrarian social organisation in Sierra Leone was a report by the Rice Commission, of which Dawe was a member, 'on its enquiry into the position of the rice industry' (Mackie et al. 1927). This report drew attention to a number of obstacles to greater productivity in the rice farming sector that are still of great importance today. One of its major findings was that rice farmers in the Scarcies region and elsewhere were severely constrained by *labour* shortages. Hitherto, reluctance or refusal to adopt labour-intensive methods (e.g. water control) in rice production had been interpreted as evidence of ignorance or 'indolence' on the part of a 'backward' population.

A second major set of findings reported by the Rice Commission concerned the importance of indebtedness (especially prior to the harvest) and litigation (especially after the harvest). These were correctly identified, perhaps for the first time, as critical aspects of peasant political economy in rural Sierra Leone (their present-day importance is discussed in Chs 4 and 7). After careful analysis of annual fluctuations in rice prices, the Commission concluded that many farmers were too deeply indebted ever to benefit from good prices for rice in the hungry season. Profits accrued mainly to rural traders and money lenders. In consequence, price incentives were by themselves unlikely to stimulate major new productive efforts (e.g. increased cultivation of swamp land).

Given this rapidly deepening understanding of both the social and ecological specificity of Sierra Leone's agricultural problems, it is perhaps surprising to find the relevance of South Asian experience being canvassed once again during the early 1930s. The stimulus came from the visit to Sierra Leone in 1929 of F. A. (later Sir Frank) Stockdale, agricultural adviser to the Secretary of State for the Colonies. Stockdale was a former Director of Agriculture in Ceylon, a country with a good record in rice research (Pain 1983). It is understandable, perhaps, that Stockdale should have felt it appropriate to recommend that 'one of our officers [Glanville] ... study rice problems in those parts of India and Ceylon where conditions prevail which are similar to those in the Scarcies area' (Department of Agriculture 1929).

Rather than rekindling an enthusiasm for the technology transfer option, however, Glanville's visit served to reinforce the importance of in-country research. From the evidence that 'isolation of the best varieties, and the distribution after careful trial, of this pedigree seed ... [had] given amazingly good results in India' Glanville drew the conclusion that a vigorous rice improvement programme along similar lines was a priority for Sierra Leone (Glanville 1933). In large measure this would build on local foundations.

'Valuable work [could] be accomplished without delay' Glanville suggests 'by assisting the rice farmers to make mass selections on their own farms'. Since some farmers were 'known to possess good strains' they were, by implication, already moving in the right direction. He cites as an example 'one of the best and most popular rices in the Scarcies area at the moment . . . Pa Fodea, which is said to be a selected strain of Pa Litoma' (Glanville 1933).

Interest in local rice varieties had been fostered earlier by Douglas Scotland at Njala. Scotland had carried out trials with two upland varieties known in mende as **jɔbɔ** and **pende** in his first full season at Njala in 1912. Perhaps on the advice of local field assistants, **jɔbɔ** had been grown interplanted with millet and beniseed. He soon discovered that **pende** (an African rice, O. *glaberrima*) tillered especially vigorously, and because it ripened quickly was well suited to planting in damp low-lying places as a hunger-breaker crop. **Pende** is still grown for these reasons in the Njala areas today (see Chs 5 and 8). In 1923, 15 types of Sierra Leone upland rice had been planted at Njala 'principally for collecting specimens for the British Empire Exhibition' and 16 indigenous swamp varieties were tried to see how they performed in inland valley swamps (Department of Agriculture 1923). Once the rice research station at Rokupr was opened in 1935 screening work of this sort could be placed on a regular footing.

By the mid-1930s, therefore, the colonial Department of Agriculture's rice policy had come to maturity. There was some measure of agreement that without adequate allowance for social and ecological circumstances specific to the Sierra Leonian setting Asia-to-Africa technology transfers were likely to prove ill advised and ineffective. The new in-country research base (at Rokupr) opened up a choice of development strategies for the rice sector: modified technology transfer based on 'adaptive' research (Screening Asian inputs for their applicability under local conditions) or R&D programmes designed to support the best local initiatives. In the main, subsequent policy favoured the second of these options.

The indigenous alternative

The Department of Agriculture's swing away from the technology transfer option reflects two important sets of circumstances. The first was that research began to suggest earlier harsh judgements concerning local agricultural and ecological skills had been misplaced (Jones 1936). The second set of circumstances, undoubtedly, was the positive way in which the farming community in Sierra Leone had responded to the problems caused by the catastrophic drop in export crop prices from 1929 onwards. To the evident surprise of a number of eye-witnesses, recession had been followed by a rapid compensatory expansion in the food-crop sector. For example, food crop railings from stations in Southern Province quadrupled between 1929 and 1935 and in 1934, after many years of near shortage, Sierra Leone resumed exports of rice.

On a second visit to Sierra Leone Stockdale noted that:

the most striking agricultural change which has taken place during the period 1929 to 1935 has been the extension of rice growing. Not only has there been a marked increase in the growing of hill rice, but there has also been the extension of cultivation in the inland swamps, and on the naturally flooded lands of the Scarcies deltaic area ... With the onset of depression the people of Sierra Leone turned their attention to the production of food for home consumption, maintained and even increased their exports of palm kernels, which are in fact a by-product of the production of palm oil for local use as food, and increased the production of piassava to make up for the loss of the kola trade [due to decline of demand in Nigeria] (Stockdale 1936).

To Glanville this was conclusive proof, if proof were needed, that local initiative was equal to the technological challenges posed by swamp development. In a paper entitled *Rice cultivation on swamps* (1938) he traces the historical trajectory of wet-rice development in Sierra Leone. 'The utilisation of inland swamps has been a natural growth ... swamp cultivation was begun by local farmers without outside assistance'. The main contribution of Government, he argues, should be to continue to support these changes with propaganda and practical assistance.

Such practical assistance, however, required a thorough understanding of what farmers were trying to do. 'Textbook' arguments and preconceptions based on experience in other parts of the world were not always helpful in this respect. For example, although transplanting was advantageous in favourable circumstances (because less seed was required, the field was more uniform, yields were higher and weeds less of a problem) it was less advisable in swamps subject to sudden flood or rapid flow of water during the transplanting season in July and August. In swamps of this second kind it was better to continue to establish the crop early by broadcasting. Glanville notes that Scarcies farmers in the 19th century may have developed transplanting without outside assistance. If farmers in Sierra Leone were capable of working out for themselves the advantages of transplanting it was equally probable that those rejecting the technique had good reasons for doing so.

Glanville also notes that wetland development in Sierra Leone had implications for crops other than rice. The popularity of swamp development, in farmers' eyes, depended as much on dry-season swamp crops such as sweet potatoes, cassava, tobacco and vegetables, as on increased output of rice during the rainy season. Local innovations in dry-season cultivation of swamps deserved support and wider dissemination for ecological as well as economic reasons, e.g. dry season crops were often grown on heaps, and the levelling of these heaps before the next rice crop buried rice stubble (thus enhancing fertility) and checked weed growth.

The key to successful R&D in the rice sector, then, was to identify and support farmers' interests. Rokupr took its early bearings from the fact that 'the Scarcies farmer is always on the look out for anything new in the rice line and is undoubtedly responsible for propagating several new varieties from field selections' (Glanville 1938). The close rapport between Rokupr and the local farming community bore fruit almost immediately. A year after Rokupr opened, Stockdale was able to report that there was 'keen demand for seed from the station.'

Improved seed was put into circulation by means of a revolving seed distribution scheme, one of the most successful development projects undertaken by the colonial Department of Agriculture. The programme was responsible for distributing 93 000 bushels of improved seed in the 13 years of its operation, and was finally terminated because the varieties concerned were by then all in general use. To Roddan, the officer in charge of the seed distribution scheme, the 'daily queue of farmers . . . waiting just to give in their names', demonstrated that 'the way to gain the confidence of the farmer is to assist him in growing his own crops' (Department of Agriculture 1936).

The return of technology transfer: the polder irrigation scheme

Notwithstanding the success of the gradualist farmer-oriented policies adopted during the 1930s, the notion that the estuaries of the Great and Little Scarcies might be developed for irrigated rice cultivation along the lines of the great river deltas of South-East Asia, first proposed by Governor Wilkinson in 1920, sprang back into prominence at the beginning of World War II. Freetown, with the finest natural harbour on the western coast of Africa, was a major strategic base for the Allied war effort. The wartime increase in Freetown's population raised the spectre of food supply difficulties on the scale experienced in 1919. In anticipation of such a contingency an irrigation and drainage unit of the Department of Agriculture established in 1941 embarked on an emergency programme to grow more rice, funded by a 'grant cum loan' from the Colonial Welfare and Development Fund of £303 000.

Work on the construction of large-scale rice polders along the Great Scarcies commenced in April 1942. Land beyond the immediate reach of freshwater flooding in the rainy season was used relatively little by local farmers because the soils were saline. The aim of the polder scheme was to solve the salinity problem by excluding brackish tidal water from these back swamps during the dry season and to keep the land under drainage (Garvie 1957). Successful rice polders are found in both Burma and Guyana (Grist 1975) and the Sierra Leone scheme may have owed its inspiration to both these examples.

Due to staffing difficulties and physical problems in constructing the polders little was achieved for the duration of the war. The bunds had to be cut in 1945 because of heavy rain and flooding. The evident lack of progress led to scrutiny of the scheme by A. E. Griffin, consulting engineer to the Secretary of State for the Colonies. On his advice further work was halted, except for the polder at Rosino which was maintained for experimental purposes, because, as noted in the Annual Report for 1948, 'the problems associated with irrigation agriculture . . . are complex and much fundamental work is desirable.'

By 1948 average yields on the monitored plots had declined to 31 per cent of their level in 1944 when the polder was constructed. Opening up the polder to regular tidal flows restored yields to earlier levels. As the 1949 Annual Report drily notes: 'the success of reverting to the utilization of natural and unrestricted irrigation by tidal river water [was] astonishing'. Clearly the whole initiative was misconceived. It had been a mistake to exclude brackish water in the dry season. The salinity problem was not solely a question of sea water incursions.

Land colonised by the mangrove *Rhizophora racemosa* becomes intensely acid upon drying, and it transpired that the most effective way to deal with this problem was to allow sea water to wash the soil throughout the dry season and for residual salt to be leached by early rain (Jordan n.d.).

During the war Glanville had taken up a post in Nigeria, but returned to Sierra Leone in 1944 as Director of Agriculture. When the immediate pressures of wartime lifted the Department of Agriculture took up once more the threads of the prewar approach towards agricultural development. The 1947 Annual Report re-states the case for a policy based on careful trials and work with peasant farmers, and stresses the continued dynamism of farmer initiatives in rice cultivation, pointing to the success of Temne migrants to the Rotifunk area in opening up mangrove swamp cultivation in the Bumpeh Creek, with the consequent adoption of this technique by Mende farmers in Moyamba District.

Determined that the lessons of the polderisation scheme should be properly learnt, Glanville commissioned the Njala soil chemist, H. W. Dougall, to carry out a thorough study of the polder site at Rosino. After demonstrating how the mangrove soils became increasingly toxic under poldered conditions Dougall turned his attention to the associated swamps and upland margins, where indigenous initiative had evolved a land-use system which he doubted could be bettered:

> A land-use system in the seep zone (which extends from the bottom of the lower footslopes to the margin of the rear area) has been evolved by the local Africans themselves. It is on this pale, brownish-grey and reddish-brown colluvium that they establish their rice nurseries, cassava and sweet potato beds and occasional small banana groves. It is doubtful if the system could be profitably improved upon ... (Department of Agriculture 1949).

This pinpointed a crucial weakness of the original polder scheme, namely that it:

> envisaged only reclaiming for the cultivation of rice, the hydrophilous marsh grassland behind the river's flood plain. It did not take cognizance of Rosino as a 'unit of landscape' of which the marsh grassland formed an integral part.

In Dougall's view, rather than treating wetland environments in isolation, it made better sense to approach land-use planning from the perspective of what he terms 'the complete landscape form'. As subsequent chapters will argue, this was an insight of the greatest significance. Survival and success in peasant households in Sierra Leone often depend on the skill with which valley and upland are integrated.

The significance of Dougall's call for integrated development of valley topographic sequences was largely lost sight of during the 1950s and '60s, due to a preoccupation first with schemes for the extensive cultivation of valley bottom lands by tractors and then with a further round of Asia-to-Africa technology transfer, this time focused on small-scale irrigation methods suited to the cultivation of Green Revolution high-yielding rice varieties. This most recent phase of wetland technology transfer is the theme upon which the next chapter focuses.

2 Bringing the Green Revolution to Sierra Leone

In 1955, G. Lacey, drainage and irrigation adviser at the Colonial Office, visited Sierra Leone as a consultant on water control and swamp development. His subsequent report summarised the major lessons of irrigation initiatives during the colonial period:

> The early attempts at [irrigated] rice cultivation on the Great Scarcies river had a somewhat chequered career ... they have taught me that every proposal for cultivation of rice in swamps must be based on firm local knowledge, and that it is a mistake not only to introduce methods of rice cultivation in swamps because they have been found successful in other countries but it is an equally great mistake to assume that within one Colony all swamps demand the same treatment. (Lacey 1957).

Conscious of these problems, agricultural policy makers during the 1950s shifted their attention from irrigation as such and concentrated on a tractor mechanisation programme for extensive cultivation of rice in the bolilands of northern Sierra Leone and the riverine grasslands of the lower Sewa and Waanje behind Turner's Peninsula. By comparison with schemes in other parts of British colonial Africa (cf. Baldwin 1957) tractor ploughing in Sierra Leone was relatively successful. It greatly extended the possibilities of rice cultivation in wetland environments where farmers limited to the use of the hoe had previously found the soils difficult to cultivate and yields discouraging. Tractor hire opened up opportunities for women to cultivate rice on their own account. Along the lower Sewa and Waanje, where labour shortages were a major constraint on output, tractor ploughing had the great advantage that it destroyed the rhizomes of wild perennial rice in the deep-flooding riverine grasslands. Local communities adapted their farming methods and social arrangements to accommodate mechanisation, and were keen for the scheme to be expanded (Jedrej 1983).

Mechanisation was not at first sight an inappropriate solution to some of the most urgent agricultural development problems posed by the rapid expansion of diamond mining during the early 1950s. From 1950 to 1956 many rural areas experienced a major exodus of farm labour as younger men moved to the diamond districts to try their hand at unlicensed mining (van der Laan 1965). Urban areas and diamond districts experienced rapid inflation in food prices. A strike in February 1955 in protest at the high cost of food in Freetown led to rioting in which 18 people died. Rice imports reached 36 800 tons in 1956. Given the severity of the food supply problem during the years of the diamond boom it was not illogical for policy makers to think in terms of using windfall revenues from the mining sector to subsidise an extensive programme of mechanised rice cultivation.

In addition to technical and managerial difficulties (Gleave 1977, Starkey 1981, Jedrej 1983) the scheme suffered from two major drawbacks. It could not be continued without major subsidies but at the same time tied up a disproportionate share of the resources available to the Department of Agriculture. Thus the scheme accounted for only about 4% of the country's total rice output while consuming 80% of the Department of Agriculture's budget. In 1956 a total of 15 000 acres was ploughed by tractor, but the Annual Report for 1957 estimated that a further 75 000 acres would be necessary to replace the 36 800 tons of rice imported the previous year. Once the flow of labour from farming to mining began to slow down during the 1960s it became clear that changes would have to be made. Subsidised mechanisation tied up resources badly needed for a more broadly based agricultural development strategy.

It was in looking to broaden the agricultural development strategy after Independence that attention once more returned to irrigation. This time, however, the emphasis was to be on small-scale farmers. The aim was to introduce a package of development measures for inland valley swamps based on intensive wet-rice management techniques practised by peasants in Taiwan and parts of South-East Asia (double- and triple-cropping of high-yielding varieties in water-controlled swamp environments). The shift in emphasis from large-scale to small-scale irrigation seems to have obscured earlier warnings about the need for local knowledge in swamp land development and the danger of introducing irrigation measures solely on the basis that they had worked well elsewhere.

The Green Revolution

Improved wetland management packages in Sierra Leone first introduced during the 1960s were elements in a broader strategy for Third World agricultural development sometimes termed the Green Revolution. The Green Revolution was a reaction to failures of large-scale development schemes during the 1940s and 1950s. It was built up around the idea that concentrated well-funded crop breeding could deliver a 'biological package' to commercially oriented smallholders in which the productivity gains would be as good if not better than results attainable by large-scale initiatives. High-yielding rice varieties developed at the International Rice Research Institute (IRRI) in the Philippines were among the early successes for this approach. Varieties such as IR 8 were fertiliser-responsive and sufficiently quick-ripening to be planted twice in one season where water control was available.

A network of International Agricultural Research Centers was set up during the late 1960s and early 1970s to extend the approach to other tropical food crops and ecological zones. This network is managed by an organisation known as the Consultative Group on International Agricultural Research (CGIAR). Development of African rice farming now depends in particular on the work of three institutions within the CGIAR network: IRRI, the International Institute of Tropical Agriculture (IITA) in Nigeria, and the West African Rice Development Association (WARDA). WARDA has headquarters in Liberia but runs regional programmes in Ivory Coast, Sierra Leone, Senegal, and Mali.

At the same time as this major international plant improvement network was established, attention began to be paid to ways of delivering these new biological inputs to small-scale farmers. Under the direction of Robert McNamara in the 1970s the World Bank announced a commitment to a greater emphasis on development programmes designed to benefit the poorest groups in society – the 'bottom 40 per cent' (World Bank 1975). It was argued that many more small-scale farmers would adopt Green Revolution technologies if they were not so badly constrained by lack of credit and problems of physical access to inputs. To solve these access problems the Bank promoted a large number of Integrated Agricultural Development Projects (IADPs). Typically, an IADP is a semi-autonomous regional development authority which supplies small-scale farmers with improved inputs (and credit for their purchase), provides extension advice, and attempts to solve physical access problems by, for example, a programme of rural road construction or improvement. Some IADPS also tackle other infrastructure improvements – e.g. rural water supplies and better health facilities – without which the benefits of 'biological' input packages might be lost. Finance for IADPs frequently comes from the International Development Association, the soft-loan affiliate of the World Bank. The World Bank (along with the Ford and Rockefeller Foundations) provides CGIAR funding and a home in Washington for its secretariat, and Bank-funded IADPs are often closely linked to component institutions in the IARC chain.

According to Binswanger and Ruttan (1978) the full Green Revolution model for small-holder development in the Third World now comprises, therefore, three levels. IARCs carry out fundamental R&D work on crops and other farm inputs. Innovations (e.g. high-yielding varieties) emanating from IARCs are then screened and fine-tuned for local application in national centres for 'adaptive research and extension'. Finally, technology 'packages' – sometimes termed 'mini-kits', and at their simplest comprising an improved variety and fertiliser – are delivered to small farmers either through the existing national agricultural extension services or through IADPs.

It has been argued that the Asian Green Revolution has exacerbated economic inequalities in peasant communities (Griffin 1979, Pearse 1980, cf. Harriss 1982) because, for example, the benefits of high-yielding varieties were often only available to farmers who could afford the additional expense of fertiliser and irrigation (Farmer 1981). Lipton & Longhurst (1985) contest this view and argue that on balance the benefits to the poor have been positive. Whatever the relative merits of the positions involved, it is clear that 'Asian' critiques of the Green Revolution have little relevance in sub-Saharan Africa partly because rural poverty manifests itself in different ways – for example, in complete contrast to most parts of Asia lack of labour power is often a more pressing problem than landlessness – and partly because, as yet, relatively few IARC varieties of African staples are incontrovertibly successful or widely adopted. Accordingly, the main criticisms of attempts to generate a Green Revolution in Africa have focused on unsolved agronomic and environmental difficulties, and the evident logistical problems associated with the input delivery process (Richards 1985).

The first set of problems reflects the inherent complexity of many African food-crop farming systems, in which a high degree of mixed cropping is common (Steiner 1982). Research progress has been relatively slow and yield gains from improved technologies modest. Innovations released before they were adequately proven under local conditions have undermined farmer confidence and morale. The logistical problems associated with the Green Revolution in Africa are especially daunting. The main difficulty, at a time of severe economic recession, is in the length and expense of the supply chain linking research institutions such as IITA to the isolated smallholder. Few IADPs operate in villages off motorable roads, and construction of new farm access roads is often prohibitively expensive. In consequence, many (sometimes a majority of) farm households remain outside the direct reach of the new technologies. Poor farmers can only afford to buy or borrow improved inputs in tiny quantities, thus imposing enormous administrative overhead costs. Seed and fertiliser are useless if not supplied on time, and yet delays are almost inevitable when roads are liable to flooding in the rains and vehicles, spares and fuel are in short supply as a result of chronic foreign exchange difficulties. These two sets of criticisms are especially apposite in the case of Sierra Leone.

Green Revolution initiatives in Sierra Leone

Because of the importance of rice in the national economy, the widespread availability of relatively under-utilised swamp land and the overwhelming predominance of peasant producers in the agricultural sector Sierra Leone was an early and obvious candidate for the Green Revolution treatment. Initiatives in Sierra Leone have been aimed in particular at small farmers with access to inland valley swamp. An inland valley swamp is defined as 'a narrow, level, valley bottom drained only by a sluggish seasonal stream and which is waterlogged for much of the year' (Land Resources Survey 1979). The standard 'package' involves clearing and levelling an area of swamp, and implementing water control by constructing a head bund, drainage channels and bunded paddies. The advantage of water control is that submergence supplies the crops with abundant additional nutrients from fresh clay particles, organic matter, nitrogen-fixing blue–green algae, etc. (Grist 1975). Drawbacks include the labour required for construction and maintenance and 'the depletion of free and combined oxygen from the subsoil, and accumulation of various organic acids which retard root development, inhibit nutrient absorption and normal aerobic respiration and cause root rot' (Grist 1975, p. 37). A developed swamp is permanently cultivated, with the aid of fertilisers and insecticides (swamps under local management often require to be fallowed for short periods from time to time). Rice seedlings are nursed and then transplanted into rows (typically on a 20 × 20 cm spacing). In principle, water control allows for the cultivation of two or three crops per year of a quick-maturing short-straw rice variety such as CCA.

The earliest attempts to introduce water control into inland valley swamps date back to the 1930s. Dr F. J. Martin, the Njala soil chemist, deputising for

Glanville as agricultural officer, Northern Province, while the latter was touring Madras and Ceylon during 1931 laid out a bunded swamp at the Makump substation 'the purpose [of which] was to demonstrate how, with simple controlled irrigation, it is possible to utilize the valley bottoms to greater advantage than is done at present.' The experiment 'clearly demonstrated that, in the rainy season, wetland rice can be successfully grown in bunded valley lands whose only water supply is derived from direct rainfall, supplemented by seepage and "run-off" from valley sides; and that in valleys where there is a perennial water supply it is possible to grow a great variety of crops in the dry season if the watercourse is directed to the side of the valley and utilized for the irrigation, by gravity, of the lower lands.' (Department of Agriculture 1931). The Irrigation and Drainage Department attempted water control on a number of inland valley swamps during the 1940s, but with mixed success because many such swamps were sandy and great care had to be exercised not to overdrain them.

It was not until the 1960s, however, that serious efforts were made to promote the more general adoption of water control measures. In 1964 a nine-man team from the Republic of China (Taiwan) visited Sierra Leone and 'successfully demonstrated that "Japonica" types of rice, which under local farming methods give poor yields, will give extremely high yields in Sierra Leone under the intensive methods for which they were evolved, and on a small area . . . obtained two high-yielding crops in the same year' (Jordan 1966, cf. Farm Demonstration Team 1964). The same report goes on to add that 'while it is not thought that large-scale irrigation works would be economic in the country *at the present stage* [my emphasis] there is scope for much minor water management in inland swamps and it is likely that the intensive method could be of considerable application. . .' (Jordan 1966). This option was then taken up by the Ministry of Agriculture in a programme (organised in conjunction with the United States Peace Corp) to extend the relevant techniques to small–scale farmers countrywide (Haas 1974). Farmers received financial assistance to cover the labour costs of swamp development and subsidised inputs of fertiliser and improved seed from the Ministry. Peace Corp Volunteers provided technical supervision.

A further boost to the small farmer irrigation option was provided when in 1970 a UNDP/FAO project identification document (Strong 1970) singled out a proposal to develop a further 15 000 acres of selected inland valley swamps and to upgrade 36 000 acres of partially developed swamp as a priority for funding. One of the major reasons given was that water control would permit cultivation of three crops a year and so eliminate dry-season underemployment in agriculture. Since the work could be done by small farmers on a self-help basis no capital would be needed for heavy machinery. The work of the Demonstration Team from the Republic of China was cited as evidence that quick results (in terms of increased output of rice) could be achieved by promoting swamp developments along these lines.

It was at this point that the World Bank made available a loan from the International Development Association to fund the first in a series of Integrated Agricultural Development Projects. This project – the Eastern Area IADP – was inaugurated in December 1972 (Airey *et al.* 1979). Swamp development

Table 2.1 Planned crop targets for Sierra Leone IADPs (Land Resource Survey 1979).

Project	Funds	Phasing	Crop	Area (ha)
Eastern (Phases 1 & 2)	IDA	1972–79	swamp rice	4795
			upland rice	485
			cocoa	740
Eastern (Phase 3)	IDA	1980–82	swamp rice	1620
			upland rice	46575
			cocoa	4050
			coffee	4050
			oil palm estate	810
			oil palm outgrowers	1620
			rubber estate	2835
			rubber outgrowers	605
Northern	IDA	1976–79	swamp rice	1215
			upland rice	10125
			groundnuts	4050
Koinadugu	EDF	1978–82	swamp rice (etc.)	2430
			upland rice	405
			livestock	8100
Northwestern	EDF	1980–84	swamp rice (mangrove)	5265
			cassava	565
Moyamba	ADB	1980–84	swamp rice	2330
			upland rice	8745
			various cash crops	1745
Magbosi	IFAD	1980–85	swamp rice	3240
			upland crops	6480

was one of its major objectives (Lappia 1980). Farmers interested in swamp development were offered a loan to cover some of the labour costs incurred in improving a swamp to this standard (repayable over five years at moderate interest) and technical advice on levelling, siting of bunds and construction of drainage channels. The project also supplied fertiliser and improved rice varieties suitable for cultivation in water-controlled swamps.

A second World Bank project, the Northern IADP, was begun in 1976. It also promoted the swamp development package, though not to same degree as the Eastern IADP (Table 2.1). Disappointing initial results led to greater emphasis on upland rice from 1977–78 onwards (Karimu & Richards 1981). A series of similar projects (funded from sources including the EEC and the African Development Bank) was subsequently established to cover the entire country (Fig. 2.1). Development of water-controlled swamps featured quite prominently among the aims of each of these projects (Table 2.1). Water control, although still an important part of the rhetoric of development, is now pursued with noticeably less vigour in the majority of IADPs owing to an

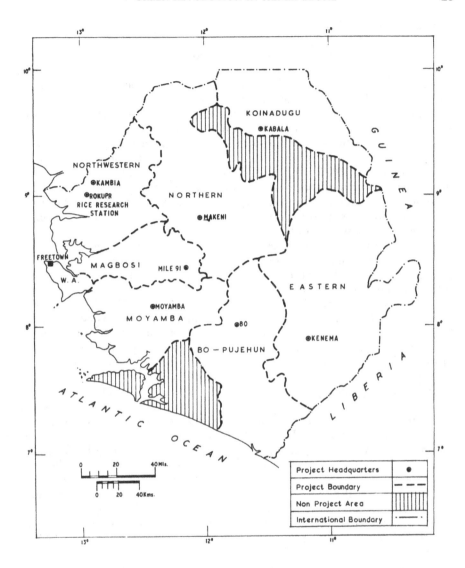

Figure 2.1 Integrated Agricultural Development Projects and the Rice Research Station in Sierra Leone.

accumulation of practical difficulties. A recent FAO-sponsored conference in Freetown (December 1984) revealed the extent to which doubts are now entertained about the viability of water-control in smallholder rice cultivation under Sierra Leonian conditions, but there were less clear ideas about where to move next (Weatherhead 1984).

Limitations to the Green Revolution swamp package

One of the earliest analyses of the adoption of water-controlled swamp cultivation practices – a study of a Peace Corp swamp development project in Alikalia, Koinadugu District (Haas 1974) – found that participants in the project tended to be titled men, Koranic teachers, and shopkeepers. At first sight this appears to be a further example of the familiar tendency for richer peasants to monopolise development inputs. Haas notes a paradox, however. Adopters had less rice available and were more likely to be short of rice in the hungry season than those who rejected the innovation. This is confirmed in other studies. Johnny (1979), Karimu and Richards (1981) and Richards (1983) report that specialist rice producers tend to be hostile to the swamp package, but that it is favoured by part-time farmers (e.g. traders and schoolteachers) or farmers with a major interest in tree-crop cultivation, because timing of operations is not so critical in a water-controlled environment.

The failure to impress full-time specialist rice producers suggests that water-controlled swamp cultivation practices are not always as advantageous as their promoters claim, and that these disadvantages are especially apparent to those with upland or 'undeveloped' swamp land to serve as a source of comparison. Recent studies (Lappia 1980, Karimu & Richards 1981, Carloni 1983, Weatherhead 1984) have documented difficulties not anticipated when the 'Asian model' was first introduced. Many swamps quickly dry out when the rains cease, and the promised benefit of double cropping proves to be unattainable. Design, layout and construction work is often carried out to inadequate standards. Surveyors and extension workers frequently give farmers inappropriate advice on the location or size of the head bund. Drainage channels are frequently over-excavated, with results in sandy swamps not unlike pulling the plug out of a bath. An overdrained swamp developed over gravelly soils is illustrated in Figure 2.2. This swamp was originally intended as a demonstration project by an IADP to silence criticisms among local farmers that swamp construction was more difficult and time-consuming than they had at first been led to believe! Swamps with insufficient water flow are vulnerable to a number of soil management problems, including iron toxicity. Farmers faced with such difficulties frequently find that their yields drop below those achieved by local management practices without water control. Abandonment rates for developed swamps are high, and recovery of swamp loans is, not surprisingly, then very difficult.

Of the difficulties faced by those adopting water-controlled farming methods in inland valley swamps in Sierra Leone the most significant, perhaps, is the problem of labour shortage. In contrast to most parts of South and South-East Asia, Sierra Leone is not densely populated. In consequence there is no large pool of landless or underemployed peasants willing to work as hired labourers. Rural labour shortages have been made worse in recent years by outmigration to Freetown and the diamond mining districts. Water-controlled swamps have high yields per hectare but labour productivity in such swamps is often less good than on upland rice farms or in swamps managed according to indigenous methods. In areas where upland fallow periods are of adequate duration (Ch. 4) a bushel of upland rice requires only two-thirds to three-

Figure 2.2   A failed water-controlled swamp rice farm.

quarters of the labour needed to produce one bushel of rice in a water-controlled inland valley swamp. Initial calculations of labour requirements for both development and subsequent maintenance of water-controlled swamps were often wildly optimistic, and IADP loans for hiring additional labour to complete such work were in consequence often far too small to be useful (Karimu & Richards 1981).

Historically, farming practices in many parts of West Africa have been adjusted to shortages of labour not land (Levi 1976, Isaac 1982, cf. Levi & Havinden 1982). As will be seen from the evidence presented in later chapters a major technique for labour conservation in Sierra Leone is to adopt a staggered planting programme making use of the different planting opportunities offered by upland and valley soils. Indigenous swamp management methods (broadcasting of flood-tolerant varieties in inland valley swamps without water control) are designed to complement other farming operations (cultivation of upland rice in particular). Water-controlled swamp farms, in so far as they were seen as part of a wider portfolio of farming operations at all, were promoted as replacements for upland rice cultivation. But given the failure rate attached to swamp development of this kind it is understandable that few specialist rice cultivators are prepared to risk a once-and-for-all switch.

Figure 2.3 shows the kind of labour bottleneck problems faced by an average farm household using different types swamp and upland cultivation methods in northern Sierra Leone. The four scenarios show the way labour inputs would be distributed seasonally in order to achieve, in each case, the

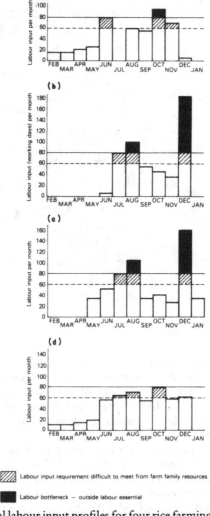

Figure 2.3   Seasonal labour input profiles for four rice farming systems; (a) upland rice, (b) local swamp rice, (c) improved swamp rice and (d) two-thirds upland one third local swamp (Karimu and Richards 1981).

same harvest output. The heavily shaded part of each column shows the extent
to which, in any month, the household would need to seek outside hired help.
Not only is hired labour in rural Sierra Leone expensive and in short supply,
but, as the subsequent case study will show, organising such labour is itself a
time consuming and risky business. Two of the graphs show the pattern of
labour distribution when all the rice is produced in swamps, using indigenous
and improved management practices respectively. The other two graphs show
the result of combining upland cultivation with swamp cultivation (water-
controlled and indigenous management practices respectively). In the case of
the combination of upland and improved swamp practices, the proportions are
dictated by the smallest size of swamp loan package offered by the Northern
Area IADP. The results, although based on rough-and-ready figures, suggest
that households minimise labour bottleneck problems when they stick to a
combination of two-thirds upland rice and one-third indigenous swamp
cultivation. These proportions first reported as typical for northern Sierra
Leone in the 1930s (Glanville 1938) are still typical today (Karimu & Richards
1981). One of the main purposes of the case study presented in this book is to
explore the logic of this combination.

An alternative to technology transfer?

The problems associated with small-farmer swamp development in Sierra
Leone illustrate once again the danger of relying on a more or less unmodified
Asian technology package without taking adequate account of local social and
ecological circumstances. Lacey's conclusion concerning the high-technology
irrigation initiatives on the Scarcies during the 1940s – that it was an error to
introduce methods of rice cultivation solely because 'they have been found
successful in other countries' – could with equal justice be applied to more
recent small-farmer oriented irrigation initiatives inspired by the Green Revolution. Practical difficulties of implementation in typical small-farmer production environments in Sierra Leone have been compounded by problems
associated with the way Green Revolution research is organised at the international level: e.g. a tendency to compartmentalise rice research into separate
mangrove, inland-valley and upland components and a relative lack of attention
to the 'adaptive' link in the research chain until relatively late in the day (the
USAID-funded Adaptive Crop Research & Extension Project in Sierra Leone
did not commence operations until more than a decade after initial attempts to
implement the Asian swamp-rice package on a national scale and in any case
focused mainly on upland crops).
    An awareness that difficulties of the sort faced by swamp development
programmes in Sierra Leone may reflect generic defects in the Green Revolution approach is currently prompting a re-assessment of CGIAR research
methodology. In recent years there has been a shift in the focus of attention
from individual crops to the farmer and farming systems. Recent emphasis on
farming systems research (FSR) has brought out the extent to which greater
agricultural productivities are dependent on the effective co-ordination of a
range of inputs. Emphasis on the integrated development of the complete

farming system has in turn stimulated a much greater awareness of the importance of ecological specificity in farming practice. Buddenhagen (1978) writes about the new philosophy in rice research in the following terms:

> The modern trend to narrow [the] great genetic diversity in rice by concentrating on only one or two types of rice culture and with isolation or protection from the biological and physiological pressures of specific environments, is ... now gradually shifting to an appreciation of environmental complexity and the utility of traits earlier unrecognized.

Buddenhagen then goes on to sample seven distinct rice ecologies from a much larger range of African rice ecosystems. 'Rice improvement programmes and rice cultural management objectives' must be focused, he concludes, on each of these 'many different combinations of conditions' in turn (Buddenhagen 1978, p. 23). It is on account of this great ecological diversity that Pearson *et al.* (1981) conclude 'most Asian technologies are not transferable [to West Africa] without substantial sacrifices in economic efficiency, and hence the successful development of rice production in West Africa will likely prove to be a highly indigenous process' (p. 394).

In institutional terms the implication of arguments such as these is that Green Revolution research must be decentralised. This means a renewed emphasis on national research centres. In Sierra Leone local improved varieties emanating from Rokupr have consistently out-performed IRRI material, especially in upland conditions (Will, Banya & Williams 1969, Will *et al.* 1969). Three of the most successful improved varieties now offered by IADPs (ROK 3, ROK 16 and LAC 23) are selections from local strains rather than HYVs developed by International Agricultural Research Centers. ROK 3 and ROK 16 were selected from local cultivars at Rokupr, while LAC 23 is of Liberian provenance (Virmani *et al.* 1978). Locally based varieties are readily recognised as such by villagers. Mende farmers, for example, recognise ROK 3 as an improved variant of **ngiyema yaka**. Part of the advantage and appeal of such selections is that, recognising their ancestry, farmers have very clear ideas about where and how to use them to maximum advantage (Ch. 8).

The argument for greater devolution within Green Revolution research programmes does not stop at the national level, however. If Buddenhagen stresses the need for research to be focused on specific and often highly localised agro-ecosystems, Maxwell (1984) points out that ecological, economic and social changes within the lifetime of a small-farmer food-crop R&D programme are liable to confound the assumptions upon which the programme was initially founded. Farming systems research must be able to pick up and respond to such changes. Research geographically and sociologically remote from the mass of the farming population is inappropriate in such circumstances. To be responsive to localised needs and often highly specific ecological circumstances Green Revolution R&D must be securely rooted in local communities and interactive in character (Byerlee & Collinson 1980, Rhoades & Booth 1982, Ngambeki & Wilson 1983).

Conclusion

This chapter has outlined the fate of the 'Asian model' for development of small-farmer rice farming systems in Sierra Leone. The problem with the technology transfer approach is that it appears to offer a short cut to progress. Recent experience underlines the point that there is rarely any substitute for solid local knowledge. Technology transfer is especially pernicious where, as in Sierra Leone, it comes replete with a set of major but untested assumptions about the extent to which specific agricultural practices are 'backward' and 'advanced'. Thinly disguised cultural evolutionist notions about the 'backwardness' of upland rice cultivation, and a corresponding confidence that farming systems must eventually evolve along Asian lines, has blocked appreciation of possible indigenous development alternatives based on what farmers are already attempting to do for themselves. It is to these alternatives that the case study in the following pages is addressed in the belief that peasant farmer experimental initiative is one of Africa's most important, if seriously undervalued, agricultural resources.

3   Mogbuama: landscape and society

A general introduction to the case study

While Green Revolution water-controlled swamp rice farming packages have been viewed by development agencies in Sierra Leone as a *replacement* for indigenous upland rice farming systems, many farmers prefer to *combine* wetland and upland rice cultivation. The aim of the following account of rice farming practices in Mogbuama, a medium-sized village in central Sierra Leone, is to show how and why this combination is so important to small-scale rice producers, and to explore ways in which existing integrated systems might be further developed.

The case-study analysis is based on fieldwork in which participant observation of farming activities throughout an agricultural season was combined with more conventional farming systems data collection procedures (e.g. soil and vegetation survey, questionnaires and input–output monitoring schedules). Participatory immersion in farming as a social and technological process brings out the importance of specific agricultural and social events, the ways in which these events and sequences of events are intertwined, and what they mean to the actors concerned. In particular, attention is drawn to the cumulative consequences of mistakes and accidents as the agricultural season progresses. Integrated use of upland and wetland is a way to ameliorate these consequences.

The account is organised as follows. The present chapter sets the case-study village, Mogbuama, in regional context, provides a sketch of village social organisation, and summarises the main features of the ecology of local rice farming systems. Chapter 4 discusses land use, land tenure and the organisation of agricultural labour, addressing the questions who can farm, what kinds of farm they can make and how they mobilise the necessary resources. Chapter 5 is an activity-by-activity account of the farming year, focusing on the way in which the main ecological and social variables interact. Chapter 6 assesses the 1983 harvest and patterns of success and failure. Chapter 7 looks in more detail at reasons for farm failure, concentrating in particular on the complex interaction between climatic hazard, indebtedness and seasonal difficulties over access to labour. Chapter 8 takes as its theme the way in which farmers experiment with planting materials and planting strategies to avoid or recover from some of the seasonal hazards discussed in the previous chapter. An alternative scenario for rice R&D in Sierra Leone, drawing on the lessons of the case study, is outlined in Chapter 9.

A common thread connecting the various aspects of the case study is the crucial importance of topographic planting strategies (following the soil catena) in the integration of upland and wetland and the smoothing out of seasonal labour supply bottlenecks. Catenary farming systems are well developed in the case study region because of the presence of a major escarpment. The basic idea of planting up and down a topographic sequence, however, is both widespread and long-established in humid-zone rice cultivation throughout West Africa (Moorman & van Breeman 1978, Moorman & Veldkamp 1978). Three among many possible examples serve to suggest the more general significance of the case study in this respect:

(a) One of the lessons of the polderisation scheme on the Scarcies during the 1940s, as noted in Chapter 1, was that it was a mistake to treat mangrove swamp farming systems in isolation from adjacent areas beyond the reach of the tidal flood, because associated swamps and colluvial footslopes were integral to local farming practices.

(b) The Dutchman Olfert Dapper described a 17th-century rice farming system in the Cape Mount area (Liberia) apparently not dissimilar to catenary farms found in Mogbuama today. Dapper's description has been summarised by the historian Adam Jones (1983, p. 165) as follows:

[A first crop] grown in 'low muddy places', was harvested as early as May. Probably the amount was small, but enough to feed the farmer and his dependents in the 'hungry season'. [Two other harvests] were similar in timing to those referred to by later writers: the intermediate crop was probably a short-duration variety, sown in 'moistland' riverain areas with a fairly low yield; and the main crop was hardly different from the upland crop grown by most farmers today . . . .

(c) Peasant farmers in Ofada (western Nigeria) make integrated use of hydromorphic toposequences in which the bulk of the rice crop is planted in seasonally flooded lowlands (*katakiti*) and (along with cassava and maize) on the uplands with impeded drainage (*akuro*). Some farmers also make supplementary use of permanent swamp land (*abata*) but this is a relatively hazardous practice without water control (Okali et al. 1980). The Ofada case (it will be seen later) is directly comparable with one of the main rice farming systems in Mogbuama.

Planting in catenary sequences is also well attested throughout sub-Saharan Africa for crops other than rice (Burnham 1980, Ruthenberg 1980, Richards 1983). The evidence that catenary farming systems are superior to irrigated use of wetland where agricultural labour is the main limitation on smallholder output helps explain the relative lack of irrigation systems in pre-colonial sub-Saharan Africa (Goody 1971). The arguments about spreading risks and easing labour bottlenecks continue to be of general relevance today in those parts of tropical Africa where population densities are light or agricultural labour is in short supply.

The landscape

The following account of the soil and vegetation resources of the case-study area forms the basis for subsequent discussion of land and labour as factors of production. A further section outlines village social structure and introduces some key socio-political issues: e.g. the importance of clientelism and factionalism in local politics, and the way in which development project inputs are channelled through patron–client networks.

Rice farming land in Mogbuama
Southern and western Sierra Leone is a plain interrupted by occasional isolated

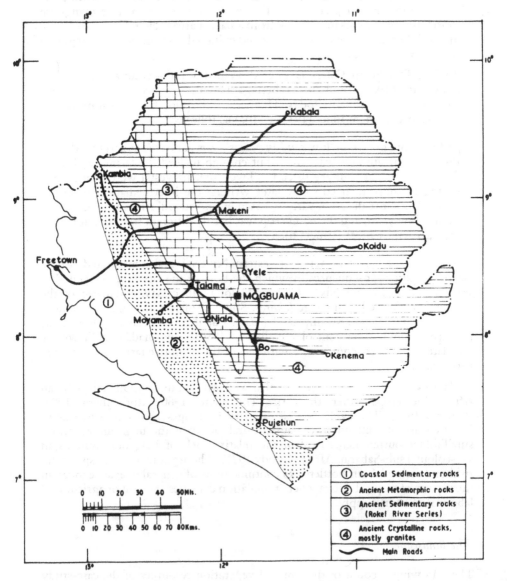

Figure 3.1 The geology of Sierra Leone.

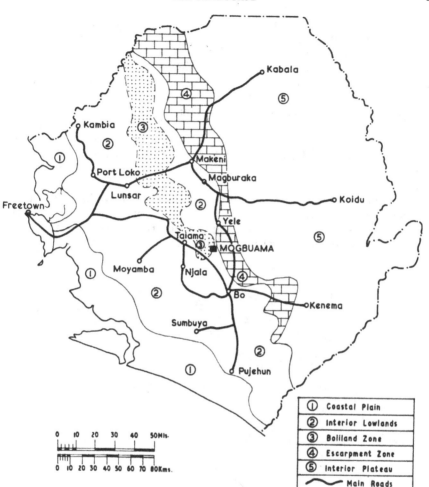

Figure 3.2 The escarpment zone in Sierra Leone.

hills. The northern and eastern half of the country is a dissected plateau of ancient crystalline rocks, mainly between 200 and 500 metres high, but reaching 1945 metres in Bintimani, the highest point in West Africa west of Mount Cameroon. An often pronounced escarpment where these two provinces meet follows the boundary between the ancient metamorphosed sediments of the Rokel River Series and the granites of the Precambrian Basement Complex. The case study focuses on farming systems in this escarpment zone. Mogbuama village is located exactly on the junction between the granite and Rokel River Series a few miles from the geographical centre of Sierra Leone (Figs 3.1 and 3.2).

Much of the lowland underlain by Rokel River Series rocks is covered by extensive seasonally flooded grassy depressions known as bolilands (Stobbs 1963). The boliland zone in Sierra Leone stretches from the area to the south of

Mogbuama north-west to Makeni, Kamakwie and the Guinea border (Fig. 3.2). Around Mogbuama the soils of the boli grasslands are interrupted by extensive tracts of more fertile and forested soils where rivers flowing off the granite escarpment have dropped much of their load. Meander changes and river capture at the foot of the escarpment have left behind a complex sequence of river terraces and former river channels, now carefully exploited by farmers, especially for the cultivation of early rice. Thus land in Mogbuama is divided three ways between boli grassland, lowland forests on old river terrace materials (both to the west of the village), and dissected forest lands in the granite zone to the east (Figs 3.3. and 3.4). Few farmers choose to cultivate the bolilands. The bulk of farming is done either on river terrace lands or in the granite zone.

Farmers in Mogbuama combine three types of rice cultivation. They plant early-ripening rices on river terraces and in river flood plains, medium-duration rices on rain-fed upland farms, and long-duration rices in swamps and water courses (making use of natural flooding). The long-duration rices are often

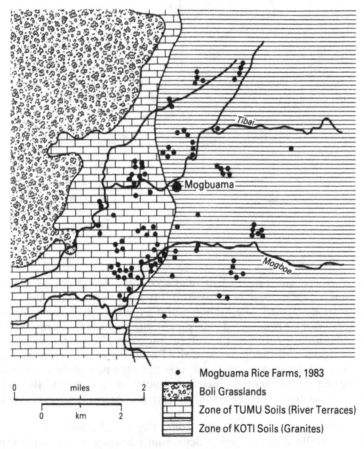

•   Mogbuama Rice Farms, 1983

Boli Grasslands

Zone of TUMU Soils (River Terraces)

Zone of KOTI Soils (Granites)

Figure 3.3   Main soil and land-use types in Mogbuama.

Figure 3.4 The escarpment east of Mogbuama. A, granite whaleback with grassy vegetation; B, mature forest on gravelly soil; C, granite hills.

'floating' or flood-tolerant types (cf. Fig. 4.1). Whenever possible farmers will look for sites where all three types of cultivation can be combined in a single farm. This can be best done by following the soil catena. A catenary farm makes good use of available labour, the scarcest factor of production in small-scale rice farming in Sierra Leone.

Of 98 household rice farms made in Mogbuama in 1983, 60 per cent were located in the river terrace zone south and south-west of the village (cf. Fig. 3.3). The mainly alluvial soils in this region are sufficiently moisture-retentive to allow rice to be planted soon after the first few storms of the rainy season in April. First, quick-ripening varieties are planted on lower terrace soils or in riverine flood plains flanking the three main rivers crossing Mogbuama territory. The main medium-duration rice crop is planted on the higher older terraces a month or so later (i.e. late May/early June). Household members fill in spare time during the planting season by broadcasting long-duration flood-tolerant rices on adjacent swampy areas. Early rices are ready for harvest in August or September. The main upland varieties are ready in October and the long-duration swamp varieties are harvested from November onwards. The farm illustrated in Figures 3.5–3.7 has these three types of rice cultivation combined in catenary sequence: medium-duration rices planted on a ridge of old river terrace materials, early rices planted in a river floodplain area at the foot of the ridge, and long-duration floating rices planted in an adjacent swamp.

Mogbuama village is sited on the crest of a slight escarpment where the granite and Rokel River Series meet. The landscape to the east of Mogbuama comprises a series of forested valleys interrupted by bare granite outliers of the main escarpment of the Kangari Hills. Typical rice farms in this zone follow the valley cross section from ridge to stream (cf. Fig. 3.16). The gravelly upper

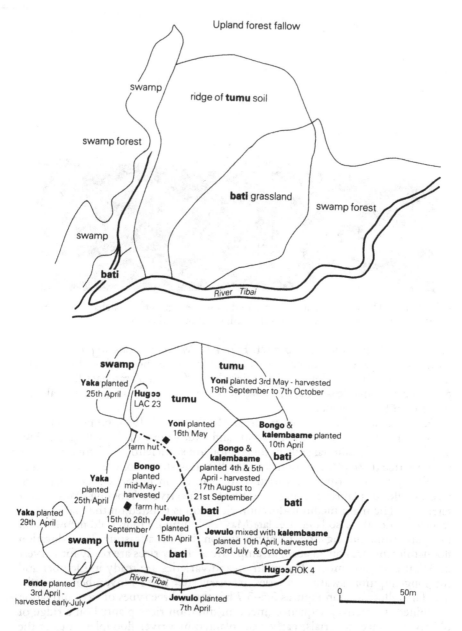

Figure 3.5 Two farms combining river terrace soil (**tumu**) and riverine grassland (**bati**).

Figure 3.6 A farm combining river terrace soils (**tumu**) and riverine grassland (**bati**) after clearing: A, **tumu**; B, **bati**.

Figure 3.7 The same farm with early rice nearing harvest (July): A, medium-duration rice (**yɔni**) intercropped on **tumu**; B, early rice (**bɔngɔ**); C, early rice (**jewulo**) on **bati**.

slope soils are planted to medium–duration rices when the rains are well set (from June onwards). Sandier soils on lower slopes, trapping and retaining runoff, can be planted with early rice at the beginning of the season (a few weeks after the planting of equivalent low-lying plots in the river terrace zone

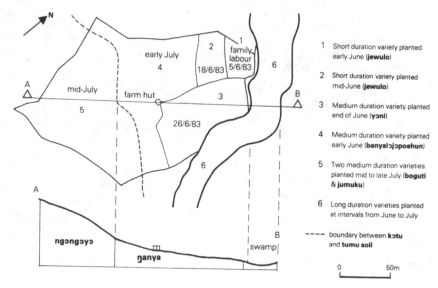

Figure 3.8   A catenary farm in the granite zone east of Mogbuama.

Figure 3.9   A catenary farm in the granite zone; A, kɔtu; B, ŋanya; C, kpete.

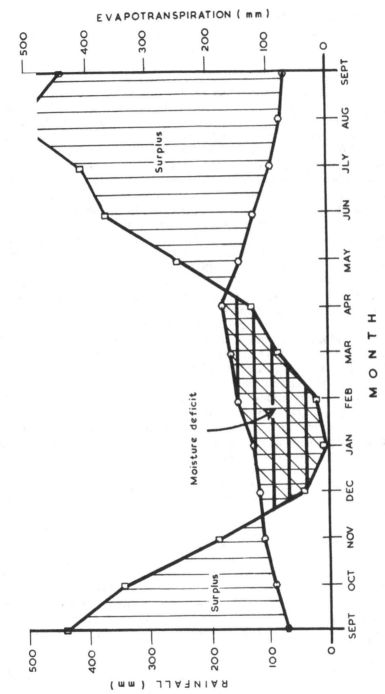

Figure 3.10 Rainfall and evapotranspiration at Njala (average annual rainfall, 1926–62, 2750 mm).

west of the village). Water courses and valley swamps are planted with long–duration flood-tolerant varieties at convenient moments any time from April to July (Figs 3.8 and 3.9, cf. Fig. 4.1).

Climate, vegetation and soils
The climate of central Sierra Leone is humid tropical, with high rainfall (averaging 2750 mm at Njala) and a strongly marked dry season of four to five months (December to April). Streams in Mogbuama are seasonal (only one, the Tibai, never completely dries, although even here flow ceases for a week or two in March and April). From July streams begin to overflow after heavy rainfall, and flooded, swampy conditions prevail in many low-lying areas until December. Although rainfall totals are high, soil moisture is in deficit for up to six months of the year, especially on the free-draining sandy and gravelly soils of the granite zone (Fig. 3.10). Agriculture (apart from cultivation of valley bottom lands) is in consequence a seasonal activity, and vulnerable to rainfall uncertainties, especially at the start of the rainy season. Drought is a less serious hazard than unseasonally early rainfall, though a problem from time to time (e.g. 1985). Early rain interferes with the burning of upland farms, and produces a sequence of adverse consequences which sometimes result in extreme indebtedness and hunger in the following year. Rainfall data relating to this hazard are examined in Chapter 5.

Farmers in Mogbuama distinguish four main vegetation types: forest and forest fallow (**ndɔgbɔ**), upland grasslands, riverine grassland (**bati**) and boli grasslands. In the bolilands a distinction is drawn between **foni** (areas of short grasses) and **ngala** (long grasses of the *Anadelphia–Rhytachne* association, cf. Stobbs 1963). On the regional vegetation map of Sierra Leone Mogbuama is in the transition zone between forest and derived savanna zones (Cole 1968). The small area of upland grassland (used for cattle grazing) around a large granite whaleback east of the village (cf. Fig. 4.2) is probably edaphically determined, as are some of the boli savannas where soils are often of especially low fertility and seasonally waterlogged. In other cases, farmers claim boli grasses are spreading at the expense of forest. Land immediately south-west of Mogbuama along the track to Senehun is an example (cf. Fig. 4.2). **Bati** grasslands result when swamp forest along the flood plains of the major streams is cleared for farming.

Soils of the river terrace zone are silty, gravel-free, occasionally waterlogged at the height of the rains, and in some cases of higher fertility than soils developed over crystalline rocks to the east of the village (Fig. 3.11). The Mende term for silty soils of the type predominating in the river terrace zone is **tumu** (literally 'dusty'). A drier, less permeable type of **tumu** found where soil-eating termites have been especially active is sometimes distinguished and termed **kɔ́kɔ́**. There are some small areas of clay soils in the river terrace zone. Farmers distinguish clay soil (**bɔbɔ**) from **tumu** because the former goes hard rather than powdery when dry.

For soils in catenary sequences in the granite zone east of Mogbuama farmers use the following terms: **bɔbɔ** or **pɔtɔ-pɔtɔ** (a Yoruba loan-word, via Krio) for waterlogged swamp soils in valley bottoms, **ŋanya** for sandy soils on lower slopes, and **kɔtu** for upper slope and hill-crest soils containing a large

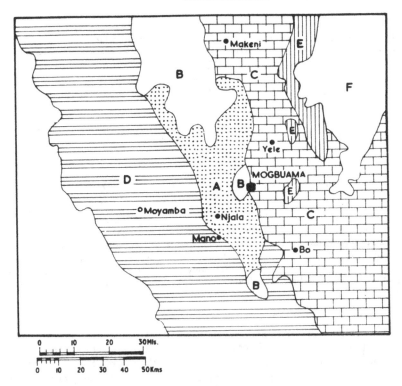

A	Soils from the Rokel River Series under secondary bush
B	Soils of the Bolilands
C	Soils of the Escarpment region from Granite and acid gneiss under savanna
D	Soils of the Interior Plain from acid gneiss and metamorphic rocks
E	Soils of the hills and mountains from the Kambui Schists
F	Soils of the plateaus from granite and acid gneiss under secondary and forest

Figure 3.11 Soil provinces in central Sierra Leone (after van Vuure *et al.* 1972).

proportion of laterite gravel. Where the gravel fraction is less coarse upper slope soils are sometimes referred to by the term **ngɔngɔyɔ**. Soils containing rock fragments are termed **gaŋa** and granite outcrops are **faama**. The hybrid term **kɔtu-ndumu** is sometimes used to describe mid-slope colluvial mixtures.

Mogbuama cultivators draw a sharp distinction between soils in the river-terrace zone and in the zone of crystalline rocks (Fig. 3.11), and see this distinction as having far-reaching consequences for rice planting strategies and other farm management decisions. Samples representing the main soil types recognised by farmers were examined in the laboratory. These samples were all taken from the surface horizon (0–10 cm) in rice farms within one to six weeks of date of planting (i.e. after burning and several weeks of exposure to heavy rain). Analysis covered pH, organic material (using the total combustion method), particle size (using the sieve and pipette method), and exchangeable bases (Table 3.1).

Table 3.1 Analytical data for ten soil samples from Mogbuama farms.

Soil type	Silt(%)	Clay (%)	pH	% C	CEC (meq%)	TEB (meq%)
ngɔngɔyɔ	9.1	0.4	6.4	6.8	6.26	4.84
kɔtu	15.9	2.8	—	6.8	—	—
ŋanya	15.8	1.9	6.7	7.3	8.86	5.72
ŋanya	13.6	2.3	—	3.9	3.08	2.71
ŋanya	14.8	8.0	6.4	6.5	—	—
tumu	16.7	6.5	6.8	5.8	5.22	3.17
tumu	23.8	3.4	6.4	4.2	5.00	3.24
tumu (kɔ́kɔ́)	27.6	4.1	6.4	11.2	10.35	1.44
bati	26.8	2.1	6.7	18.7	13.34	4.48
kpete	50.7	4.9	5.9	30.2	20.94	7.77

Key to Mogbuama soil categories: **ngɔngɔyɔ/kɔtu,** upper slope gravelly soils in granite zone; **ŋanya,** sandy colluvial soils in granite zone; **tumu,** soils derived from old river terrace materials over Rokel River Series rocks; **bati,** river flood plain soil, river terrace zone; **kpete,** swamp soil, granite zone.

In local perception, the main characteristic of **tumu** soils in the river terrace zone is that they retain moisture. In consequence they can be planted earlier than freer-draining soils in the granite zone. On the other hand these moisture-retentive properties are a handicap when trying to burn felled vegetation on a farm caught by unseasonally early rainfall. The much less extensive **ŋanya** soils in the granite zone are also suitable for cultivation of early rice, but more by virtue of their position on the lower part of the soil catena, where they trap runoff, than because they are especially water-retentive. It is recognised that **kɔtu** soils are prone to drought and cannot be planted until the rains are well set (cf. Land Resources Survey 1979).

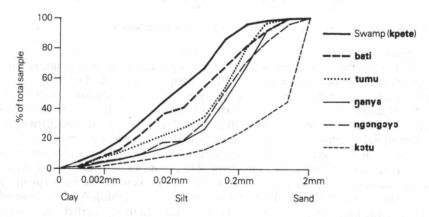

Figure 3.12 Sediment analysis for six Mogbuama soil types.

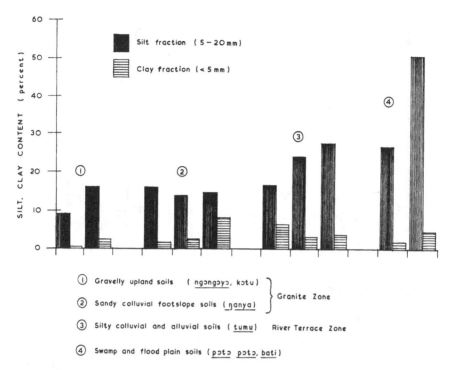

Figure 3.13 Fine particle fractions for major soil types in Mogbuama.

These distinctions are confirmed by the samples analysed for particle size (Figs 3.12 and 3.13). The 5–20 μm silt fraction is the most important determinant of water availability in tropical soils (Pitty 1978, pp. 133–5). **Tumu** soils have the highest proportion of silt of all the upland soils analysed, thus confirming the distinction farmers draw between soils in the river terrace and granite zones. The data also confirm that the suitability of **ŋanya** soils for early rice is probably largely a question of location. The samples examined were not markedly different from **kɔtu** and **ngɔngɔyɔ** soils in terms of silt content. It should be added that all samples examined were unusually low in clay because of exposure to heavy rainfall for a number of weeks prior to collection.

Most Mogbuama farmers believe that yields from rice farms in the river-terrace zone are generally better on average than yields from farms in the granite zone. Harvest data (Ch. 6) tend to confirm this proposition. Local opinion is agreed, however, that the issue is a complex one, and that it would be difficult to say how much better results are due to soil moisture conditions on the one hand and greater intrinisic fertility on the other. Mogbuama farmers are conscious that the harvest is very dependent on the extent to which a cleared farm burns well. Farms in the granite zone are generally fallowed for longer than farms in the river-terrace zone and the greater bulk of vegetation increases the ash available from a good burn. Conversely, farms in the river-terrace zone

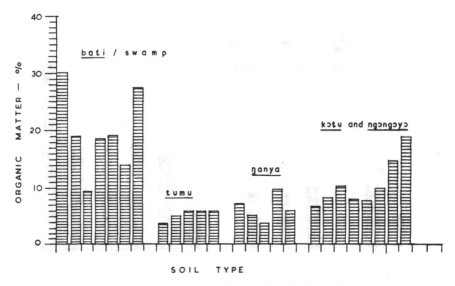

Figure 3.14 Organic matter content, samples of four major soil types.

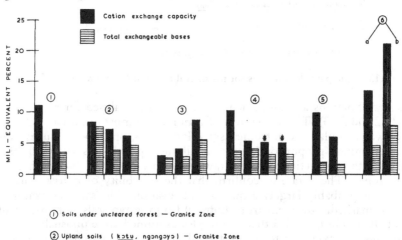

① Soils under uncleared forest — Granite Zone

② Upland soils (k<u>ɔtu</u>, ngɔngɔyɔ) — Granite Zone

③ Sandy colluvial footslope soils (<u>ŋanya</u>) — Granite Zone

④ Silty colluvial, alluvial soils (<u>tumu</u>) — River Terrace Zone

⑤ Silty colluvial soils extensively modified by soil-ingesting termites (<u>kɔkɔ</u>) — River Terrace Zone

⑥ Flood plain and swamp soils (a. <u>bati</u>, b. <u>kpete</u>)

✳ <u>tumu</u> soils identified by farmers as below average in fertility

Figure 3.15 Soil fertility – various Mogbuama soils compared.

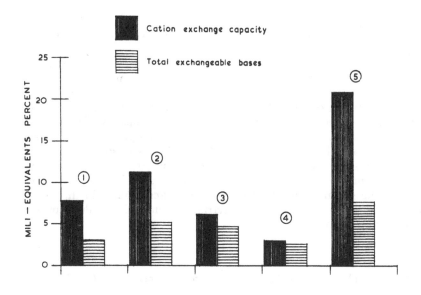

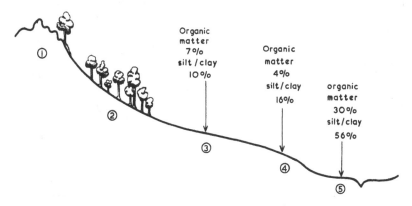

① Forested hill crest with bare granite outcrops

② Bush fallow (c. 15years)

③ Upland rice farm, gravelly soil (ngɔngɔyɔ) over granite

④ Early rice farm, sandy soil (ɲanya) on colluvial footslope

⑤ Water course planted to floating rice

Figure 3.16 Variations in soil fertility across a catenary profile in granite zone.

caught by early rainfall sometimes hardly burn at all, and sometimes do very badly as a result. All Mogbuama farmers would agree that swamp and **bati** soils are especially fertile.

Swamp and **bati** soils have the highest organic content. The greater average length of fallow and more reliable burn on farms in the granite zone are reflected in the figures for organic material (Fig. 3.14). It is less easy to draw any clear distinctions between **tumu** soils in the river terrace zone and **ŋanya** and **kɔtu** soils in the granite zone on the basis of cation exchange capacity (CEC) and total exchangeable bases (TEB), except to note that the samples of **ŋanya** soils are particularly poor in bases (Table 3.1 and Fig. 3.15). Two **tumu** soils sampled because farmers had identified them as especially infertile proved to be below average in terms of CEC (Fig. 3.15). The poorest sample of all (in terms of TEB) was the soil modified by soil-eating termites (**kɔ́kɔ́**). In the catenary profile illustrated in Figure 3.16 soil fertility declines down slope until the swamp portion is reached.

Table 3.2 Sample data for Soil Series represented in Senehun boli (van Vuure *et al.* 1972).

Soil series*	% silt	pH	% carbon	Cation exchange capacity (me/100g)
Upland				
Njala	21.7	4.5	2.78	13.22
Upper river terrace				
Bonjema	38.7	4.6	2.36	8.43
Mokonde	22.7	4.5	1.7	7.29
Middle river terrace				
Taiama	33.5	4.4	3.24	14.15
Kania	23.5	5.0	2.73	11.07
Nyawama	14.6	4.3	1.26	6.72
Lower river terrace				
Pujehun	17.0	4.4	2.71	8.86

* All data for A-horizon (0–10 cm) samples.

The soil survey for the Njala area (van Vuure *et al.* 1972) makes it clear that the low to very low fertility of Mogbuama soils is typical for central Sierra Leone. Data for river terrace soil series in Senehun boli, adjacent to the southern border of Mogbuama, are summarised in Table 3.2, and confirm that although as a group the river terrace soils are very varied, some are of above average agricultural potential. On the other hand, these silty **tumu** soils often suffer from erosion risks, especially at the junctions between terrace levels (cf. Millington 1985b). This is a point of which Mogbuama farmers are not unaware.

Administration and politics

Administratively, Mogbuama is a section headquarters in Kamajei Chiefdom, Moyamba District (Fig. 3.17). Kamajei Chiefdom was created in 1950 from two smaller chiefdoms, Kamagai and Maje. The northern border of Kamajei Chiefdom is also the boundary between Southern and Northern Provinces, and the ethnic and linguistic divide between the Mende and the Temne. A significant number of Mogbuama residents speak Temne, and several features of social organisation – especially agricultural work groups – appear to reflect Temne influence.

The village is seven kilometres north-east of the Chiefdom headquarters at Senehun. The main footpath from Senehun north to Gondama (the head-

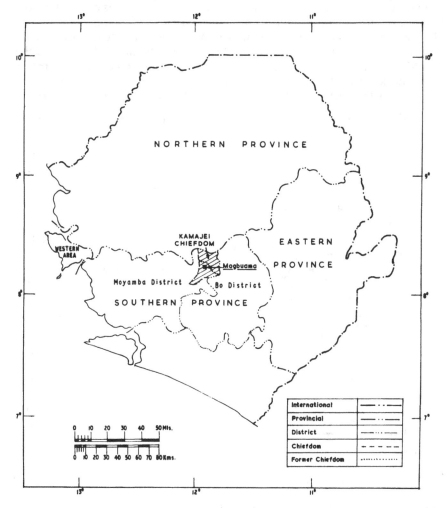

Figure 3.17   The Mogbuama and Kamajei chiefdom.

quarters of the former Maje Chiefdom) runs through Mogbuama. A former major 'hammock road' from Senehun into the highlands of eastern Sierra Leone once ran across Mogbuama territory three kilometres to the south of the village. Prior to the opening of the Bo–Taiama road across the southern part of Kamajei Chiefdom in 1974 the main external connection was by dirt road (constructed 1945) southwards from Senehun to Pelewahun (near Njala) and then onwards to the railhead at Mano. In 1977 the development agency CARE built a farm-access track from Mogbuama to Fala junction on the Taiama–Bo road. This track allows vehicles access to Mogbuama during the five months of the dry season. Two substantial bridges would be needed to keep the road open in the rains. When the road is closed Mogbuama is reached by walking either from Senehun or Fala, or if coming from northern Sierra Leone, from Yele, 20 km to the north. The region from Mogbuama northwards is one of the most extensive roadless tracts in south-central Sierra Leone (cf. Fig. 3.2).

In the 19th century the area around Mogbuama was affected by three main political influences: the affairs of the polity which Abraham (1978) terms the Kpaa Mende State, of which Taiama, 15 km west of Mogbuama, was a major centre and at times the capital (Fig. 3.18), the activities of warlords in the highlands to the east (several prominent Mogbuama families claim eastern

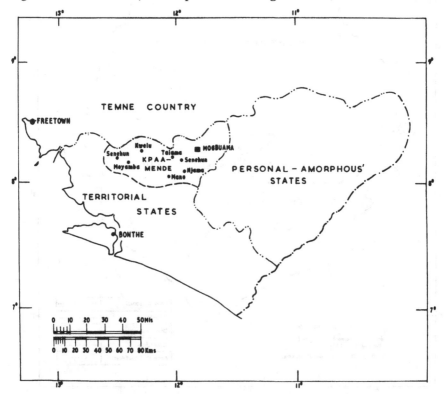

Figure.3.18   The Mende country and the pre-colonial Kpaa-Mende state (Abraham, 1978).

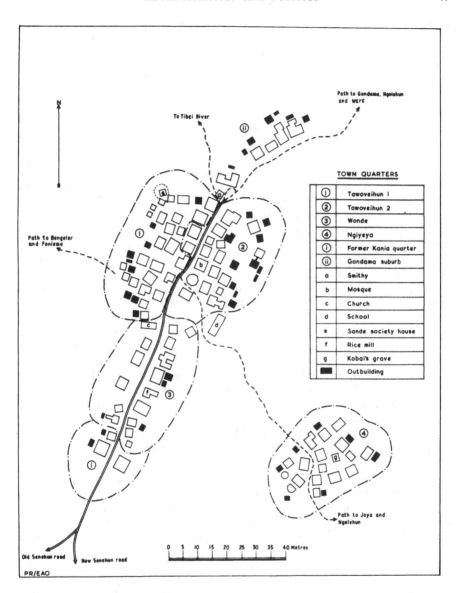

Figure 3.19 Mogbuama village.

origins, i.e. from Kono, Kailahun and Guinea), and finally, British trading, missionary and military interventions from the coast. Opposition to the extension of British administrative control to the Sierra Leone interior culminated in the uprising of 1898, in which Taiama played a major part (Abraham 1978). In the period immediately prior to British colonial control, Mogbuama, in common with other agricultural villages in the region, came under the patronage and protection of various warriors, one of whom, Kobai, built a stockaded settlement, Ngiyeya, now one of the four quarters of the present village (Fig. 3.19). Inaccessible and with few export resources, the region north of Senehun was only lightly incorporated into wider regional and international systems during the colonial period.

Today the bulk of production is still for subsistence and local exchange and direct interventions by central government are few and limited in impact. Apart from three primary school teachers in Mogbuama and one in Gondama, whose salaries are paid by the Ministry of Education, central government has little if any direct contact with Kamajei Chiefdom north of Senehun. In the past there has been the occasional agricultural extension effort directed to the development of tree crops, and Maje and Kamagai Chiefdoms were both designated as areas for soil erosion control in the 1940s (Millington 1985a). Sustained contact with agricultural development agencies began as recently as 1982, when some Mogbuama farmers registered with the Moyamba Integrated Rural Development Project. This project, part of the IADP network discussed in Chapter 2, is funded by the African Development Bank, and offers the normal range of inputs to rice farmers: improved seed, fertiliser, agricultural implements and a credit package for swamp development. Understandably, its impact had only been slight at the time of fieldwork. The farming systems described below are largely if not entirely the result of indigenous initiative and informal diffusion processes.

Local government, by contrast, is very active in the Mogbuama area. Chiefdom officials visit all section towns regularly to arrange tax collection and supervise court proceedings. The paramount chief is also a frequent visitor, pursuing chiefdom political matters and arranging the upkeep (through communal labour) of local infrastructure, especially footpaths and footbridges.

The political system in rural Sierra Leone is organised around patron–client relationships. A prominent villager will be referred to as **numuwa** or **kpako** (literally, 'big person'). In Mogbuama these terms would apply to 10 or 15 men and four or five women. Each, to a greater or lesser extent, acts as a political patron to both ordinary citizens (**tali**) and to migrant 'strangers' (**hota**). The major patrons at village level are likely to support and in turn be protected by a patron at the chiefdom or national level. Cartwright (1978) shows that the system is general throughout rural Sierra Leone and extends from village to ministerial and cabinet level. In this way local grievances are often quite actively and rapidly aired at the national level, even if scope for subsequent action is limited.

Mogbuama patrons control between them the main village political and legal offices and chief position in the Poro, Wunde and Sande societies (see below). Some hold office as chiefdom councillors. In typical cases patrons also frequently lend money and negotiate crop sales. Some Mogbuama patrons have land, houses and business interests in other settlements in Kamajei chiefdom and further afield (Freetown, Bo and Moyamba, for example). Wealth and patronage go hand in hand. In many respects control of a patron–client network is as important a 'capital' asset as investment in property, cattle and tree-crop plantations, three of the main ways in which material wealth is accumulated in Mogbuama.

Although a patron–client relationship is inegalitarian it is possible to argue, nevertheless, that it is useful to both parties (Gellner 1977, Scott 1977). Mogbuama has land in relative abundance, but labour and capital are in short supply. In effect patrons gain access to labour, and clients to capital, through such relationships. Patrons turn to clients to provide, say, political support during a chieftancy contest and timely labour at crucial moments in the farming cycle. Clients look to patrons for subsistence support (rice when the hungry season is severe), financial and other kinds of help with disputes and court cases, and brokerage services, e.g. assistance in coping with government departments, schools and other external agencies (Murphy 1981). Where both sides reap real benefits from the association, patron–client relationships, despite their inegalitarian character, continue to enjoy popular moral force and political legitimacy (Scott 1977). Poorer villagers in Mogbuama expect (even demand) that those with a little wealth or good fortune should begin to act as patrons.

Gellner (1977) argues that clientelist political relationships tend to be important where the state is weak or remote. The durability of clientelism in Sierra Leone (and the apparent lack of any strong rural class consciousness, by contrast with parts of northern Nigeria, say) might best be explained by the fact that for many years the state has derived the bulk of its revenues from an enclave mining sector, and in consequence has not found it necessary to intervene very strongly in rural affairs. Rural clientelism (to follow Gellner's argument) has thrived in an atmosphere of relatively benign neglect.

Settlement pattern and population characteristics

The rural settlement pattern in central Sierra Leone is predominantly one of small to medium-sized nucleated villages, with the village farmlands forming a contiguous block around a centrally located settlement site. Mogbuama follows this pattern (cf. Fig. 4.2). With one or two exceptions, those who farmed Mogbuama land in 1983 were also resident in Mogbuama, and vice versa (the exceptions incuded two patrons, one a man, the other a woman, who had household farms, and households to go with them, elsewhere in Kamajei chiefdom, in addition to their farms in Mogbuama). As might be expected, however, the long-term picture is more complex. Some Mogbuama descent groups own land at a distance and are divided between members resident in Mogbuama and members resident in outlying villages. Even so, the situation is simple by comparison with the tangled web of farms, residence and land ownership described by Hill (1982) in Hausaland and Karnataka. Her reservations about 'the village' as a valid unit of study are not applicable in the Mogbuama case.

In the course of surveys of all 98 household farms in Mogbuama in 1983 I enumerated 549 people: 142 male adults, 184 female adults and 223 children. The farm household is a seasonal 'economic' subdivision of the residential household, **mawɛɛ** (see later). Some older members of residential households have no direct attachment to any household farm, but maintain themselves from private farms of groundnuts and swamp rice. I know of about 25 such adults. Allowing for the addition of this last group, therefore, a reasonable estimate for the population of Mogbuama during the farming season in 1983 might be 575 persons. This makes Mogbuama a medium-sized village by Sierra Leonian standards.

Chiefdom tax is paid by all residents deemed to possess a taxable income: i.e. most adult males and some adult females (e.g. widows and divorced women who support themselves by trade or farming). Chiefdom records list 142 taxpayers in Mogbuama town. This is exactly the number of adult males listed in my farm household survey (note, however, that one or two males listed as adult are not yet quite old enough to be taxed and that some females are liable for tax in their own right). Taxpayers constitute 25% of the estimated total population, therefore. Figure 3.20, based on tax return data, shows the size and distribution of all settlements in Kamajei chiefdom, assuming the same ratio of taxpayers to total population throughout. On this basis the chiefdom population total would be about 7500 (1812 taxpayers), with 16% of the total in Mogbuama section, and about 50% of the total population of the section in Mogbuama town.

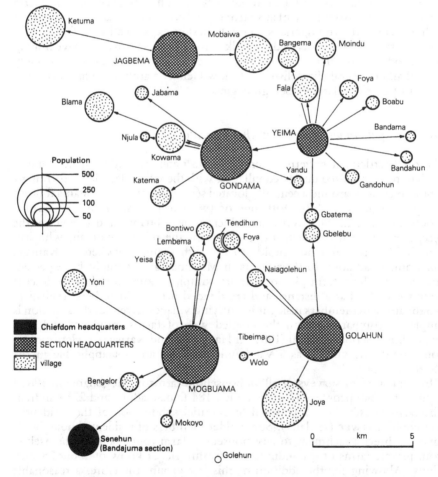

Figure 3.20 Settlement size and distribution, northern Kamajei chiefdom.

In terms of taxpayers, Mogbuama is second in size only to Senehun, the chiefdom headquarters. Gondama, headquarters of the former Maje chiefdom surpasses Mogbuama in numbers of buildings, but because of its isolation has many absentee landlords. A number of Gondama people with trading interests base themselves in Mogbuama, because it is closer to the main road. Intervillage migration within Kamajei chiefdom is common and straightforward. Migrants from within the chiefdom are not considered 'strangers'.

Throughout the chiefdom, population densities range from 10 to 20 persons per square kilometre, a low figure by national standards but not untypical of some of the more isolated parts of south-central Sierra Leone (12 out of 52 chiefdoms in Southern Province had population densities in this range in 1974). The 1974 census total for Kamajei chiefdom was 6557, an increase of only two persons over the 1963 census figure. Kamajei is one of 28 chiefdoms nationwide to show either decline or no increase in population between 1963 and 1974. Low rates of *rural* population growth in Sierra Leone (typically 0.5–1.0% per annum for the period 1963–74, as distinct from a national rate of 2.8%) are the result both of high infant mortality and outmigration to cities and the diamond mining areas. An estimated current population for Kamajei of 7500 would be consistent with a slowing of outmigration in recent years due to decline in the mineral sector and worsening economic conditions in urban areas (Airey *et al.* 1979). Despite possible modest increase in population density during the period 1974–83 there is as yet little sign of undue pressure on land resources locally.

Heads of farm household were in 94 cases male, and in four cases female. The majority (64%) of heads of household were Mogbuama citizens but 26% were strangers from outside the chiefdom and 10 per cent came from other villages in Kamajei chiefdom. Of the 48 adult males who were not heads of household, 27 came from Mogbuama, 11 from Kamajei chiefdom and ten were strangers. Married women comprised 69% of all adult women, but only 48% of married women came from Mogbuama. Of the remainder, 31% of wives came from other villages in Kamajei chiefdom and 20% were strangers.

Marriage is a means whereby alliances are cemented among the major descent groups in the chiefdom. Whereas it is common for a Mogbuama man to have a wife who was born elsewhere in the chiefdom (or outside the chiefdom if the man in question has spent time as a migrant) male strangers are frequently married to Mogbuama women. This is one of the main ways in which strangers become fully established clients (the landlord of a trustworthy stranger may be willing to help pay bride wealth on his behalf). The majority of unmarried women in the survey (89 per cent) were from Mogbuama. They were mainly either young and not yet married or older women (some divorced, some widowed) assisting on the farms of relatives. In four cases, however, older women controlled the farm household. Two of these women had recruited male strangers to assist with the work.

Social organisation

Households and descent groups
It is useful to distinguish three levels of household social organisation in
Mogbuama. The first level is that of the farm household: the group that works
together on the farm in any given year. The second level is that of the residential
household. This group may contain several farming households. This happens
where, say, brothers are economically dependent, making separate farms, but
still reside with and accept the authority and protection of their father in 'town
business' (i.e. political matters), or where 'strangers', although requiring a
patron's accommodation and legal protection, are sufficiently well established
to make their own farms. The most appropriate designation, therefore, for the
head of a residential household is 'landlord' (**mamɔ**).

The third level of household organisation is that of **bondaa**, the family
reckoned in terms of descent. The patrilineal descent group, **ndehu**, is a
primary focus in land tenure matters, for example. 'Family business' of this
kind is transacted in periodic meetings, often held at holiday times, and in some
cases involving rituals at a shrine dedicated to a founding ancestor. In some
circumstances, the Mende also give considerable attention to matrilateral
kinship. the mother's brother, **kenya**, is an important source of help and
patronage to many young people, for example. Younger married women
appear to be especially concerned to maintain these matrilateral links.

The main significance of the levels of social organisation distinguished above
is that farm households may be re-negotiated annually, residential households
have a development cycle lasting several decades, and descent groups endure
from generation to generation. The 'annual' level, often neglected in previous
accounts of Mende social structure, is crucial to an understanding of the
relationship between social and agricultural change.

Secret societies and the court
Much of everyday life in Mogbuama is handled within the context of the
'household' structures just described. Inter-household conflict and 'public
affairs' are handled by the so-called 'secret societies' and the chiefdom courts. In
addition, town elders are involved in *ad hoc* policy making, e.g. informal
dispute settlement, and schemes involving community labour.

Two of the three main societies, **Pɔɔ** (Poro) and **Sande**, are especially
concerned with the transition from youth to adulthood. In some respects they
are not unlike British public schools. The 'secrets' acquired during initiation are
as much a question of tone, style and convention as of factual information (cf.
Murphy 1980). **Pɔɔ** initiation (for boys) takes place every 10–12 years (the most
recent session was December 1983). Fees for joining are modest and all
Mogbuama adult males, with the exception of the members of one prominent
household, are members. This exception proves that although membership
is said to constitute a minimum requirement for participation in adult affairs
and village political life 'objections of conscience' can be successfully
accommodated.

Little (1967) and Jedrej (1980) regard **Sande** as a type of 'finishing school'.
Here, girls learn practical and social skills which enhance their value as wives.

Household and family heads aspiring to social advancement are often prepared to invest heavily in a daughter's training in order to cement an advantageous marriage alliance with a powerful descent group. Initiation fees are high by village standards and the instructors are often women of some consequence. **Sande** initiation takes place annually.

The third society, **Wunde**, which operates on a chiefdom basis, is a political club of major significance among the Kpaa Mende. Membership is open only to men and, unlike **Poo**, is restricted to those who can afford the not inconsiderable fees. It is said that advancement among the senior grades of the society can cost as much as Le 1000 at a time, a large sum by village standards. The society also levies substantial fees from the family of a deceased member before burial can take place. Through fees and subscriptions of this sort the society is able to maintain its own resources for the pursuit of politics independent of powerful descent groups.

Chiefdom courts mainly deal with infringements of local bye-laws (e.g. evading community labour), petty criminal cases (e.g. theft of crops and animals), debt and breach of contract (e.g. failing to turn up for work after being paid to do so), and a range of personal disputes (e.g. slander, defamation, adultery, divorce). A typical example would be a case in which a husband sought damages and the return of bride price for a wife eloping with a lover. The court pays its expenses out of sureties deposited by plaintiff and defendant and any fines then levied. The court also oversees the administration of 'swears' (cases in which plaintiffs will require a defendant's testimony to be given in the presence of 'medicine' thought to have the capacity to harm the untruthful).

Litigation is an important medium of clientelist politics through which patrons jockey for position and seek to undermine their rivals (cf. Finnegan 1963). Knowing how and when to pick a quarrel with a rival and how to pursue it successfully through the courts involves a finely developed sense of political and legal brinkmanship. A lost case may reduce a patron to debt and client status.

Patrons and their sources of power
The patrons who dominate village politics in Mogbuama have various sources of power. Some hold local government office (Mogbuama has a section and a town chief, two assistant chiefs, and five chiefdom councillors, one of whom is a woman). Others enjoy seniority in descent groups and secret societies. A third group bases the exercise of political patronage on wealth built up through trade. members of a fourth group – literate men such as the imam, pastor and primary school teachers – enjoy influence as brokers between the community and the outside world, both in spiritual and political matters, and also in the more mundane field of letter writing and record keeping (cf. Murphy 1981).

Women suffer certain important handicaps in competing for status and political power. The most serious is that they remain, in effect, legal minors while they continue to bear children. Under the control of a husband, few women can accumulate the resources to embark on an independent political career. Nevertheless, from middle age onwards some women begin to compete on more level terms with men (some are able to build up resources through farming and trade, perhaps using part of this wealth to sue for divorce, others are able to 'inherit' clients and capital, both economic and social, from a deceased husband). The Mende accept women as chiefs. The members of a ruling house would prefer to see an able and energetic woman present herself as a candidate, if the house has no man of equal political ability, rather than lose the nomination to a rival descent group. The paramount chief of Kamajei in 1983 was a woman, Madam Boteh Sovula.

Politically, there are two or three distinct factional structures in Mogbuama each with a major patron at its apex, supported by second rank 'big persons', some of whom once led factions in their own right and others who are clients in a more formal sense, e.g. 'strangers' made good or successful former apprentices (**makɛlo**, 'a child sent for training').

Factions survive through the leader's efforts to retain the loyalty of existing supporters and recruit new members. Mogbuama, despite the diamond boom, would appear to have been more successful than many rural communities in Sierra Leone in keeping a significant proportion of its young people, in recruiting residents from elsewhere in the chiefdom, and in attracting 'strangers' from neighbouring chiefdoms (26% of heads of farm households in 1983 and 20% of wives were born outside Kamajei chiefdom). A loyal stranger is encouraged to settle by his landlord's assistance in marrying a local woman (often a woman from the landlord's own descent group). Returned migrants and traders frequently bring in wives from other chiefdoms. The population figures suggest that these inflows barely serve to balance migration losses. Given this steady-state demographic environment, it is not unreasonable to predict that the success or failure of individual factions will be predicated on a good deal of internecine struggle.

Faction leaderships in rural Sierra Leone are constantly alive to the need to mobilise new resources to sustain their networks of followers and beat off challenges. In recent years typical sources have included cash advances on commodity purchases from Lebanese traders, resources from the national political system (e.g. allocation of government-imported rice to Members of Parliament for distribution during the hungry season), and loans and other inputs from agricultural and rural development projects. Village and chiefdom patrons often act as 'loan brokers' between their clients and IADP projects. This is explicitly encouraged by IADP managements (Karimu & Richards 1981) and is mutually beneficial to patron and project. From the patron's point of view, the ability to fix a loan for a client helps retain the client's loyalty. From the point of view of hard-pressed IADP officials, beset by often quite unrealistic targets for subdividing large capital sums into tiny packages and disbursing them over huge and inaccessible terrains, two or three willing village agents able to line up sizeable followings (and chase them up when repayment is due) are a godsend.

Community labour
Although factional competition is often intense, Mogbuama can also unite to carry out projects on a town or section basis. All tax payers, except the handicapped and infirm, traders, teachers, chiefs, chiefdom councillors, **makayia** (town messenger), **helemɔ** (town crier) and some young people, under full-time training (e.g. a blacksmith's apprentices), are liable for **ta yenge** (town work). Altogether about 50–60 men from Mogbuama town (and a

similar number from the rest of the section) can be mobilised for community work under these arrangements. Heads of household with non-taxed male dependents will nominate one of the latter to work on their behalf.

Once community work has been decided upon by the chiefs, they notify the town foreman (**ganga**), who in turn informs four 'headman' one for each quarter, whose responsibility is to ensure that all those liable for work turn out at the right place and time. Whether the work is called by town or section chief depends on the nature of the project. Clearing paths and building stick bridges across streams in the rainy season are section projects, for example. The community is responsible for five such bridges in Mogbuama section (but not the temporary palm-log bridging necessary to open the Fala track to vehicle traffic in the dry season: this was constructed on the basis of subscriptions from the town's 27 traders). Rebuilding the primary school – a self-help project undertaken in 1983 – was also considered a matter for the whole section.

Town, section and paramount chiefs are sometimes able to 'beg' community labour to help in their private ventures (farm work and house building, for example), but they would be expected to give generously in return. Such work is not compulsory, whereas proper community work very definitely is. Failure to turn out for legitimate community work carries a stiff fine, though this might be 'begged down' depending on the circumstances.

Religion
Mogbuama has a mosque and a UMC (Methodist) chapel. The majority of residents would claim allegiance to Islam or Christianity, with Christians perhaps slightly in the majority. Mosque and church are vigorously supported (each day evening prayers in the chapel are attended by 20–30 people). Some youths and younger adults belong to an Aladura church, a denomination of Nigerian origin (Peel 1968). There is little evidence of rivalry between the two major faiths. Religious allegiance appears not to be a factor of consequence in local politics. The Mogbuama primary school was a joint venture between Muslims, Methodists, and the Catholic Mission (although there are, apparently, only a few Catholics in the village).

Moyamba Integrated Rural Development Project
Mogbuama lies in the sphere of operations of the Moyamba Integrated Rural Development Project, one of the component projects in the national network of IADPs (cf. Fig. 2.1). This project, funded by the African Development Bank and administered through the Ministry of Agriculture, began operations in 1980. It first registered farmers in Mogbuama in 1982. An extension agent covering Mogbuama is stationed at Senehun.

In common with other IADPs in Sierra Leone it offers small farmers credit (both seasonal loans and loans to develop swamps for rice cultivation) and a range of material inputs (principally fertiliser and seven or eight 'improved' rice varieties). These inputs can be supplied as part of a credit deal or bought for cash. The standard seasonal loan is Le 91.50 per three acres, and a swamp loan is Le 300.00, paid in three instalments. Ten Mogbuama farmers (all male) registered with the project in 1982. All took seasonal loans, and three took swamp loans in addition, although they have yet to develop such farms. Of the ten, two farmers dropped out in 1983 (one because of difficulties in repaying his loan). The eight farmers who continued their membership in 1983 were joined by 16 new recruits (including four women) all of whom applied for seasonal loans.

So far, then, about 20% of all Mogbuama households are represented on the project. It is interesting to note, however, that only one stranger farmer has qualified for membership. As already noted, the project requires local patrons to vouch for potential members, with the consequence that clientelist politics and project operations become intertwined. No farmer has yet applied to the project for fertiliser or 'improved' seed. All rices currently grown in Mogbuama are indigenous varieties or long-standing introductions which have acquired Mende names.

External linkages
During the dry season one or two commercial vehicles reach Mogbuama each day. At other times, road transport to Freetown or Bo begins at Senehun or Fala junction on the Bo-Taiama road (Fig. 3.12). One of the produce traders in the village once had a hand cart, but otherwise there are no wheeled vehicles. There are few, if any, bicycles in Mogbuama.

There is no regular or periodic market in Mogbuama or environs. Retailing (principally of necessities such as rice and kerosine) is done as a side-line by Mogbuama's resident produce merchants. Women petty traders sell one or two luxuries, e.g. cigarettes. Travelling traders – drug peddlers and cloth sellers, for example – visit the village from time to time, but for most purchases (and for most types of medical treatment) Mogbuama residents would have to travel to Bo (40 km) or Njala (25 km). Senehun, the chiefdom headquarters, is a little larger than Mogbuama but offers only a restricted range of facilities.

Until 1976 children had to be sent out of Mogbuama to attend primary school. Gondama has had a small primary school since the 1920s, but most Mogbuama children would be sent to relatives in Senehun or Njala to attend school. The first intake of children to Mogbuama's own primary school graduated in 1983. Seven boys sat for secondary school entrance, two or three then leaving the village to take up places in Bo and Njala.

Between a quarter and a third of Mogbuama children under eleven currently attend school. Parents see education as the key to entering the relatively privileged world of urban, formal sector, employment. Only a few have the resources, however, to gamble on success in the educational race. For their children to sit the secondary school entrance examination, for example, Mogbuama parents had to find Le 10.00–15.00 per child to cover fees, transport to Njala (the examination centre) and overnight accommodation. In 1983 the West African Examination Council common entrance examination paper was cancelled at short notice due to a breach in security but the news did not reach Mogbuama until too late. Parents thus had to find extra money to cover transport and accommodation for the rescheduled examination. This was at a time, just prior to the onset of the 'hungry season', when all available financial resources were needed for farming (Ch. 7).

Despite these kinds of obstacles a number of Mogbuama citizens have achieved educational success and are well established in formal-sector urban employment (the invitation to a Christmas dance arranged by one of the leading descent groups in Mogbuama named sponsors from places including Njala, Bo, Freetown, and Abidjan). In some cases successful migrants are active in re-investing their wealth in Mogbuama. Two substantial cemented houses have been built by migrant big men, for example. Some outmigrants have invested in small coffee plantations. Others sponsor strangers and clients to manage rice and groundnut farms. I noted two such cases in 1983, and expect the trend to increase as urban living costs continue their rapid rise.

Success is much harder to achieve for outmigrants without formal educational qualifications. Some Mogbuama citizens are labourers, traders or artisans in Bo, Freetown, and the diamond fields. I have no data on remittances to the village from such migrants but since many Mogbuama farmers send rice to their urban kin in return it appears unlikely that any large positive balance accrues to the village account from such sources.

Summary

This chapter has provided an introduction to the farming-system case study by describing landscape and social organisation in the case-study village, Mogbuama, a medium-sized settlement on the western edge of the escarpment zone in central Sierra Leone. Attention has been drawn to the importance of soil catenary sequences and of the differences between the moisture-retentive soils of the scarp-foot zone of river terraces to the west of Mogbuama and the freer-draining upland soils of the granite zone to the east. The story unfolded in subsequent chapters concerns the way in which farmers exploit the potential of these different soils for rice farming purposes, and the difficulties they encounter. From the social perspective, particular attention has been drawn to the significance of patron–client relations in village politics. Subsequently it will be shown that the material on clientelism is important in understanding local approaches to risk avoidance and agricultural innovation.

4 Land and labour

Types of farm

Household farms and early rice

The most important category of farm in Mogbuama (as in any Mende village) is the **kpaa wa**, the household rice farm. A few wealthier or older people – merchants, office holders and independent-minded old women – support themselves from business or savings, but the great majority of the population has an active involvement in a household rice farm. The **kpaa wa** is invariably an intercropped upland rice farm cultivated according to bush fallowing techniques.

Subsequent discussion turns on the issue of the significance of early rices in local farming systems. Early rice on moisture-retentive soil is (arguably) a type of wetland cultivation (in strict terms it is transitional between wetland and upland cultivation, cf. Moorman & Veldkamp 1978). However, it is appropriate to consider the early rices in conjunction with the upland farm since they are planted as part of the household farming effort (with the prime purpose of alleviating hungry season rice shortages).

The terminology for places where early rices are planted presents one or two complications. Where the **kpaa wa** occupies a catenary sequence then the early rices will be planted as part of the main farm, and the area in question will tend to be referred to by soil type, i.e. as the **tumu** or **ŋanya** part of the farm. An alternative term in English would be 'runoff plot' because the early rice crop appears to benefit from heavy runoff from the cleared upper slopes of the farm as they await planting. Sometimes, however, early rice is planted in a separate farm (**bulu**) cleared for this purpose alone. I only came across one such farm in Mogbuama in 1983, though in a sense the category might have been applied to many of the farms in the river-terrace zone (since much of the rice planted here was early rice). Deighton (1957) mentions that **bulu** plots are especially common in the Bumpe region (Moyamba District). Where the lower part of an upland farm terminates in a seasonally flooded grassland bordering one of the main streams, this is referred to as a **bati**. Bati lands are also used for early rices, and are known to be very fertile, but difficult to manage because of periodic flooding from July onwards. There were about half a dozen **bati** rice farms in Mogbuama in 1983 (cf. Figs 3.6 and 3.7).

Private farms and swamp rice

The household head sometimes sets aside a portion of the main farm for an adult dependent (e.g. a wife or adult son). This portion is known as **gbɔɔ**, and the harvest is the private property of that individual. There are a number of other types of private farm. Anyone with the money, time and access to suitable land may plant groundnuts on the previous year's rice farm. Watercourses of seasonal streams and inland valley swamps (**kpete**, or **yɛngɛ gbete** for deep swamps with water all year round) are planted with long-duration flood-tolerant varieties known as a group as **yaka** rices (Fig. 4.1). Adult dependents, both men and women, find groundnuts and **yaka** rices important as sources of income independent of the main farm. The head of household may also have a private farm of this sort, or (in about a quarter of all cases) a small tree-crop plantation (most commonly, coffee). Dry-season plots of cassava, sweet potatoes and vegetables in dry swamps also count as private farms. Farmers occasionally make private plots of cowpeas on the main rice farm immediately after the rice harvest. Private farms comprised between a quarter and one third of all farmland cultivated in Mogbuama in 1983. It needs to be kept in mind in subsequent discussion that household farm activities always take precedence over private ventures of this sort.

Figure 4.1 **Yaka** (flood-tolerant) rice planted in a seasonal water course.

In summary, priority attention in Mogbuama rice farming is paid to the upland **kpaa wa** on which dry rice predominates, but two types of wet rice are also cultivated: first, early rice planted on runoff, **bulu** and **bati** plots (all associated with the **kpaa wa**) and secondly, **yaka** rices broadcast in inland valley swamps and waterways. Early rices are part of the household farming effort, whereas **yaka** rice farms are individual projects. Taking both early and **yaka** rices together about one third of all rice planted in Mogbuama could be classed as 'wet rice'.

Who can farm?

The **kpaa wa** is directed by the head of the farm household (the definition and composition of this group is discussed later). In Mogbuama in 1983 there were 94 male-headed and four female-headed farms of this sort. A number of male-headed farms were jointly managed: e.g. a father working with one or more adult sons, an older man working with his adult nephew, or two or three brothers working together. This is similar to the Hausa concept of a gandu farm (cf. Hill 1972). It seems to be a convenient arrangement for an older man perhaps lacking the physical strength and a younger man the financial strength to cope alone. Three female-headed **kpaa wa** illustrate the range of circumstances in which women come to control such farms. One is the household farm of a successful and influential woman trader/political patron. She is a leader of the local migrant community in Freetown, but returned to farm in Mogbuama, partly to re-assert her land rights and partly to reduce the cost of the food she needs for her dependents and clients in Freetown. A second farm is that of a widow who is responsible for a number of youthful dependents, who work with her on the farm. The third is the farm of a single woman without dependents. With only herself to look after she does not have to make an upland farm. A private swamp farm or groundnut farm would do. She prefers upland intercropped rice, however.

Since there is an abundance of land in Mogbuama (see later), there are few if any restrictions on a stranger who wishes to make an upland farm. Permission to farm is granted by the head of the appropriate land-owning lineage in return for certain token payments, typically Le 4.00 and two bushels of rice. These payments will also be required from farmers from elsewhere in Kamajei chiefdom who wish to farm on Mogbuama land, though farmers in the latter group are not considered strangers (they do not require to be guaranteed by a landlord). Strangers made 20 out of 98 farms in the **kpaa wa** category in Mogbuama in 1983. Anyone with the resources and interest – citizen or stranger, man or woman – is free to cultivate groundnut or **yaka** rice, subject to the approval of the land owners. I recorded 63 groundnut farms in 1983, 27 belonging to women, and 56 farms of **yaka** rice, 12 belonging to women. strangers are not allowed to plant tree crops, however.

Land types and land tenure

Household farms can be made on any one of the three major land types in Mogbuama: the river-terrace zone, the zone of granitic rocks and the boli grasslands (cf. Fig. 3.3). The boliland is farmed only occasionally. In 1983 48 household farms were located in the river-terrace zone and 50 on the granite (Fig. 4.2). Given the significant differences between the main soil types in these two zones, farmers have to weigh up the possibility of earlier rice and higher yields in the river-terrace zone against the greater chance of being unable to properly burn the farm when caught by early rain on moisture-retentive **tumu** soils. By contrast, **kɔtu** soils in the granite zone give lower, slower, and safer yields. The farm management implications are explored in greater detail in the next chapter. The question to be raised here is to what extent do farmers have a genuine choice between **tumu** and **kɔtu** soils? The answer requires discussion of the land tenure system.

Land rights are vested in family groups (**bondaa**). Family membership is not rigidly determined by descent, however. In a society where fostering, strangerhood and clientship are common it is accepted that a powerful political figure might wish in later life to 're-work' humble or stranger origins into a more respectable family history. Although this history will be couched in terms of 'descent' this is in many cases a polite sociological fiction, and is one of the reasons why family histories and land rights are closely guarded secrets.

Some people even claim that land rights and associated family histories have been 'bought' and 'sold' in the past. I was given the following rags-to-riches story on a number of occasions (it is an archetype with details drawn from several distinct cases). The founder of such-and-such a land-holding group came to the area two or three generations ago (typically from the Kono or the Guinea Highlands) and was given land and permission to settle. By refusing to become embroiled in local politics and concentrating on farming the recently arrived stranger amasses considerable wealth. Meanwhile, the local 'big men' have run into economic difficulties (by neglecting their farms for politics, losing expensive cases and accumulating gambling debts). The quietly industrious hero of the story then steps in with a loan, for which his reward is a wife or wives and secure title to the land he works. In one account the landlord sits down with his financial saviour and while in his cups offers him 'unto half his kingdom'. In another account the established families of the town, ruined by recession and heavily in debt to a merchant or craftsman, offer their banker, in return for the cancellation of their debts, a complete family history, authenticating it to such effect (in the eyes of the British colonial authorities) that the purchaser is able to contest chieftancy elections.

Thus descent and history follow the distribution of power and wealth not the other way round. When fortune, misfortune, or clever dealing alter the balance of power and resources within the community, history and descent are adjusted to accommodate the new *realpolitik*. This point is made not to denigrate Mogbuama principles of land tenure (the invention of tradition is a stock-in-trade of politics in all societies, cf. Hobsbawm & Ranger 1983) but to help account for the very great flexibility with which apparently cut-and-dried principles of land tenure are implemented when farmland is allocated.

A number of smaller and less powerful descent groups within Mogbuama continue to exercise residual land rights embedded within the rights of more powerful groups. Where a family fallen on hard times has 'sold out' to a powerful outsider, or where a family weakened by out-migration seeks another stronger group to act as its caretaker, 'submerged' land rights will be quietly recognised. It would be foolish to act otherwise when so many people know that so many public versions of origin and descent are based on political and legal fictions.

The land tenure picture is further complicated by informal recognition of land rights traced through the mother's brother (**kenya**), and a clientelist political system which benefits from encouraging strangers to settle (benefits which are enhanced by the fact that labour is in shorter supply than agricultural

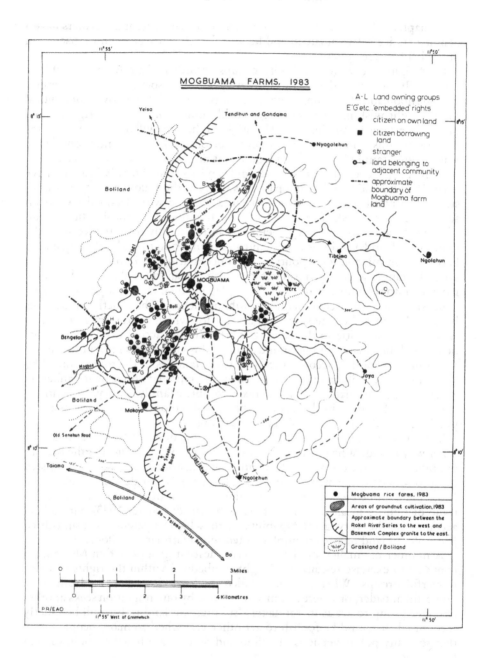

Figure 4.2 Mogbuama farms in 1983, by land-holding group and land type.

land: see below). In such circumstances it is not easy to answer even simple questions such as 'how many land-holding descent groups are there in Mogbuama?' One (not uncontroversial) answer would be 12. I have attempted to illustrate this version (the correctness of which is an issue for local politics not scholarship) in the form of a map (Fig. 4.2). The map shows, in relation to the major land types, the descent group affiliations of each farm in 1983 (including the patronage affiliations of strangers) and the embedded rights of some of the smaller descent groups.

I ought to add that stranger status, like land tenure rights, is a political variable, not a fixed sociological category. Sometimes I would be told 'so-and-so was a stranger', only to have this contradicted on a later occasion (depending on the speaker's political purposes) on the grounds that 'so-and-so has been here so long that he is really a citizen'. Strangerhood in Mogbuama is what in American academic parlance would be called a tenure-track appointment. There is a promise of a permanent position, provided the candidate is prepared to work hard and keep to the rules of the system: to 'keep the secrets of the town', as one informant put it. It is not the purpose of my map (or the business of my research) to take any positions in this delicate area. Where a farm is marked as belonging to a stranger it simply means that someone (generally the farmer himself) has at some time and for some purpose claimed or admitted to stranger status. Strangers will normally farm on land to which their landlord has rights. In the nature of things, however, a person capable of offering patronage and protection to a stranger will tend to have very extensive rights, not only in Mogbuama but also via marriage alliances in surrounding settlements as well. Thus the real choice of land types open to a stranger, through his landlord, is often quite varied. In some cases, however, it appears that the stranger's position is close to that of farm manager. In this case, it may be presumed that the stranger concerned has little choice about where to farm.

Two families settled at Mogbuama have the bulk of their land beyond the northern limit of Mogbuama territory. Members of these families frequently prefer to borrow land within village limits and lend their own farm land to strangers and residents in villages further north. Allied by marriage to Mogbuama land-holding groups with abundant land within the village limits, they experience little difficulty in securing farm land of their choice.

Taking into account access to land on the mother's side and through marriage alliances, and a stranger's access to a wide range of land types through his landlord, heads of Mogbuama household farms appear to have considerable freedom to choose to farm either in the river-terrace zone or on the granite. The merits of the two zones are frequently debated, and whereas some farmers told me they had access to only one type of land, others have found it easy enough in practice to change from one zone to the other. I would conclude that the majority of farmers are free to exercise a real choice between **tumu** and **kɔtu** soils.

Land availability and fallow periods

The 98 household farms in Mogbuama in 1983 occupied, in total, approximately 150 hectares (about 4–5% of a total cultivable area of some 30–35 km^2

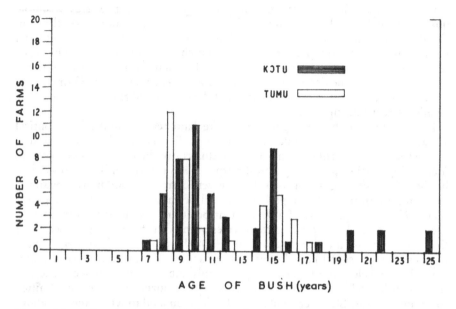

Figure 4.3   Fallow intervals (1983 farms) on **kɔtu** and **tumu** soils.

[Fig. 4.2]). At this rate of bush clearance, fallow intervals should average 19–20 years. There are two main reasons why the actual averages (Fig. 4.3) are somewhat lower. Not all land is regularly in use in the fallow cycle, and farmers believe that an 8–15 year fallow interval is optimum.

Mogbuama has a number of quite mature forest islands uncultivated for upwards of 30–40 years, partly because these are distant from the village, partly because some are adjacent to the grassland area used for cattle grazing (and farms would be subject to cattle damage), and partly because the farmers concerned cannot mobilise enough labour to clear high forest. Similarly, farmers find the grasses of the boli land difficult to clear and boli soils, except for some well-watered depressions, of low fertility and difficult to work. So farms are made in this zone only occasionally.

Mogbuama farmers deny that they are short of land. They insist that in relation to fallow intervals, each case is judged on its merits. They examine the colour and texture of the soil to assess its organic content (looking particularly at depth of rotted leaf litter) and at the character, composition and dimensions of the vegetation cover, before deciding a bush is ready to be re-farmed. There is said to be no virtue in leaving a bush to fallow for longer than the period judged necessary to ensure a good harvest, since this only compounds problems of clearing. The local view is that **tumu** soils are often adequately fertile after eight or nine years of fallow, and that the tangled swamp forest in the river terrace zone is especially difficult to clear if left too long. **Kɔtu** soils in the granite zone, on the other hand, are said to require longer periods to regain their fertility (typically, 12–15 years). Forest regrowth on **kɔtu** soils is less impenetrable to the clearers than forest regrowth on **tumu** soils.

Bush left for longer than 25–30 years requires special techniques for its cultivation. Not only does it require much more labour for clearing, but it also needs to be cultivated for two years in succession, because it is said not to give of its best in the first year. The soil is described as 'having too much manure' (an excess of nitrates? cf. Grist 1975). The rice is said to grow strongly but panicles are poor. Planting in the first year is delayed for as long as possible to maximise leaching and so overcome the problem. A more abundant harvest is expected in the second year. There was only one farm cultivated on this system in Mogbuama in 1983. Unfortunately, since the farm failed due to neglect at weeding time, my attempt to measure the harvest came to nothing.

Data concerning the length of fallow on household farms in 1983 is presented in Figure 4.3 (this excludes one or two cases where a farm had been made on **loba**, i.e. land cleared but not used the previous year, and cases where the area of bush chosen had proved too small for the farmer's needs and available labour, thus necessitating taking in an adjacent patch of under-fallowed bush, known in Mende as **kpokpo**, to make up the area). The average for the 90 farms for which I have data is 11.9 years. The average for farms in the **tumu** zone is 10.8 years and for farms in the **kɔtu** zone is 12.7 years. In both cases, however, the distribution is quite strongly bimodal (Fig. 4.3) so averages are misleading. In the river-terrace zone fallow periods peak at 8–9 years with a secondary peak at 14–15 years. In the granite zone the first peak occurs at ten years and is followed by an almost equally sharp peak at 15 years. Eight farms in the granite zone had been fallowed for between 16 and 25 years. It would be difficult to conclude from data such as these that Mogbuama farmers suffered from any major degree of land pressure.

The farm household

Rice farming requires both regular inputs of household labour for routine activities and periodic inputs of hired labour to cover the most urgent and demanding tasks. A typical household unit comprises one or two adult men, one or two adult women, and two to four children in the age range 8–15 years old. There is, however, considerable variation over the 98 farm households in Mogbuama in 1983 (Fig. 4.4). The smallest unit was a middle-aged woman farming alone. The largest unit contained 24 persons. The maximum number of adults in any farm household was 12. The distribution of adult workers was as follows: 62 households contained from one to three adult workers (accounting for 42% of the total workforce), 31 households contained four to six adult workers (accounting for 40% of the total workforce) and the balance, seven households (18% of the adult workforce), contained from 7 to 12 adult workers. Mean household size was 5.6 persons. Adult females outnumbered adult males by 184 to 140 (an average per household of 1.9 adult females to 1.4 adult males).

In Mogbuama in 1983 only two households approached in size the very large farming households still to be found in Mende land 40–50 years ago (cf. Little, 1948a, 1948b). Both these households, each with over 20 members, were headed by prominent Mogbuama patrons, and comprised younger affines,

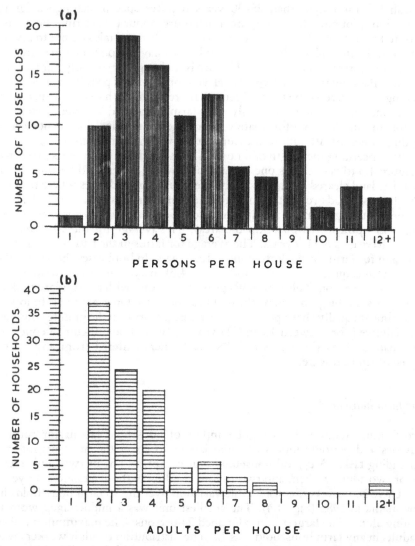

Figure 4.4 The size and composition of Mogbuama farm households, 1983; (a) household size, and (b) farm adult workforce.

wives, children, 'apprentices' (**makɛlɔ**), and 'stranger' clients. A large household unit permits the cultivation of a large farm, but the returns to the head of household may not be all that great. It is difficult to supervise activities on a very large farm, and to provide adequately for all its members, who are apt therefore to seize the chance to provide for themselves. I found it almost impossible to assess the efficiency of such farms because it was obvious that 'unofficial' harvesting and sales of rice were rife. The quiet early evening negotiation for the purchase of a 'surplus' pan or two of rice from the wife in charge of food preparation for the day is a regular feature of the life of the Mogbuama produce trader. Powerful and busy heads of large households are prepared to wink at this (they have no time or opportunity to stop it) but it means that they often have little precise knowledge of the state and productivity of their farms. Some larger farms given an illusion of inefficiency therefore.

From May or June to the end of the rice harvest in November the life of the farm household centres around the **kpowa** (the farm hut). Quite often during this period all daylight hours will be spent in the farm, and since the meals are prepared and taken here, the farm hut rather than the village residence becomes the focus for everyday social activity. Under these conditions, at meal times especially, many farm households take on the appearance of 'nuclear' families. This appearance of domesticity can be misleading, however, since the farm group is by no means necessarily a regular or permanent 'family' unit. Whereas some household units are stable for season after season, other farming households are short-term arrangements, perhaps for a single season only. Although those who work together are often linked by kinship or marriage, there are other cases in which the main or even sole link between the adults sharing the farm work is the farm itself. Thus, against farm households composed of husband, wife and their children, or an uncle, nephew, their wives and elderly relatives, I have records of households along the following lines: a politically influential woman who has recruited a younger male client to act as farm manager, a man and a woman who found it convenient to come together to make a farm because both had recently divorced, and a woman trader from Bo, who came to Mogbuama to assist a friend on his farm rather than see her trading capital depleted in the pre-harvest slack season. Any appearance of domesticity in these cases is limited to the farm hut, and the individuals concerned go their separate ways upon reaching the town in the evening.

Much literature on peasant economy makes the assumption that subsistence production is inextricably embedded within longer term issues of family organisation and household reproduction (cf. Fortes 1949, Goody 1958, Sahlins 1974). Bloch (1973), for example, treats kinship as a medium of account through which subsistence producers build up and discharge long-term debts and obligations. Whereas it would be wrong to disregard the long-term perspective altogether, it is also important to understand that each year's rice farming in Mogbuama is to a significant degree a free-standing unit of account. Not all households are embedded within 'the development cycle of the domestic group'. Those that are not, pay off their members at the end of a season like sailors at the end of a voyage. In cases of this sort the 'farm husband' or 'farm wife' will have agreed at the outset to work for a fixed reward, e.g. all their food needs during the year and so many bushels of rice when the harvest is in. At this point the household is dissolved. Undoubtedly, transactions of this kind are facilitated by the fact that computations in terms of rice bushels are a widely accepted 'currency' for assessing loans, debts, fines, and farm productivities.

Household work – the roles of men, women, and children

The farm household unit copes with the routine business of the farm. The work is to some extent specialised by gender and age. Men clear, plough (hoe), and make fences to protect the rice from rodent pests (notably the cane rat). Women take responsibility for cooking, weeding, tidying up the farm after ploughing, and prepare the rice for the barn after the harvest (including parboiling when there is sufficient early rice to be sold). Children assist the women, and carry out a multitude of fetching and carrying tasks. From age 8–9 girls help with weeding and boys assist with ploughing.

Cooking is a major item, and is especially important on those occasions where a large labour group is necessary. The taste and quality of the food influences the amount of work done. A work party may abandon its task if the food is not well prepared. During the early part of the farming season when the majority of streams are still dry, supplying work parties with drinking water and obtaining enough water for cooking requires considerable effort on the part of the women. Fetching and carrying water, and taking water to the workmen when required, is a task often assigned to children. Bird scaring – necessary both in the week after the rice has first been ploughed and then for about a month or six weeks between panicle emergence and harvest – is the concern of all available members of the household, but is an activity in which children and old people figure prominently. It is not uncommon to meet children normally away at school who have been recalled for bird scaring and harvesting work.

Gender specialisation is not hard and fast. Some women and girls help with ploughing. Men help out with weeding if the women cannot cope alone, and everyone works together on bird scaring and harvesting. In the relative privacy of life based around the **kpowa**, men (especially young men) will cook if they have to, and it is not uncommon to see boys as well as girls helping prepare the family meal. I once shared a meal prepared by a man in front of his wife in the farm hut. Having quarrelled with her, he cooked food to assert his independence, but I doubt he would have dared try on such a demonstration in town (at least I hope not, since the results were nearly inedible). I was told about a woman in a neighbouring settlement who was willing to go brushing farms. This was an unusual case, however. Brushing and tree felling were the most exclusively male preserves of all Mogbuama farming activities.

My data and observations of daily household farm work suggest that men and women work equally hard (cf. Spencer & Byerlee 1976). Male farming duties tend to be concentrated in the earlier part of the year, however. Men are hardly ever seen in the village in daytime between February and the end of ploughing (July). From then onwards they are much more 'visible' off-farm. Older men have more time for court and politics. Younger men more frequently travel to Bo to sell produce once the early rice harvest has commenced, or spend time out and about on the farm tracks and byways hunting or setting and inspecting traps. Women are at the farm day-in day-out from June onwards, but spend considerable amounts of time earlier in the season on their own specialist interests, notably cotton spinning and fishing. In the late dry season it is a daily occurrence to meet large parties of women –

sometimes 50 or more – off to fish in the surviving pools on the nearly-dry Mogboe and Tibai rivers.

Work rhythms for children tend to follow those of the women, but the older boys may be quite heavily involved in the miscellaneous tasks associated with brushing, felling, and clearing the farm. It always surprised me how important the labour of children was in terms of routine farm operations. They 'fill in' in so many useful ways; laying fires, fetching firewood, stirring the pot, collecting vegetables for the meal, collecting water, taking it to the labourers while working, pounding rice, chasing off stray goats and cows, scaring birds, and generally supplementing adult activities in ways too numerous to measure, but which clearly must add quite significantly to the productivity of the household farming unit.

While gender specialisation in routine agricultural labour is an important aspect of current agricultural practice in Mogbuama, I have little direct evidence that the burdens fall disproportionately on women and children (an argument often made for other parts of Africa). Mogbuama farm households are generally too poor, and too constrained to fit all the vital tasks in on time, to permit any major degree of male 'exploitation' of female labour, in the simple sense of male 'leisure' consumed at the expense of women's work. This comment is perhaps less true of the household of a prominent political patron with numerous wives. Even here, however, it can be argued that wives are recruited to the household more because marriage alliances are an important element in local politics, than because the head of household has any economically motivated plans to exploit female labour. Some patrons appear to be quite pushed to sustain their large households, and their first interest is to ensure that any new addition to the household, whether wife, stranger, apprentice or foster child, is self-supporting. There can be no doubt that young wives are expected to work very hard. I think I would conclude that this is more because they are young than because they are women (cf. Bledsoe 1984). Participating in brushing and ploughing (Ch. 5) made clear to me the enormous labour demands placed on young dependent males.

Finally, I suspect it might be easy to overstress gender specificity in agricultural task allocation as a cultural obstacle to technological change. Men and women stress their belief that certain tasks belong properly to men or to women, but my study uncovered some evidence that these proprieties are abandoned if the need arises. The best example of this is the number of men in poorer households who said they helped women with weeding when time to complete the work was running short.

Non-household labour

There are several points during the farming year when the farm household is unable to cope on its own. Non-household labour is most important in the case of brushing, ploughing and harvesting. These activities require either casual hired labour, or more commonly, the assistance of a work group. Outside labour is also required to help control the burn, and is frequently called upon for weeding and for fencing the farm against rodents. The organisation of labour in these cases, however, tends to be informal.

Previous studies (Njoku & Karr 1973, Spencer 1975, Johnny 1979, Njoku 1979) have established that average labour inputs into upland rice farms in central Sierra Leone are of the order of 80–90 work-days per bushel of rice planted. In the course of fieldwork I was able to compile a detailed record of all labour inputs from non-household sources (the data for work groups are complete, but are estimates for casual hired labour). Work groups supplied 3251 work-days of labour, distributed as follows: brushing 11%, ploughing 36%, and harvesting 53%, and 300–500 work-days are estimated to have come from casual sources. In total, 300 bushels of rice were planted on household farms in Mogbuama in 1983. Thus, taking an aggregate input of 80 days labour per bushel planted as a standard, 13% of all labour came from work group sources, and a further one or two per cent from casual labour.

Hired labour
There are no full-time hired labourers in Mogbuama, but a number of younger and poorer farmers, both male and female, work for wages on an occasional basis. In 1983 a typical contract for a day's work was Le 1.00–1.50 cash and a meal. The cash payment is generally made in advance. Direct hired labour is most important during the hungry season, when a number of poorer farmers are willing to postpone their own farm work for the price of a meal and a few cigarettes, and then again at the beginning of the dry season when produce traders recruit carriers to headload rice and other commodities to the Bo road at Fala. I doubt that direct hired labour accounts for more than 10–20% of all non-household labour in Mogbuama (see discussion in subsequent chapters).

Tee
The simplest kind of labour group, **tee** ('by turns', cf. **teelee**, 'to go from place to place' [Innes 1969]) is an informal arrangement among neighbours or kin to join together to work on the farms of members according to a rota. One such group had five members (with adjacent farms) who reciprocated labour for ploughing and fencing. No financial transactions or legal commitments are involved but the workers expect to be provided with food by the recipient of the day's labour. Women sometimes form **tee** groups for weeding.

Bɛmbɛ
A second category of labour company is the special purpose work group. Where such a group is formed to hoe broadcast rice it is known as **bɛmbɛ**. A **bɛmbɛ** is a co-operative in which the members agree to work together for a fixed number of days. The days available are divided equally among the members. The host for the day is responsible for feeding the group. Members in need of money may decide to sell one or more of their turns for cash to the highest bidder. In addition, it is common for members of a **bɛmbɛ** to agree that they will work a set number of days for general hire. Average hire rates were Le 1.50 per worker in May, the early part of the ploughing season, rising to about Le 1.80–2.00 in late June. Some groups have written constitutions, and defaulting members can be taken to court for breach of the rules. Others are

wary of formality. All co-operatives are supposed to be registered with the chiefdom authorities, and this involves a registration fee.

In Mogbuama in 1983, three **bembɛisia** (pl.), with memberships of five, eight and eight respectively, were formed by adult workers, mostly heads of households working on their own account. A fourth group with 14 members comprised mainly dependent youths, and two other groups, with ten and 13 members respectively, were formed by children about 10–12 years old. Two of the three adult groups worked for each member only twice. The other group worked four times per member. In this last case, 20 out of a total of 32 turns were sold (the group had eight members). Several men in this group were quite badly affected by the hungry season and indebtedness (Ch. 7) and, for them, the possibility of raising a reasonably large sum (Le 12.00–16.00) by selling one or more of the days when they were due to receive labour was a major attraction of work-group membership.

The 'youth' **bembɛ** and the two groups composed entirely of children employed a drummer to speed their work. The first of the children's groups was organised by the teachers in the primary school from among their senior pupils. The group worked first on the teachers' farms, and then on the farms of the households to which the pupils belonged. Spare turns were sold for the 'school fund'. The second group comprised some very young boys, most not at school. Despite the youthfulness of its members, this outfit had a strong self-help orientation. In fact, having appointed a literate teenager to manage their affairs, the precocious *co-operants* later decided to sack him on the suspicion that money earned from the sale of 'spare' days supposedly banked with an elder, had been misappropriated. This group did much of its work on groundnut farms.

Gbɔtɔ

The **gbɔtɔ** is a special type of **bembɛ** for youths from about 10 to 15 years old, reflecting elders' control over the labour of dependents. Each member is nominated to the group by his head of household. Since **gbɔtɔ** work is full time for the duration of ploughing (April to July) it is only heads of larger households who can afford to spare a teenage dependent for this length of time. For Mogbuama heads of household the question of whether they could afford to nominate one of their dependents to a **gbɔtɔ** was made even more difficult by the fact that no such group was based in Mogbuama in 1983: those interested in mobilising **gbɔtɔ** labour had to send their nominees to Tendihun and Mobaiwa. The latter place is 20 km from Mogbuama on the northern boundary of Kamajei chiefdom. Nevertheless, the head of one Mogbuama household had enough children and apprentices to participate in both groups in 1983.

The **gbɔtɔ** is organised by an elder who acts as manager, supervising the work and negotiating hire contracts. The work is carried out to drumming provided by a three-piece band led by a player of **kele**, a tuned slit-drum. The group manager and the older boys together mark out work portions (**mawu**) for each session, and these are completed in a competitive spirit. The music spurs on the work, with the **kele** by turns praising the energetic and chiding the slow.

Working hours are long, typically from 7.00 a.m. to 6.30 p.m., and work closes each day with a session in which punishments are handed out for lateness and laziness. A late arrival may find himself dressed in the equivalent of a dunce's hat (made from palm fronds) and subject to a verse or two of a mocking chorus, or nominated to carry home all the hoes. This combination of music and discipline is said to ensure that a **gbɔtɔ** will achieve more in one day than any similar group, despite the youthfulness of the workers. The group is capable of ploughing an average size household farm of approximately 1.5 ha in two days. In consequence, **gbɔtɔ** labour is especially eagerly sought after, and many household heads without nominees in the group are prepared to pay quite heavily to obtain it. **Gbɔtɔ** work is often done to a low standard, however, leaving much subsequent covering up and filling in to be done by household members (up to two weeks per day worked), a fact which organisers of other kinds of **bɛmbɛ** hasten to point out.

Hire rates for a **gbɔtɔ** with 13 workers varied from Le 19.00–20.00 per day earlier in the ploughing season (mid-May) to Le 28.00–30.00 at the end (late June) when the work is harder due to weed growth and farmers are anxious to complete their farms due to the advance of the rains. The money is generally saved by the manager and divided among the participants in the group at the end of the ploughing season. Some heads of household will insist on claiming some or all this money, but in other cases the boy will be allowed to keep his earnings.

Mbele

A work party organised specifically to harvest rice is known as **mbele**. Two such groups were formed in Mogbuama in 1983. Both had 16 field workers claiming two turns each, and a 'town chief' (a political patron) and two drummers. The town chief and assistant drummer qualify for only a single turn. Each group works a basic stint of 36 days, therefore. One group then decided to work three extra days for hire.

Women work alongside men in an **mbele**: one group had two women members, the other, seven. Only two of these women were married. Generally, a married woman will only join **mbele** if her husband has at least two wives. Group rules are as follows: working hours are from 7.00 a.m. to 6.30 p.m., and the member for whom the work is performed, in addition to providing food for the day, is required to give the group half a bushel of husk rice, a pan of clean rice and a 'hand shake' of 30 cents. The value of these 'presents' is approximately Le 7.90 per day. The group meets every day, excepting Fridays, until its work is completed, and at the end of this period has about Le 250 to divide among the members (not counting earnings from any extra days sold). The earnings are divided equally among members, after token payments for services rendered have been made to the officers of the society – group leader, those who allocate stints, and the musicians.

The work routines of the **mbele** are not unlike those of the **gbɔtɔ**. When stints have been allocated an official known as the **pɔɔvɔ** starts to cut rice and gives one lash to the first person to join him who then does the same to the next person until the last one to start has no one to hand the beating on to. Stints are shared out up to ten times a day. The last to finish gets six strokes of a special palm thatch 'whip' or pays a fine (e.g. not to eat sauce for a week). Each day there is a special competition in which the last to complete the stint earns the 'privilege' of carrying the group's kerosine tin of rice back to town. Sometimes the **mbele** is divided into two groups of eight to harvest a measured portion. The winners are empowered to administer a thrashing to the losers (but they will go easy for fear of losing the next such competition!).

Some join **mbele** because the discipline means the work is done speedily, and they stand to benefit from money earned, but others (e.g. junior relatives) will be obliged to join. Where the household farm is small the **mbele** may finish the work in one day. In such cases the second day will be offered for sale. In late September 1983 the cost of hiring the group was Le 22.00, plus the 'presents' mentioned above (valued at Le 7.90) and the cost of feeding. One farmer's expenditure on rice, fish, oil, and condiments for one day's work was Le 29.50 (Le 1.64 per capita). Altogether, then, the total cost of hiring **mbele** for one day is approximately Le 52.00. The group is capable of harvesting between 25 and 30 bushels per day, according to whether the crop is sparse or abundant. If a young dependent wants to sell a turn it should be with the permission of the head of household. Women are also expected, in theory, to offer money from such sales to their husband or guardian.

General purpose work groups
Two general purpose work groups (**kɔmbi**) were active in Mogbuama in 1983. Mbla Kombi (**mbela**, father-in-law, from the days when such groups were formed to carry out bride service) allocated one turn each to its 20 members, meeting six times for brushing, and seven times each for ploughing and harvesting. A lottery was held to decide the allocation of turns: in effect, to decide which activity any individual member should receive group assistance with. Most of the members of Mbla Kombi were household heads, and several also belonged to special purpose work groups.

The group is explicitly egalitarian, laying much stress on 'self help'. This is clearly seen in the attempt to involve as many members as possible in 'official' positions. In addition to a literate secretary, whose job it is to write down the constitution and keep records of attendance, and a political patron (a 'town chief' who represents the group to the local government authorities, mediating and resolving any disputes or conflict of interest in return for work done on his farm), Mbla Kombi has a number of 'field officers' – e.g. timekeeper, judge, foreman, and 'doctor'. The job of the last is to test and pronounce fit for consumption the food provided by the member receiving the work group. Any failings in this last respect – inadequate portions, too little salt, not enough meat or oil – are punished by a series of fines, as are other evasions of the egalitarian norm, e.g. not turning up on time, quarrelling at work or skipping a work day. Shorter working hours (from 9.00 a.m. to 4.00 p.m.) is a further manifestation of egalitarianism, the group saying, in effect, 'we can be trusted to do a full day's work without all the disciplinary hocus pocus needed in the case of **gbɔtɔ** and **mbele**'. As with other types of work group, a member is free to sell his turn should he so wish. Mbla Kombi worked no extra turns for cash in 1983.

The other group – One-way Kombi – began as a dance society, formed by some of the younger people in the town to cater for their entertainment. It has both male and female members, since in Mende entertainment music of this sort men drum and women sing. From this base One-way Kombi evolved into a savings and credit society. Members pay in a small subscription each Friday evening, and are entitled to borrow from the society's funds from time to time. Loans are repaid with interest, and society funds may be used for welfare, as well as credit, in deserving cases. Thrift and credit societies of this sort are popular and widespread throughout rural Sierra Leone and Liberia (cf. Seibel & Massing 1974). Sharing these established common interests the members of One-way Kombi then began to organise agricultural work parties. In 1983, 24 male members of the group joined together for brushing, working one day for each member. The group was formed again at harvest time, this time incorporating some women members. Their working practices are similar to those of Mbla Kombi. In some years, the women of the group organise a weeding work party, but this was not done in 1983.

Another savings group, Ngiyeya Kombi, with 20 members (16 women and four men) also arranged group work in 1983, but in this case only for harvesting. Each member received one turn. Group working rules were as follows: working hours from 9.00 a.m. to 4.00 p.m., no punishments (loads are carried by the most junior), hire rates of Le 22.00 plus food for the group for the day and half a bushel of husk rice. This group met for harvesting every day except Fridays over a period of three and a half weeks from late September, and then reverted to being a savings club.

Summary

This chapter has outlined the way in which land and labour are utilised for rice production in the case-study village. The bulk of rice for subsistence is produced on the household farm. Lower slopes and moisture retentive soils are utilised for an early rice crop, important both as a hunger-breaker and for cash income. In addition members of the farm household often have private farms for personal cash income. Most swamp rice production is private business of this sort. Population density in Mogbuama is not high, and there is little evidence of land shortage or an undue reduction in fallow intervals. Land tenure rules operate in a flexible manner. 'Stranger' farmers are encouraged to settle and are readily granted land for rice farming purposes (but not for the planting of tree crops). The typical household farm is a joint venture between one or two adult men and women in which the participants are usually but not necessarily linked by kinship or marriage. Some agricultural tasks on the household rice farm are gender-specific (only men do brushing and women do the bulk of the weeding) but the overall labour burden appears to be shared roughly equally between men and women. Contributions from children are important in some tasks, e.g. weeding and bird scaring. Labour shortages are the main constraints on rice production, and few household farms can be completed without bringing in outside help. Such help is especially important in dealing with planting and harvesting bottlenecks. In the absence of a landless labouring class or a seasonal migrant workforce, most outside labour is provided by a range of reciprocal work groups. These groups are organised and operate in various ways, but fall into two main categories – self-help co-operatives and brigades of young workers organised by elders. The elaborate complexity of labour group rules intended to ensure a high work output is eloquent testimony to the strategic significance of seasonal labour scarcity in the case-study village, a scarcity common in many specialist food-producing communities throughout West Africa (Karimu 1981, Levi & Havinden 1982, Sharpe 1982).

5 The farming year

The key to understanding rice cultivation in Mogbuama is to be found in an analysis of how farmers cope with a specific sequence of seasonal risks and timing constraints. This chapter is a blow-by-blow account of the way these risks and constraints present themselves and how they are dealt with.

Choosing and brushing a farm site

Most farmers had an idea where they would make their 1983 farms before the 1982 harvest was completed. There is a preference for a new farm adjacent to the old one when possible. It is convenient to be able to make use of the old farm hut and to have a ready supply of vegetables and other farm produce at hand. Farmers with access to land both east and west of the village must weigh up the relative merits of **tumu** and **kɔtu** soils. Strangers must negotiate a site with their landlords.

Consideration is given to any special advantages or disadvantages of sites under consideration. If the bush is especially old the farmer must assess whether enough labour is available to clear the site in time for it to dry out and burn well. Old bush – fallowed for upwards of 25 years – may take twice as much labour to clear as a bush which is only 8–12 years old. As a general rule, Mogbuama farmers believe a tract of fallow land is worth considering for recultivation as soon as tree regrowth and shade have eliminated all grassy species. Many examine the soil, however, before committing themselves to a final decision. Leaf fall is described as 'the bush's own fertiliser'. Age is less important than leaf litter or soil colour as a guide to an auspicious site. An abundance of certain tree species, e.g. **mbeli** (*Harungana madagascariensis*), **tijo** (*Phyllanthus discoideus*), **ndɛwɛ** (*Macaranga* spp.), **koba** (*Sterculia tragacantha*), and **bɔbɔ** (*Irvingia gabonensis* or *Funtumia africana*?), indicates that rice will do especially well. Farmers try to avoid planting rice near **kandi** (*Anisophyllea laurina*) because the rejuvenating stumps are said to dehydrate the surrounding soil. This was clearly demonstrated in the case of a farm in the river-terrace zone where the rice crop was thin and droughty even though it had been planted on **tumu** soil in mid-June when the rains were well set.

The December holiday period provides a good opportunity for the announcement of farming plans, for family meetings to co-ordinate activities and if necessary resolve any competing claims to the same piece of land (said to be an unusual occurrence), and for interested parties to meet and plan labour groups for the following season.

Brushing of farm sites began in the last week of January. The work was carried out exclusively by men and boys. Getting and keeping a good cutlass is a topic of some concern at this time of year. One Mogbuama blacksmith makes especially fine specimens. He is able to reshape the thickest of lorry leaf springs, and once allowed me to try the one he uses in brushing. It was exceptionally heavy, but beautifully balanced and springy – a Stradivarius among cutlasses. A poor cutlass jars the arm and is quite literally a pain in the neck.

A blacksmith's output is constrained by the availability of suitable scrap metal. W visited Njala on a number of occasions during the dry season while the road remained open to bring back scrap. A good cutlass cost about Le 6.00 to Le 8.00. This and a set of hoes and harvesting knives represents quite an investment by local standards, and a number of poorer farmers may find themselves hard-pressed to find the cash. There are two blacksmiths in Mogbuama. Both will supply implements in return for labour on their farms. W's 1983 **kpaa wa** was one of the largest in Mogbuama (on which he planted 12.5 bushels of seed rice, i.e. about 5 ha). The other blacksmith had a smaller but still above average sized farm (about 2.2. ha against an average for the village as a whole of 1.26 ha).

Brushing is cheerful and not uncongenial work. Everyone is rested and well-fed after the holiday break. Rice is abundant at this time of year, and most men have a little cash to burn (mainly on cigarettes) from post-harvest crop sales. If the deeply indebted are a little apprehensive about what the year might have in store, even they are willing to be convinced that this time things are going to be different. The weather is hot, but not yet oppressively humid, and the work takes place under shade, initially at least.

Brushing involves cutting down saplings and small trees up to about 150 mm in diameter with a cutlass, and hacking through undergrowth. As they go, the workers need to keep an eye on one or two especially hazardous plants. **Nyɛbu** (*Anthostema senegalense*), if slashed incautiously, sprays a latex which irritates the eyes. **Kokaa** (? *Uncaria africana*) tangles and tears clothing, and **njewɔ** (? *Guarea leonensis*), aptly called the 'bush razor', cuts like a sharp knife.

Some of the larger trees are left to prop up the brushed material so that it dries thoroughly underneath. This is to ensure a good burn, and is especially important on the damper, moisture-retentive, **tumu** soils. These larger trees then require to be felled by axe – a separate operation when drying is well advanced. 'A farm which has been cleared but in which the big trees have not yet been felled' (Innes 1969) is known as **ndoka**.

The more promptly brushing is completed the better is the chance that the trash will dry properly and burn well. The male members of each farm household go to the farm each day to continue with the work steadily. However, it is reassuring to be able to draw upon the resources of a labour company and brush the greater part of a farm within a day or so when the flash of distant lightning in the evenings serves to warn of the impending return of the rains. In 1983 three labour companies undertook brushing work in Mogbuama – Mbla Kombi and One-way Kombi from Mogbuama and Rainbow Kombi from Joya. This last group, founded as a dance society and savings co-operative, visited Mogbuama to brush the farm of a schoolteacher who, as a skilled wood carver, makes dance masks for the group and receives agricultural work in return.

I worked with Mbla and One-way labour groups on three occasions during brushing. On 26 January, 11 members of One-way were at work in thick riverain forest along the banks of the Tibai on behalf of P, the secretary to the company. Working from 9.00 a.m. until 4.00 p.m. they managed to brush about half of what was subsequently to become a **bati** farm of 0.75 ha. One-way Kombi divides into a first and second team for work purposes. This was the second team in action, having been hired for cash to allow P to make an early start with a farm known to be potentially high-yielding but difficult to manage due to the uncertainties of the Tibai flood later in the year. The cultivation history of every plot of fallow land in Mogbuama is known in detail, and this history is often recounted during brushing.

On 9 February, both units of One-way Kombi (about 25 workers in all) brushed an area of 13-year forest on **tumu** soil belonging to W, the blacksmith. He is 'town chief' (i.e. patron) of One-way Kombi and claims to have first stimulated the formation in Mogbuama, a few years ago, of labour companies of this sort along the lines of groups he had seen in Makeni and Torma Bum. W makes a public point, for my benefit, of the fact that the second team is working better today, than the elite group. One member asserts, in answer to a question about the reason for forming a work company, that 'we all do it to help ourselves', but W is anxious for them not to waste time chatting, claiming that Mbla Kombi is a less effective group because the group is too big and argumentative. Sorting out disputes wastes much time as a result. In return for working on his farm, W supplies all members of One-way Kombi with their agricultural implements free.

On 29 January, 21 members of Mbla Kombi (three had permission to be absent) brushed an area the farmer thought would take between two and three bushels of seed rice (i.e. about 1.0 ha). The bush was nine years old, on **kɔtu** soil, and markedly less thick and difficult to clear than the forest along the Tibai or the land worked on by One-way Kombi in the two cases described above. Mbla Kombi proved to be a much tougher, louder, more aggressive group than One-way. Stints are allocated and the group divides into two halves competing to finish. Each stint takes about 45 minutes, and is accompanied by singing, shouting, banter, and quarrels. From time to time during the afternoon scuffles break out as the tense, competitive workers, geared up like boxers for a big fight, press towards the final bell. The farm owner, a young trader who rates a turn because his assistant (a Temne 'stranger') belongs to the work group, is worried whether they will complete the area he has in mind by 4 p.m. P, who leads this group as well as being clerk of One-way Kombi, quietly reassures him during a break for water, palm-wine, and cigarettes. His managerial style is different from that of the blacksmith. He listens a lot and stays out of the banter and quarrelling over the distribution of cigarettes. Nevertheless, his confidence that the work will be completed proves to be accurate, and is testimony to his ability to motivate an apparently 'difficult' group, in which there is a greater proportion of strong-minded adult members farming on their own account than in One-way Kombi.

Despite the need to complete the work before the rains start in earnest, brushing does not appear to represent a major labour bottleneck. This appears to be reflected in the fact that only 12 per cent of all group labour in Mogbuama in 1983 was devoted to brushing. There are no specialist brushing groups equivalent to **bembe** (ploughing) and **mbele** (harvesting) groups. Many farmers manage with household labour supplemented by the occasional hired labourer. Anxious farmers can bring their start date forward. Money from the recent harvest is available for jobbing labour as necessary, whereas later in the year cash shortage proves a major constraint. Per hectare, brushing requires fewer man-days than ploughing and can be undertaken at any time within the appropriate period. By contrast, rainfall and soil type closely determine when it is best to plough any given farm and exact sizeable penalties on the untimely and disorganised farmer.

It seems probable that brushing was much more of a labour bottleneck in the case of 'long-fallow' farms, where felling a single large tree might occupy a labour force for a whole day. When I once asked a man who had land rights to a patch of forest unfarmed for over 25 years why he no longer farmed there, he told me that he no longer had the labour resources to do so. He reckoned that clearing a 10-year bush required less than half the labour input, so confirming a point made in a survey, *Soil conservation and land-use in Sierra Leone*, undertaken over 30 years ago, that 'small sections of bush appear to be going back to forest because the farmers are unwilling to make the heavy effort involved in felling' because 'either the return is not considered by the rising generation to be adequate for the effort involved in brushing, or . . . older farmers are unable to make the effort with so many of the younger men away from home' (Waldock *et al.* 1951).

The burn

A good burn is crucial to the success of the upland rice farm. The ash, rich in phosphates, fertilises the soil, a fact farmers acknowledge when they choose to try out new or unfamiliar rice varieties in those parts of the farm where they have made bonfires of unburnt sticks and branches. Phosphates are frequently the limiting soil nutrient factor in forest zone agriculture in West Africa (Ahn 1970, Piggott 1954). Burning also raises soil pH.

A badly burnt farm is problematic in two major respects. First, the farmer is faced with the laborious task of piling unburnt branches into bonfires and burning them piecemeal. Many of the felled trees have to be further chopped up before this can be attempted. This can double or treble the normal workload at this time of year, and seriously delay planting. Secondly, a badly burnt farm is often very weedy, because more weed seeds survive to germinate and because the rice competes less strongly with weeds in conditions of reduced fertility.

The major cause of a poor burn is unseasonally early rainfall. Two or three heavy rainstorms in February and early March can wreak havoc on a recently brushed farm, especially if spaced at ten-day to two-week intervals. The rain prevents the felled vegetation from drying out thoroughly, and at the same time encourages early germination of the weed seeds surviving in an abundance in the soil of a mildly burnt farm. In years when the early rainfall problem is severe, farmers sometimes find themselves only able to plant half to two-thirds of the area originally brushed because of the additional labour required in clearing the farm and subsequent difficulties experienced as a result of luxuriant weed growth.

Early rainfall, then, is the most significant climatic hazard affecting farmers in

Mogbuama. According to agricultural records at Njala the rice crop was
seriously affected by early rainfall on six occasions between 1912 and 1957. The
years in question were 1918, 1923, 1932, 1936, 1939 and 1951. There have been
two occasions since when the combined totals for January and February were
three times the expected average – 1959 and 1963 (Fig. 5.1). Apart from the case
of 1918 (discussed in Ch. 1) the worst year on record seems to have been 1936,
when early rain was described by the Annual Report of the Department of
Agriculture as 'catastrophic' in its impact. Over 100 mm fell in February alone
(compared with a 27-year average of 18 mm). It would appear that serious
problems from inadequately burnt farms might, therefore, be expected to occur
as frequently as one year in seven.

The most recent year in which farm burning in Mogbuama was hindered by
early rainfall was 1981. Njala rainfall records show only moderate rainfall in the
nine weeks from the beginning of February (a cumulative total of 75 mm
compared with a long-term average for the period in question of 89 mm). Since
Njala is 25 km from Mogbuama these records may not be an altogether
adequate guide to local conditions. It is important, however, to note how the
rainfall was distributed, with 15 mm falling at the beginning of February and
88 mm in the five week period from 8 March during which the majority of
farmers burn their farms (Fig. 5.2). The graph of cumulative rainfall for this
period (Fig. 5.3) is an almost perfect logistic curve, with the rainfall events
distributed in such a way as to create the maximum uncertainty in farmers'
minds about when to time their burn. This is in contrast to 1983 when, despite
heavy rainfall in mid-March (45 mm at Njala) few farmers complained of a poor

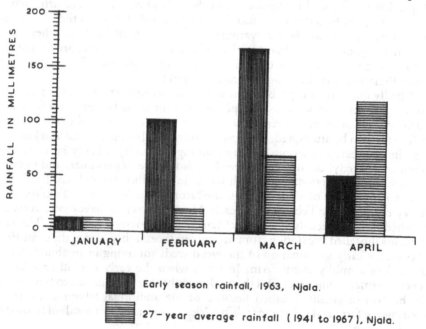

Figure 5.1   Early rainfall at Njala, 1963.

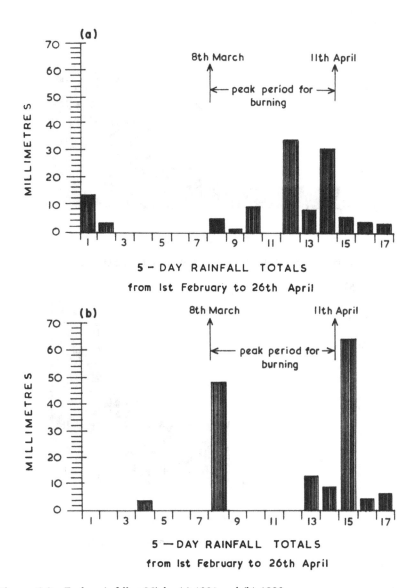

Figure 5.2   Early rainfall at Njala; (a) 1981 and (b) 1983.

burn. In this case the cumulative rainfall curve is noticeably stepped (Fig. 5.3). Early rain was followed by several weeks of settled conditions and most farmers were able to find a space in which to fire their farms successfully.

In years with excessive early rainfall the majority of farmers are liable to be affected by the problem of a poor burn. At other times the problem of a poor burn is an individual misfortune. Some farmers complete their brushing too late

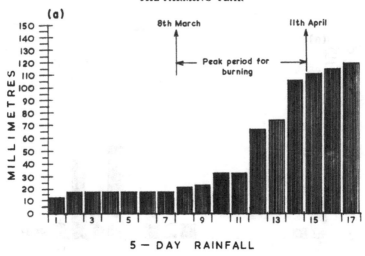

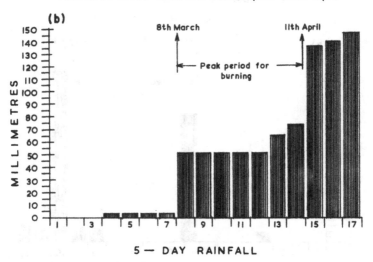

Figure 5.3 Cumulative totals for early rainfall at Njala; (a) 1981 and (b) 1983.

for the farm to dry thoroughly. Others find that a young bush (fallowed for less than seven years, say) is too meagre to burn well. This latter problem is unusual in Mogbuama, but is more common around Njala where fallow periods are shorter (especially in the case of accessible bush along motor roads where much of the felled vegetation is sold for firewood). The chances of a poor burn are heightened where species of wood-eating termites (notably *Macrotermes bellicosus*) have been especially active. Some farms in the river-terrace zone west of Mogbuama have up to 50–60 *Macrotermes* termitaria per hectare. The vegetation in this zone needs to be left longer to dry out thoroughly because of the·

moisture-retentive character of **tumu** soils. This gives *Macrotermes* time to cause trouble by eating a significant proportion of the bottom layer of combustible material and plastering with damp mud runs much of the remainder. It is this bottom layer of material that determines how well the fire catches hold and spreads when the farm is first ignited. I have heard farmers credit poor burns largely to the voracious appetites and mud-spreading habits of this species of termite. The problem is less likely to occur in the granite zone east of the village because farms there are fallowed for longer, and *Macrotermes* termitaria cease to be active in thick bush due to lack of sunlight (cf. Lee & Wood 1971).

Other cases of individually poor burns occur when farmers simply 'guess wrong'. There are a number of different theories about when to burn. Some choose to burn at night to catch the best of the breeze. Others favour the afternoon. The majority aim, if possible, to set fire to the farm before there is any heavy rain, and in 1983 all but one farm had been fired before the end of March. This exception proved to be an instructive case. The farm belonged to an old man, Q, who (because he had been ill) only finished brushing on 29 March. Friends, having completed their brushing before he had even begun, urged him to fire his farm at the first possible moment. Q did not share their sense of urgency. He reckoned that on a **kɔtu** farm the essential factor was to leave the felled vegetation for a month or so irrespective of whether it was raining or not. The sun at this time of year is still hot enough to dry out the effects of a rainstorm within a day or two, he argued, irrespective of whether the rains have begun or not, provided the leaves, trunks, and branches have been thoroughly cured, and the sap has all dried up. In the old days, he claims, no one ever hurried to burn a farm. Nowadays more and more people panic at the approach of rain. Q described burns 50 years ago in which the fire regularly consumed even the standing tree stumps. His 1983 farm, fired on the 26 April after heavy rain twice within the previous 48 hours, certainly bore out his claims (especially since it had only been fallowed for eight years). I doubt I saw a better burn anywhere in Mogbuama. Felled trees were nothing more than outlines projected in white ash on a general background of blackened soil. Even brushed stumps were thoroughly charred, so fierce had been the fire.

There is no argument that farms in the river-terrace zone are altogether a different proposition. Q concedes that delaying tactics are no help in the case of **tumu** soils. One man with such a farm, L, was so badly affected by early rain and a poor burn in 1981 that he was unable to plant more than about half of the total area brushed. Subsequently he moved his farming operations to the granite zone, vowing never to farm **tumu** soils again.

Some farmers combine to brush a sizeable block of land and burn everything at one go. The advantage of block burning is that it is particularly valuable in dealing with the problem of securing a good burn in the river-terrace zone. Once a sizeable block of brushed land has caught hold there is a better chance that everything will be thoroughly burnt because the fire is sustained for longer. (Block clearing also minimises the amount of fencing later needed for pest control.) By contrast, it may prove difficult in a single isolated plot to rekindle a fire wrong-footed by a random shift in wind direction. If farmers with adjacent plots cannot co-ordinate burning, however, there is a serious risk that the firing of one farm will ignite the neighbouring farm before it is ready. Each year there are some inadequately burnt farms to be accounted for in this way.

G, a woman cultivating a household farm in her own right, suffered from this problem in 1983. The area cleared (twice the average for Mogbuama) had already provoked some hostile comment, and G felt the premature burn was no accident. She was away from Mogbuama on the day in question, and her neighbours failed to give her advance warning. On the other hand she decided not to sue, since the court is said to allow damages only where the farm accidentally burnt is separated from other farms by a cordon of unfelled bush. Farmers wishing to enjoy the benefits of block farming must also bear its risks.

The largest area to be burnt as a block on a single day (23 March) contained 17 farms covering about 25 ha of moisture-retentive soils in the river-terrace zone. Only seven Mogbuama farms had been burnt prior to this date, six on the previous day. The threat of rain on the evening of 22 March persuaded the 17 farmers concerned that they should act straight away, even though the final felling on one of the farms in the block had only been completed two or three days earlier (and G was away). Heavy rain now, it was argued, might delay the burn for another week. No formal meeting was called to make this decision, but consultation among neighbours had produced a consensus during the morning. There was a good deal of coming and going as farmers each recruited volunteers to help manage their section of the burn. The number of auspicious days for firing farms is limited, and other groups had also decided today was the right moment. In consequence, help was at a premium. Having agreed to assist on the farm of a friend, J then had to refuse requests from three other people including his brother.

Shortly after midday, 50 or 60 volunteers begin to make their way out of town towards the block of 17 farms in the river-terrace zone, separating into individual farm parties as they reach the area to be burnt. The various groups assemble in the farm huts of the last year's farms to collect long torches made of palm ribs, and to check other essentials such as matches and palm-oil libations. With the fertility of their farms and thereby so much of their welfare and prosperity for the coming year at stake over the next 90 minutes, no one makes any pretence of hiding the tension and excitement of the occasion.

Our group moves out to take up its station. Other farms are being fired as we go. Each person lights his torch from a bundle of kindling. The only access to the farm is from the downwind side, through the last year's farm. Our job is to run the rim of the farm, setting fires every 40–50 feet or so, picking out where possible, **mambo** (*Dialium guineense*) because it is especially inflammable. Meanwhile, the owner is attempting to set fire to as much as possible from the inside the farm, getting as close as he dare to the unbrushed, upwind margin. His only line of retreat is through the fires we have already started. So vital is a good burn that farm owners are sometimes prepared to take quite outrageous risks, and accidents are not uncommon. No one was trapped inside a burning farm in 1983, but there have been deaths from such accidents in previous years.

After about 20 minutes the whole brushed area has roared into flame, and the heat forces us to retreat to watch from a nearby farm hut. The whole block of 17 farms is ablaze, and a huge column of flames and black smoke slopes up over us, completely blocking out the sun. Great flocks of hawks and kites circle overhead. The breeze is now strong and gusting, as the fire creates massive local turbulence. A cumulus cloud is forming overhead. One area to the east of us has not caught alight as it should due to a sudden shift in the wind from south-west to south-east. The farm owner is screaming dementedly to invoke the fire to burn, remembering perhaps that at the farm hut the women had argued with him about where to best start the fire in relation to the prevailing wind. But he need not have worried, since all the surrounding farms are now truly alight and the eddy currents so volatile that after a few moments the fire is blown back and his farm is consumed like the rest.

We wait on, despite the choking smoke and small outbreaks of fire all around us in the last year's farm, because people back in town will want to know how well the farm burnt. Over the next week or two the enquiry **kpaa mɔilɔ kpɛpɛngɔ?** (has the farm burnt completely?) will assume the status of a greeting. After a further 30 minutes we are able to venture into the scorched farm to check the results. The burn in this case has been good. In many places felled trees have crumbled entirely to ashes, and are marked by nothing more than powdery white outlines on the charcoal background of the soil. Friends congratulate the farmer with the eagerly awaited benediction 'it has burnt completely'. In fact, almost everywhere the burn has been good, except for some isolated patches where farmers are already beginning the tedious work of piling branches into bonfires. Even the most recently felled farm has burnt well – almost as well as the rest, to the owner's evident relief – thus emphasising the advantages of block clearing.

Finally, after congratulating or commiserating with their neighbours, the participants begin to collect up the incidental benefits of the afternoon's activities. Two boys are digging out a ready-roasted rat from its hole. One man has a fine pair of duiker. Others have collected a variety of small game (rats, birds, a snake or two). Practically everyone ends up at a central, fire-blackened, palm tree where a huge honeycomb has been temporarily abandoned by its occupants. The aggrieved evicted bees gather round us as we begin, stickily, to turn for town, the burnt stumpy farmland – to a visitor perhaps invoking images of the aftermath of a nuclear explosion, but to Mogbuama people a source of considerable satisfaction in anticipation of a heavy harvest to come – stretches to the skyline. A mixture of ribald and sympathetic comment is invoked by the sound of felling from a farm not yet ready for burning.

Clearing

The weeks between the end of March and mid-April are a time of hot tedious work as farmers gather up (**nglangla**) and make bonfires of unburnt material, and generally arrange the farm so that those hoeing the rice are able to work relatively unimpeded. A start is made on the new farm hut. A few lucky farmers on the motorable part of the track to Fala are able to arrange to sell firewood from the cleared farm.

Most of the work at this time is done by the household group. Although some farmers hire casual labour to help with clearing, work groups will not be reconvened until it is time to start to plant the rice. Where the burn has been poor, farmers now have to assess the extent of their difficulties and decide if they can afford labour to recover their position. Committing too much in the way of resources at this stage may prejudice later operations. Some decide to cut their losses and abandon the least well-burnt portions of the farm without further ado. Brushed but unplanted land of this sort is known as **loba**. Formerly, land wasted in this way sometimes incurred a fine from the chiefdom authorities.

Rice planting

There are three stages to rice planting. First the seed has to be broadcast. This is a skilled operation, and sometimes a ham-fisted farmer will ask a friend or relative known to have a good 'touch' to do this. Research by Douglas Scotland in the early days of the Njala research station confirmed that on the prevailing light soils of central Sierra Leone local broadcasting rates (0.75–1.0 bu per acre) were about optimum. A broadcaster's first concern is to obtain an even spread of seed. Any subsequent bare patches are an embarrassment. Never loth to miss an opportunity, however, farmers fill in such patches with, for example, cassava or heaps for sweet potatoes and vegetables. Beyond this, broadcasters have different theories. Some reckon to spread seed more thickly on **tumu** soils because of their greater fertility, others claim more seed is needed on **kɔtu** to account for greater losses to birds and baking sun on stony ground. All broadcasters seem to use more seed per unit area as the planting season progresses (Fig. 5.4). Measurements (Table 5.1) confirm the approximate equivalence between an acre and the area covered by one bushel of seed once allowance is made for intercrops, rocky areas, etc., but whether from such figures one could discriminate random variations from variations reflecting different soil conditions is open to doubt.

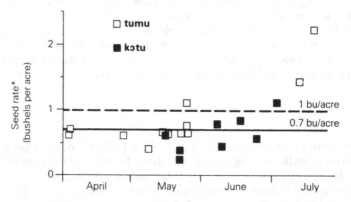

*Unadjusted seed rates. With allowance for bare rock, termite heaps, land taken by intercrops and tree stumps etc. a gross seed rate of c. 0.7 bu/ acre (the average for the the plots represented above) is equivalent to a net seed rate of 0.8 to 1.0 bu/acre.

Figure 5.4 Variations in broadcasting rates according to date and soil type.

Table 5.1 Broadcasting and 'ploughing' rates on different soil types.

Soil type	Rice variety	Bushels planted	Area (acres [ha])	Date
Bati	**pende★**	0.13	0.21 (0.09)	3 April
	jewulo, bɔngɔ	2.00	2.87 (1.16)	4 April
Tumu	**yɔni**	1.50	2.63 (1.06)	27 April
	yɔni	1.00	2.46 (1.00)	5 May
	yɔni	1.25	2.01 (0.81)	16 May
	gbɛŋgbɛŋ	0.88	1.40 (0.57)	17 May
	gbɛŋgbɛŋ, tɔkpɔehun	1.50	2.35 (0.95)	23 May
	bogutu	1.50	1.36 (0.55)	25 May
	baikɔ	2.00	2.65 (1.07)	25 May
	baikɔ and filiwa	2.25	3.42 (1.38)	26 May
	wonde yaka	0.50	0.35 (0.14)†	14 July
	gobe★	1.00	0.45 (0.18)†	20 July
Kɔtu etc.	**gbɛŋgbɛŋ and maiga**	1.50	2.26 (0.91)	15 May
	pende★	0.08	0.32 (0.13)	22 May
	bɔngɔ	1.50	4.14 (1.68)	22 May
	gboekondo	1.00	1.29 (0.52)	8 June
	bɔngɔ	0.25	0.57 (0.23)	10 June
	kɔ́kɔ̂	3.50	4.24 (1.72)	18 June
	gboekondo	1.00	1.78 (0.72)	25 June
	gboekondo	1.50	1.34 (0.54)	3 July

★Dense tillering variety.
†Excessive weed before ploughing.
Unadjusted average seed rate = 0.7 bu/acre. Net rate (corrected for land not planted due to stumps, branches, termite heaps, farm pathways, rock outcrops and farm structures) is of the order of 0.8–1.0 bu/acre.

Table 5.2 'Ploughing' work rates (m²/person/hour), with and without the assistance of drumming.

	Mobai **gbɔtɔ** (26 May, **tumu** soil)	Tendihun **gbɔtɔ** (23 May, **tumu** soil)
session with drumming	99.6 m²	90.8 m²
session without drumming	79.8 m²	—
work rate per full day (including rest periods)	66.0 m²	60.4 m²

Typical work session with drumming lasts for about 40–45 minutes, with 10 minutes lead-in, 20–25 minutes drumming, and 10 minutes for laggards to complete their stints. In the above table both sessions with drumming were measured in the late afternoon. In the case of work done by Mobai **gbɔtɔ** the measurements relate to consecutive sessions (with and without drumming).

'Ploughing' (hoeing) immediately follows broadcasting. To plough (**pu**), in the context of upland rice farming in Sierra Leone, means to scratch the soil surface lightly with a long-handled narrow-bladed hoe (**kali**). Some farmers prefer short-handled types, particularly at the beginning of the ploughing season, and change from narrower to broader blades according to soil and seed conditions. The ploughers divide their day into a number of working periods (typically 45–60 minutes at a time), and the broadcaster is required, after consultation, to mark out (with seed) the area to be covered (**mawu**) within each of these periods. Work groups often like to divide and compete against each other to complete such sections. Drumming improves work output by up to 20 per cent (Table 5.2).

The third stage is to cover any seed still exposed, fill in obvious bare patches, and collect together any weeds uprooted by the ploughers. Sorting out the farm in this way is a major responsibility for the women and children of the household, and after the visit of a work group this may occupy them fully for a week or more. This is the first point at which women play a major part in field work. Up to now their main labour input to the farm has been to prepare food and supply drinking water for work parties. The period of brushing and clearing is perhaps the nearest the women come to having a 'slack season', many of them joining regular afternoon parties to fish dry-season pools in the main rivers. Later in the year, when women are preoccupied with weeding, the men are able similarly to take time off from the farm to hunt and trap.

Ploughing in the upland rice farm is perhaps best described as 'minimum tillage', since the soil is worked as little as possible. Indeed it could be argued that 'tillage' as such is not the main purpose of ploughing. The principal purpose is to cover freshly broadcast rice seed as quickly as possible with a thin layer of soil, largely to protect it from direct sunlight and attack by birds. A secondary reason for ploughing, but one which is increasingly important as the rainy season progresses, is to rid the cleared farm of weed.

Different types of ploughing groups work in different ways. Mbla Kombi ploughs from 9.00 a.m. until 4.00 p.m. On a good day – that is one on which the members can motivate themselves and avoid disputes sometimes so serious that the group's officers have to settle cases and levy fines on the spot – its 24 members are capable of ploughing up to a hectare (approximately 2.0–2.5 bu. of rice). Mbla Kombi is composed entirely of adults. The members of **gbɔtɔ** groups are more youthful. Because such groups work longer hours (7.00 a.m. to 6.30 p.m.) under the firm discipline of a managing elder, a **gbɔtɔ** of 13 members (plus three musicians) can plough as much as or more per day than a 20-man co-operative. An adult **bɛmbɛ** with eight members – a group where the workers were mainly interested in selling labour for cash – rarely managed to plough up to one bushel of rice per day. However, the quality of their work was much higher than that of the **gbɔtɔ**, leaving much less subsequent clearing and covering for the household workforce.

Two **bɛmbɛ** groups (one organised by the school teachers) were made up entirely of small boys (some no more than 9–10 years old). On average they would achieve only one third to a half of the area ploughed by an adult group in a day (see later), a fact reflected in the charges they levy. Even so, their contribution to ploughing in 1983, considering their size and age, was far from insignificant.

Table 5.3 'Ploughing' work rates (m²/person/hour) on different soil types, group and casual hired labour compared (surveyed by compass traversing).

	Group labour	Casual labour
tumu soils	60.8 m² (n = 4)	50.3 m² (n = 6)
kɔtu soils	96.1 m² (n = 3)	85.5 m² (n = 3)

Towards the end of the ploughing season I undertook a survey of 22 farms (nine on **tumu** and 13 on **kɔtu** soils) to assess progress. By the date of this survey (mid-July) ploughing on these farms was effectively complete (only 6% of their total area remained to be finished, and in the event most of this was abandoned). An earlier survey of 15 farms showed that for an average farm (3.7 bushels of rice planted) 62% of the work had been completed by 8 June. These two surveys showed that work on **tumu** soils in the river-terrace zone starts on average four weeks earlier than on **kɔtu** farms in the granite zone. From early August onwards any further ploughing, whether on **tumu** or **kɔtu** soils, is reckoned to be a waste of time. Many **tumu** soils are by then waterlogged. On **kɔtu** soils moisture will be inadequate in the later stages of plant growth (medium-duration varieties planted in August would not flower until November).

The data from the ploughing surveys also allowed me to estimate the work rate of different labour groups (additional to the small sample of direct measurements reported in Tables 5.1–5.3). In per capita terms and averaged throughout the ploughing season adult work groups and hired labourers ploughed 2.5–2.6 'threepence pans' of rice per capita per day. (At 24 pans of rice to a bushel, one pan is sufficient for 170–240 m².) The equivalent rate for household members ploughing alone was 1.8 pans (confirming evidence from direct measurements (Table 5.3) that work groups are more efficient than isolated workers). The two groups of small boys averaged 1.4 pans per capita per day.

Work rates fall as weed cover thickens. I made a record of ploughing work rates on **tumu** soils on 30 separate occasions (seven times in April, 13 times in May and ten in June–July). The average number of pans of rice ploughed per man-day amounted to 2.3 in April, 1.9 in May and 1.5 in June–July. In two

Table 5.4 Impact of pre-planting weed emergence on 'ploughing work rates (m²/person/hour); surveyed by compass traversing.

	Adult work group (**tumu** soils)*	Pre-teenage work group (**kɔtu** soils)†
without weed	71.4 m²	21.1 m²
heavy weed	19.6 m²	10.4 m²

*Same farm, April and July.   †adjacent farms in July, one plot cleared in advance with herbicide (STAM F-34) for experimental purposes.

Figure 5.5   Weed growth on a **tumu** farm after clearing but before planting.

cases for which I have direct measurements, work rates on weedy farms at the end of the ploughing season in mid/late July were half the rate achieved on comparable weed-free plots (Table 5.4). **Tumu** soils are invariably worse than **kɔtu** soils in this respect because their moisture-retentive properties encourage rapid and luxuriant weed growth from the moment the first rains fall (Fig. 5.5).

A further problem caused by thickening weed cover is that the weeds make nonsense of the broadcaster's art. The seed is swept up as the ploughers dredge through the matted weed cover. Many bare patches are caused in this way and much seed is lost altogether when the weeds are piled up and removed from the farm. In one case I watched a farmer re-broadcast half a bushel of rice (on an area on which he had previously planted a bushel) in order to fill in bare patches caused by ploughing (this is why broadcasting rates increase towards the end of the season, Fig. 5.4). This was right at the end of the ploughing season when hunger was at its height and seed rice Le 20.00 per bushel, the maximum price reached in Mogbuama in 1983. Clearly then, if **tumu** soils are to be farmed successfully it is important to be able to organise labour for timely ploughing.

There can be little doubt that ploughing is a major labour bottleneck for Mogbuama farmers, and that the problem intensifies as the ploughing season progresses. Of the 78.7 bushels of rice planted by 22 farmers covered in my July survey, 87% of the work was by hired labour (work groups supplying 77% and casual hired labour 10%). By comparison with many peasant food-crop farming systems in Africa this is an unusually high figure. In one sense it is misleadingly large. Cash payments constitute only one third of the real wage, the balance being consumed in meals. This latter is a fixed cost, more or less, and accrues to all classes of labour, including household labour (though women often say with sarcasm that men belonging to work parties, a uniquely voracious breed, eat twice as much as normal). In addition, the figure takes no account of the follow-up work done by women and children. For every man-day's worth of ploughing there is a woman- or child-day's worth of tidying up to follow. In all probability then, the cash wages bill represents only a fifth or a quarter of the overall labour requirement for ploughing. Even so, where the farm is of average size this sum might amount to Le 30.00–40.00, not counting the cost of any ingredients the farmer needs to buy for workers' meals. This is without doubt a major sum for most farmers to find. The farmer who is obliged in addition to buy or borrow rice for feeding workers because his own rice is finished is, indeed, in deep trouble. Le 100.00 might not be enough to rescue him. At no other time of the year are farmers under this degree of extreme pressure to find cash in order to proceed with their farms.

The nub of the matter is that in addition to being more efficient than solo labour, group labour allows a farmer to pursue the most effective planting strategies (to pick the best moment for ploughing, in relation to the arrival of rain, to get in a sizeable area of early rice, or to beat the weeds). Not surprisingly, then, demand for ploughing labour outstrips supply. From data relating to all 98 farms in Mogbuama I have calculated that in order to plough just over three bushels of rice the average household needed to mobilise 34 man-days of labour, but my detailed records of labour group activity indicate that only a third of ploughing labour (12 man-days per household) could have come from such sources. By implication, the 22 farms surveyed in mid-July (where over two-thirds of all ploughing came from labour-group sources) were representative only of the more successful households in the competition for labour.

For many farmers the only way to get hold of group labour when it is most needed is to buy it. Even the 49% of households where one or more members belongs to a labour group find a third of all their ploughing needs outside the group. The largest households with several adult males may manage this entirely from their own resources, but others are forced to hire, mainly from labour-group members willing to sell their turns for cash. Just over 20% of group labour is sold in this way, and constitutes a major source of hired labour in Mogbuama. Averaged over the 51% of households without direct access to group labour this amounts to five man-days of ploughing time per farm, i.e. 15% of requirements.

Only **bati** farms are ready for ploughing in early April. The majority of.

farmers in the river-terrace zone (with **tumu** soils) aim to begin ploughing in late April. They are joined by farmers in the granite zone with the arrival of reliable rain during May. Planting is begun on the ɲanya soils at the foot of the valley slope and proceeds up slope as the rains become heavy. The first ploughing I recorded on **kɔtu** soil took place on 15 May. From this point in the calendar onwards, competition for labour between farmers in the granite and river-terrace zones becomes intense, reaching its peak in mid-June. In 1983 farmers in the river-terrace zone needed a longer period to complete their work than farmers in the granite zone because they were managing a greater area in total (61% of all rice was ploughed on **tumu** soils and 39% on **kɔtu** soils). By July **kɔtu** farmers have the field more or less to themselves, except for some **tumu** farmers delayed by lack of money or other misfortune.

The picture is further complicated by competition for labour to plant groundnuts. Groundnuts are an important subsidiary cash crop in Mogbuama. Women and young people find this an especially important way of acquiring some cash income and savings. If groundnut planting is too long delayed (into late June and July) yields drop sharply (Department of Agriculture 1959). Groundnut cultivators are often prepared to re-invest their savings in labour to ensure that this does not happen.

Yaka rices – long duration 'floating' or flood-tolerant types planted in water courses and valley swamp lands – constitute 15 per cent of all rice planted in Mogbuama in 1983. Like groundnut cultivation, a plot of **yaka** rice is a means whereby individuals (again women and young people especially) are able to raise a small cash income without any arguments as to the disposal of the produce. Although planting **yaka** rices begins in April the work is less time-constrained than groundnut work. Successful planting is possible as late as August. Since it is private work it is fitted in when convenient. Some farmers adopt the agronomically interesting practice of planting **bati** farms with a mixture of quick-yielding 'upland' rices (which they harvest before the August and September floods) and a **yaka** rice which is left in possession of the farm when the early rice is harvested (this is discussed more fully in Chs 8 and 9). It should be noted that in any case of conflict of interest between swamp work and work on the 'household' farm on the uplands, the argument is resolved in favour of the upland farm.

Sharply mounting pressure on labour for ploughing is reflected in hire rates. Hired labour used between 1 April and 31 May (32% of all hired labour recorded in my mid-July survey) cost on average Le 1.03 per man-day. Labour hired between 1 June and 17 July (68% of the total) cost on average Le 1.30 per man day. Irrespective of the complication of more rapid weed growth, farmers agree that it is more difficult to plough silty **tumu** soils than stony **kɔtu** soils. This is borne out by my field measurements of rates of ploughing (Table 5.1). Taking all types of adult labour, average work rates on **kɔtu** soils were 2.37 pans per capita per day, 28% higher than the figure for **tumu** soils (1.85 pans per capita per day). Because ploughing of **tumu** soils can begin earlier (when there is less competition for labour and hire rates are lower) the average cost of labour on all farms in the river-terrace zone worked out at Le 1.11 per man-day, compared to Le 1.34 on farms in the granite zone. The disadvantage of having to start later when rates are higher is more than compensated by the greater efficiency of labour on farms in the granite zone. Ploughing on **kɔtu** soils costs only 56 cents per pan of rice planted, compared with 60 cents per pan on **tumu** soils. Perhaps this is the point to note that the cost per pan of rice ploughed by children's work groups (averaged over both major soil types) works out at a very competitive rate of 57 cents.

At times, competition for ploughing labour leads to panic buying. S came to Mogbuama to farm on land belonging to his mother's family, bringing with him a friend K. They both joined a **bembɛ** group but since K had no farm of his own he planned to sell all his work turns. On 7 June he went to five people in turn, offering to sell his remaining work day for Le 13.00 instead of the prevailing price of Le 15.00 (for a nine-man group). Labourers and labour groups are always paid in advance. Desperate to hire labour and sensing a bargain, all five paid out Le 13.00 in expectation of receiving the work-group the following day. K disappeared from Mogbuama that night, Le 65.00 to the good, and has not been seen subsequently.

Towards the end of the ploughing season it becomes clear that a number of farms are not going to be completed because of hunger, poverty and misfortune. In some cases the unused portion is abandoned as **loba**. In other cases an attempt will be made to sell it as a going concern. Two cases are described below.

T, farming jointly with his father, had an accident while brushing and required hospitalisation for three months. There was insufficient money to pay both for hospital treatment and for enough labour to complete the ploughing of the 'four bushel' farm they had cleared. By early July the father, A, decided to cut his losses and offer for sale the half of the farm yet unploughed. Two of the wealthier men in the village, a trader and one of the blacksmiths, were said to be interested. In the end, however, A sold the portion to a divorced woman V at less than the asking price because she was a relative. V then borrowed some rice for ploughing, and arranged to hire two or three days of labour from one of the children's ploughing groups. In this way she rescued about two-thirds of the incomplete portion of the farm.

The case of Y was rather different. He neglected his farm for so long in pursuit of other interests that in the end most of it was wasted. A notable gambler, his appetite for cash was such that he sold three out of four of the turns accruing to him from membership in a ploughing group and was unable to make much progress with his own farm as a result. He rarely if ever missed any opportunity to take up casual labouring, e.g. head-loading farm produce to Fala after the road became impassable in July. It would be little exaggeration, therefore, to say that his own farm died of neglect.

Weeding, pest control, and bird scaring

Weeding

The upland rice is weeded, once, about six to eight weeks after ploughing. By convention, weeding is women's work, but I noted a number of occasions when men helped out in an emergency. Young girls are especially good at weeding and work for long periods without feeling the strain of bending as much as some of the older women. Weeding is the main labour bottleneck for women. This bottleneck is not quite so crucial to the fate of the farm overall as is the ploughing bottleneck. An unweeded farm may produce something. An unploughed farm produces nothing.

The bulk of weeding is done as unpaid household labour, with some informal collaboration between neighbours and kin. Where there is a prospect of a major surplus of rice for sale a household head may sometimes decide to put up the cash to hire women to complete weeding quickly. S, for example, paid for seven women to weed a **bati** farm for four days in early June. One way to arrange such a contract is to purchase palm oil in the dry season and to use it later in the year to recruit women labourers when oil is scarce. S offered 0.6 litres of oil in return for a day's work weeding. Women are said to be more reliable than men as hired labourers. They turn up when paid to do so, and waste no time in arguments and fights.

Women sometimes form co-operative groups for weeding. These can be either **tee** groups to facilitate work on household farms, or larger **kɔmbi** groups (perhaps formed with the intention of working for hire). At one stage it was thought than the women who belong to Mbla Kombi for savings purposes might form a weeding party. In the event this plan fell through.

Timing is as important for weeding as for ploughing. Nyoka (1980) reports detailed investigations of the weed ecology of upland rice farms in central Sierra Leone. Among his findings he observes that although weed infestation began three days after soil tillage, 'rice plants grew (in height) well ahead of weeds' initially, and 'little or no competition occurred during the first 20 days after sowing'. He concluded that any weeding carried out within this period simply served to remove potential competitors rather than 'save the crop from the competition taking place during that time'. In economic terms a single hand weeding at six weeks (in effect, the normal practice in Mogbuama) proved to be among the most effective of the experimental treatments investigated (especially on short-fallow bush). Late weeding (after nine weeks) 'produced lower yields than zero weeding'.

At the end of August I made a survey of weeding strategies in Mogbuama, based on a random sample of 30 farm households. Although the enquiries were intended for women many of the answers were supplied by male heads of households, not because the issue was in any way controversial but because the women were at the time busy weeding. In several cases I was able to check the answers by taking part in weeding. One of the questions asked was 'How many weeks after ploughing is it best to weed?' Answers ranged betweeen four to eight weeks, with the two most popular choices being six weeks (seven responses) and eight weeks (ten responses). Whatever the choice of the optimum point to begin weeding, the majority of persons inteviewed (21) said that in fact they were late. The explanations for this lateness amounted to a catalogue of the accumulated problems facing Mogbuama farmers at this time of year: 'My husband hasn't finished ploughing and so we are still busy covering the rice', 'There is no food or money to hire helpers', 'We have been busy doing groundnut work', 'My wife gave birth', 'Our daughter fell sick and has been taken to hospital', 'My wife left me', 'The early rice started to ripen so we have had to divert to bird scaring', 'We are busy finishing off the fencing of the farm'. The three most frequently cited factors were problems in finishing ploughing, lack of food or cash to support helpers, and sickness.

In 16 cases it was reported that in addition to starting late there were also difficulties in finishing the work. In half these instances the reason was given as lack of food and money. In two cases the women concerned had fallen sick. One woman had no farm hut under which to do the cooking – her husband was so behind on the farm that he had not yet built the **kpowa** – so she had been driven back to town by the sometimes almost continuous August rain.

Eight households had been able to hire labour to help with weeding (an average of 5.4 woman-days per household at Le 1.00 per day plus food). In one case where I was able to measure the work done, seven women weeded 0.2 ha of **tumu** farm in one day (working from 8.00 a.m. to 4.30 p.m., for Le 1.00 each plus food). It took 28 woman-days to weed 0.5 ha. of S's heavily weed-infested **bati** farm. In 20 cases households reported that they drew on informal help from friends and relatives. Unpaid reciprocal help of this kind was generally on a very small scale but in two instances involved eight and 15 persons respectively.

The bulk of weeding labour came from household sources. I recorded the names of 68 women in this category (an average of 2.3 persons per household). One important and interesting finding was that as many as 18 of these names of regular weeders were either new to the list of farm household members I had compiled when interviewing heads of households earlier in the season or had originally been listed as belonging to different households. Some instances were to be accounted for as cases of close collaboration between female relatives, e.g. between sisters, or mother and daughter, in which for weeding purposes the household production units had become temporarily merged. Other instances related to older female relatives (widows and divorcees) responsible for their own upkeep but without an upland rice farm. Women in this category generally supported themselves by growing groundnuts and **yaka** rice, and in some cases by lending money or rice. I eventually came to know of at least 15 women in this category in Mogbuama who went unrecorded in my earlier farm-based census. Such women were often asked to help hard-pressed younger relatives with weeding. Some were paid in rice at the harvest. Others demanded to be paid cash there and then. The importance of these cases is that they underline the point made earlier about the fluidity of the concept of 'farm household'. Women do not necessarily draw the boundaries of social units in quite the same way as men. The 'farm family' does not have definite form but is responsive, even in the short run, to farming conditions and shifts in the balance of male and female economic interests.

Almost certainly weeding requires as much if not more labour per hectare than ploughing. It is worth asking, therefore, why forms of co-operation and competition for labour are less formal than in the case of ploughing. The fact that weeding coincides with the most intense period of the hungry season is of major significance. Few households have food or money to spend on work parties. Secondly (as noted above) the penalties for failure are not quite so severe, in the sense that neglect of weeding (as the work of Nyoka confirms) does not necessarily ruin the harvest entirely. Thirdly, each household has a

THE FARMING YEAR

Pest control

Table 5.5 Main weeds on 30 Mogbuama rice farms.

Mende	Botanical identification	Times reported
hèlú	*Sida stipulata, S. corymbosa*	27
sɔ̀gbɛ́	*Urena lobata*	27
túgbéè	various sedges	
	(e.g. *Cyperus rotundatus, Mariscus alternifolius*★)	23
ndǒndókɔ̀	various convolvulaceous weeds, including	
	Ipomoea involucrata★ and *Merremia umbellata*★	21
'ndondanguli'	?*Paullinia pinnata*	20
kàpiâ	*Paspalum commersonii*	17
'manjo'	*Spigelia anthelmia*★	13
kpòkpò	various colvolvulaceous climbers including	
	Ipomoea reptans and *I. hispida*	12
'ndandei'	*Dichrostachys glomerata*	9
gòngò	the grasses *Rottboellia exaltata*	
	Pennisetum subangustum, P. hordeoides	7
kpǎgɔ̀	*Acroceras zizanoides*, but cf. **kpángé**,	
	Celosia argentea	7
ndúlúgbé	general name for various small annual weeds	6
'kpɔhu'	*Hibiscus owariensis*★	5
ndɔ́pá yéŋglé	*Corchorus fascicularis*	3
ngàlá	tall grasses, especially *Chasmopodium caudatum*,	
	Pennisetum purpureum, Andropogon gabonensis	2
'ngotawe'	*Solanum nodiflorum*★	2
ndɔ̀gbɔ́ nìkílì	*Desmodium adscendens*, also *Hypselodelphys*	
	violacea	2
'butɛ'	*Croton hirtus*★	1
kúmù	?*Ocimum viride*	1
kɔ̀mígbé	?	1
kándí	*Anisophyllea laurina, A. meniaudii*	1
ndìwì	various small grasses	1
'kpɔmu'	?*Anopyxis klaineana*	1
yánì	*Axonopus africanus*	1

Herbarium identifications asterisked. All others are based on Deighton (1957). Orthography and tone markings follow Innes (1969). Words not in Innes' dictionary are placed in inverted commas without tone markings.

greater pool of labour to call on for weeding than for ploughing. My farm household census gave figures of 140 adult males and 184 adult females for Mogbuama as a whole, i.e. 30% more females than males. In addition it is probable that young girls are even more productive weeding (by comparison with adult rates of work) than are small boys ploughing (though as already noted small boys' efforts in this respect are not to be despised), and because the work is not so demanding it is more common to meet old women weeding than old men ploughing.

The ethno-ecology of weeds of upland rice in Mogbuama reflects the

Table 5.6 Farmer rankings of weed problems on Mogbuama rice farms between clearing and planting and after planting.

Weed	Pre-planting*	Post-planting*
sɔgbɛ́ (*Urena lobata*)	1	3
ndɔ̌ndókɔ̌ (especially *Ipomoea involucrata*)	2	5
hèlú (*Sida* spp.)	3	3
ndondanguli (? *Paullinia pinnata*)	4	2
túgbɛ́ɛ̀ (various sedges)	5	1

*Aggregate of 30 responses ranking five most severe weeds.

importance of the contrast between the river-terrace and granite zones. Nearly every farmer asserted that **tumu** soils were more difficult to weed than **kɔtu** soils. The main explanations given were that weeds were less firmly rooted in gravelly and stony soils and that the greater moisture-retentiveness of silty soils encouraged weed germination. In nine cases where farmers had been unusually bothered by weeds in 1983 this was accounted for by reference to a poor burn, too short a fallow interval, or delay in ploughing. Some farmers also noted that **yɛngɛ gbete** (swamp land with water throughout the year) and catenary footslope **ŋanya** soils were easy to weed and that **bati** farms were often exceptionally difficult 'because the weeds have not yet appeared when ploughing takes place and so the seeds still remain in the soil'.

The distinction between two types of weeding – that done by the men through the process of ploughing and the later rooting out of weeds competing with the standing rice done by the women – is an important one to the Mogbuama farmer. Farmers were asked to rank their five most important weeds before and after ploughing. In total, 24 weeds were named (Table 5.5). Relatively few weeds were assigned the same significance in both ploughing and post-ploughing periods. Among the five most frequently reported weeds (cited by two-thirds of all farmers interviewed) positions changed as follows: **sɔgbɛ** (*Urena lobata*), **helu** (*Sida* spp.) and **ndondokɔ** (various convolvulaceous species including *Ipomoea reptans* and *Merriama umbellata*) were given reduced ratings in the post-ploughing period, **ndodanguli** (? *Paullinia pinnata*) maintained its position, and **tugbɛɛ**, the Mende name for a variety of small sedges (including *Cyperus rotundus*, and *Mariscus alternifolius*, 'male' and 'female' respectively in local terminology) rose in rank to become the single most widely cited post-ploughing weed problem (Table 5.6).

The distinction between **kpaa ma luwa** ('weed that springs up in newly burnt farm' [Innes 1969]) and post-ploughing weeds is one that seems rarely to have been made in the scientific literature on West African rice farming systems. The detailed study by Nyoka (1980) comes close to recognising the point at issue by noting the significance of ploughing as a type of weed control. It would be interesting for future work to look at the trade-off between thorough timely ploughing and control of later weed growth, or the utility of chemical weed control for easing the earlier weed problem. This might be an important way of tackling a major constraint to the further development of early rice cultivation on moisture-retentive soils (Chs 7 and 9).

Pest control

After ploughing is completed, and while the women weed, the men turn to a number of jobs in and around the farm, of which building a low perimeter fence to exclude rodents is the first priority. This fence is made out of farm brush wood, and has traps set in it at intervals, principally to catch cane rats (*Thryonomys swinderianus*). The cane rat is an unpredictable pest. Averaged out over a number of years and all farms the losses it causes may not be all that great. At times, however, it can single out a farm for an exceptional amount of damage; so much so, in fact, that the farmer so visited may be driven into a degree of indebtedness comparable to that associated with major illness or early rainfall. Fencing reduces the chances of such a catastrophe and helps trap animals valued for their high-quality meat. Cane-rat meat is especially welcome in households beset by pre-harvest hunger.

Once the rice is germinated it is advisable to get the fence round the farm as quickly as possible. Men frequently co-operate in fencing farms on a 'by-turns' basis. It sometimes happens that a member of a ploughing group may be owed some labour – e.g. if the group finishes his farm more speedily than expected. Spare ploughing turns of this sort may be used up on fencing work. An advantage of farming on the block system (as in the case of the 17 farms described in the earlier section on burning) is that the ratio of fencing to farm land is more favourable than for isolated farms. In Mogbuama in 1983 there were only nine such isolated farms: five in the granite zone and four in the river-terrace zone. Farmers in the middle of an extensive block manage without any fencing at all.

Other jobs at this time include building platforms (**mbamagbema**) in the farm for bird scaring. Birds are without doubt major pests on upland rice farms. Early rice is especially badly affected. Towards the later part of the harvest season the bird problem abates, perhaps because they have a much greater range of targets to attack. There are two key periods for bird scaring – just after broadcasting and then the 30 days or so leading up to the harvest (in effect, the period from flowering to ripening).

Household members keep watch on newly ploughed fields until the rice has been completely covered and germination has taken place. Bird scaring while the rice is ripening is a more long-drawn-out affair. If as is usually the case the rice has been planted in batches over a period of four to six weeks bird scaring will take the better part of two to three months. Throughout this period the platforms, mostly roofed over against sun and rain, have to be manned from dawn to dusk. Some farmers rig up a network of ropes to operate sets of rattles and alarms. Others rely on slings and stones (or on **tumu** farms, where there are no stones, on specially prepared mud pellets). Any household member is liable for this work and in some cases outside help may be recruited as well (for the price of a meal). If there is no one else to turn to the head of household will do the work himself rather than risk the heavy losses typical of an unguarded farm, but mostly it falls to the lot of children, teenagers and old people. The long school holiday is well placed in relation to bird scaring and a number of farmers draw on help from schoolchildren home for the holiday. Bird scarers wile away the tedium of their task and warn off birds at the same time by singing, often to the accompaniment of a rudimentary three-key xylophone.

Some local rice varieties are reputed to be resistant to bird attack (Ch. 8). These include both long-awned varieties, e.g. **ngolo-yombo** and **filiwa**, and varieties with long outer glumes. The general descriptive name **kalɛmbaama** (cf. **kalɛ,** 'bone', **mbaa,** 'side of the jaw') is sometimes applied to rices in the latter group (examples include 'Madam Yebu' and **gbondobai**).

In addition to bird scaring platforms, some farmers also build sleeping platforms – huts two metres or so off the ground, high enough to evade the worst of the mosquitoes – so that they can stay in the farm overnight. A well-favoured farm of early rice may attract as much attention from human thieves as from birds and rodents. In the run-up to harvest a truly dedicated farmer sleeps in the farm to give maximum attention to all aspects of crop protection, and in consequence may not be seen in town for several days or weeks at a time. The farm hut becomes the centre for the trapping and tapping operations that are the other main interest in the weeks before the harvest.

Harvesting

It is logical first to describe harvesting as a labour and organisational 'input' to the farming system before turning, in the next chapter, to a fuller assessment of the harvest as an outcome of the year's agricultural activities and a discussion of the principles underlying the distribution of harvest rewards.

Some **bati** farms planted with quick-growing rice varieties such as **jewulo** and **bɔngɔ** are ready for harvest from the end of July onwards (cf. Fig. 3.7). Early varieties on farms in the river-terrace zone are ready three or four weeks later (i.e. towards the end of August). By mid-September farmers in the granite zone have begun to harvest a little early rice from the lower slopes of their catenary farms. The main varieties in the river-terrace zone come to full harvest by late September/early October, with the bulk of the harvest in the granite zone following about three or four weeks later. The **yaka** varieties ripen from November onwards. The harvest is to all intents complete by mid-December.

Harvesting is done with a knife, panicle by panicle. Handfuls are tied together into bundles (cf. Fig. 9.2) for initial storage and drying in the farm hut. There are approximately 15 such bundles to a bushel. When convenient, the rice is taken down and 'thrashed' (a misleading term since the grain is removed from the panicle by a process of trampling). Although this kind of harvesting is slow and labour-intensive by comparison with harvesting by sickle, an implement used in some parts of northern Sierra Leone, it has the advantage of selectivity. It accommodates uneven ripening, and facilitates the roguing of off-types in the harvest. Not only is the purity of the seed stock better maintained thereby, but knife harvesting also allows for the ready identification and conservation of interesting new planting materials (Grist 1975). The significance of this is more fully explored in Chapter 8.

Harvesting work rates average between one and two bushels per person per day. Given typical input–output ratios for Mogbuama (about 18 bu. per bushel of rice planted) harvesting works out as one-and-a-half to three times more labour intensive per hectare than ploughing. It is not surprising to find, therefore, that 52% of all labour-group time in Mogbuama was devoted to harvesting. According to my estimate, total rice output in 1983 would have been of the order of 5500 bushels, and harvesting required 8250 days of labour input (i.e. between one quarter and one third of all available labour time in Mogbuama for the period between September and November).

Although this must seem a quite phenomenal effort, harvesting is much less of a 'bottleneck' than either ploughing or weeding. The work is much more pleasant. The labourers operate as a close group, and the flow of conversation, gossip, jokes, political scandal, and tall stories is uninterrupted. Men and women, working side by side for the first time in the farming cycle, clearly enjoy the company (though this is not without its hazards for some – A lost his wife when she joined a harvesting co-operative and fell in love with its drummer). There is now food in abundance, and few farmers have any immediate problems recruiting labour since rice can be sold to pay for it. This last point suggests that the labour shortages earlier in the year may be more apparent than real – the outcome of lack of purchasing power rather than an absolute incapacity of the system to offer up more effort.

The organisation and operation of specialist harvesting groups has been described in detail in Chapter 4. There were three such groups in Mogbuama in 1983. In addition, Mbla Kombi and One-way Kombi both undertook harvesting work. Just over 21% of labour-group harvest work was sold, compared to 20% of ploughing labour. Unlike ploughing, few sales of harvest labour appear to have been forced by indigence. In some cases, sales were requested (or allowed) by the head of household because the farm was too small to require the full work-party complement. M, working for her father, was allowed to sell a 'surplus' turn and keep the money for her needs over Christmas. B sold a turn and shared the money with her husband. J and P are brothers with a joint farm. Both worked for a harvesting group, but P's turns were sufficient for their farm. They sold J's turns and shared the money. Of 22 cases of sales of harvest labour for which I have details, 16 were amicably arranged sales of 'surplus' labour along these lines.

In four other cases, however, household dependents on the verge of divorce, transfer of clientship or setting up to farm for themselves, took their own decision to sell a turn and keep the money. K sold one of her turns and kept the money 'by force' because she was convinced her husband, an overcommitted polygamist, would provide her nothing for Christmas. L, a stranger working for P, sold one turn without his landlord's knowledge. P sent him packing as a result. S sold both his turns without his father's permission, but lost the money gambling. In only two out of 23 cases were sales of harvest work said to be forced by poverty. E sold both his turns because he needed cash badly, but his farm suffered because he was unable to harvest everything when it was ready. Poverty forced W to sell both his harvest turns, but then he stole some groundnuts and was able to buy the turns back.

Conclusion

The critical hazard facing farmers in Mogbuama is the hazard of early rainfall, because of its impact òn prospects for burning the farm. The two crucial management problems farmers have to address are when to time the burn and how to solve labour constraints at the height of the farming season. A poor burn involves the farm household in a series of additional labour demands. These are cumulative in their impact and may finally threaten the viability of the farm. The central concern of rice farmers in Mogbuama is to balance the advantage of being able to harvest early rice from moisture-retentive soils against the risks of being 'squeezed' by mounting labour supply difficulties.

6 The harvest

Data sources

The harvest data in this chapter derive from three main sources:

(a) interviews with all Mogbuama heads of farm households in May/June to estimate sales of rice and other crops from 1982 farms;
(b) observation of the 1983 harvest;
(c) post-harvest interviews with a sample of 33 male and female farmers to record their explanations of success and failure in the 1983 season.

Mogbuama is a volatile and competitive society. Although harvest yields and farm income are not formal secrets like lineage histories or land rights, there are no particular advantages, and several obvious disadvantages under conditions of competitive poverty, in revealing details of the harvest and of crop sales to a stranger such as myself. The partners in the farm enterprise – husband and wife, father and son, two brothers – may be trying to conceal important aspects of the business from each other. On several occasions when reported results did not tally with direct observations it transpired that one of the partners had been harvesting on the quiet. A polygynist head of household is not keen for his wives to know the amount of rice sold since it increases the pressure on him to provide them with money for clothes and other expenses at holiday times, e.g. Christmas and Pray Day. An indebted farmer will be under maximum pressure from creditors at harvest time so is unlikely to want to add to this pressure by advertising the success of his harvest.

There are a number of other factors which further undermine the quality of harvest data. Many farmers quite honestly do not know how much rice they have harvested. Where kinsfolk have provided informal help with the farm they will be invited at harvest to come and help themselves. An elderly female relative who has helped with weeding might be asked to harvest what she can in one day, for example. The Mende particularly admire open-handed generosity. The suspicion that the donor might be counting the cost would altogether spoil the gesture. Consequently many farmers are not quite sure how much rice they might have cooked for friends and relatives or given away on impulse. For reasons of this sort harvest data may be reported to the best of a farmer's knowledge but, nevertheless, tend systematically to underestimate agricultural output. I would estimate that this might be as much as a third in some cases.

A further complication, in the case of my enquiries, was that I was asking too soon after the harvest, at a time (December 1983) when the village was pre-occupied with Pɔɔ initiation, and before most farmers had thrashed their rice. Not everyone remembers how many bunches have been put up into the barn to dry, especially when the harvest period has been protracted. The crucial point, in terms of the farmer's own input–output calculations, comes after Christmas when the dried rice is thrashed and bagged, the bushels counted, and

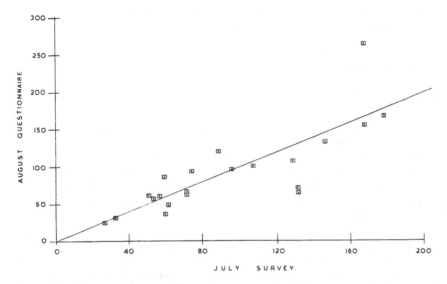

Figure 6.1 Farmer estimates of farm size: a cross-check between two data sources (in Threepence Pans of rice planted).

important decisions made about disposal of any surplus. The exceptions to this rule are the farmers who lend early rice. S had a very clear picture of the output from his **bati** farm when it became ready for harvest in July because he was besieged by would-be borrowers from throughout the chiefdom. Within a week the farm had been completely harvested and after deductions for the immediate requirements of the household the balance of the crop – 41 bushels – was sold or loaned.

In some cases it proved possible to cross check figures for internal consistency. When interviewing farmers about the harvest I asked for data on inputs (bushels of rice ploughed) as well as outputs (bushels harvested). The input figures could then be checked against measurements and observations made during the ploughing season. The two sets of results are graphed in Figure 6.1, and show a good measure of agreement. Where I was able similarly to check reported harvest figures against direct measurements made by myself or my research assistant no major anomalies were apparent. Asking about rice yields on a plot by plot or variety by variety basis seemed to be relatively uncontroversial. Most farmers seemed to have the relevant figures in mind and I never forced the issue with any who were obviously ill at ease.

The other figures, relating to non-rice crops and cash sales, are less reliable. There was little if any chance to check them against any other data or measurements of my own. In cases where questions relating to the private crops of dependents were answered by households heads, I know (from follow-up work) that a number of errors have been introduced, e.g. serious underestimates of the importance of women in the cultivation of **yaka** rices due to wrong attribution of ownership. The figures are probably no worse than data commonly used in other studies of this kind and are useful in providing an 'order of magnitude' picture of the Mogbuama agricultural economy. Care should be taken in pressing analysis beyond this point.

Mogbuama agricultural output

On the basis of data from 32 rice farmers interviewed in December, after harvesting had been completed, I estimate that total rice output in Mogbuama in 1983 was about 6000 bushels. This amounts to an average of 61 bushels per farm household and 20 bushels per bushel planted (very approximately 1350 kg/ha). If rice is to supply about half to two-thirds of daily energy requirements, a Mogbuama farm-household population of 549 persons needs something like 4500–5000 bushels of husk rice per annum for subsistence purposes. This suggests that about 20–25% of total rice output is available as a disposable surplus.

Early rice comprised 16% of all rice harvested. The remainder of the harvest came from medium-duration varieties (68 per cent) and long-duration swamp varieties (16%). Yields were of the following magnitude: early rice about 20 bushels, medium-duration upland rice about 17 bushels, and swamp rice about 40–50 bushels, per bushel of seed-rice planted (approximately 1200, 1000, and 2500–3000 kg/ha respectively). Typical village prices per bushel in 1983 were: early rice (July/August), Le 18.00–20.00; main-crop rice (October), Le 9.00–10.00; swamp rice (mid-December onwards), Le 14.00, but set to rise to Le 16.00 over Christmas. Village prices in late December 1982 were Le 10.00–12.00, so secular changes as well as seasonal price swings are apparent in the 1983 data, in response perhaps to reduced levels of rice imports resulting from severe foreign exchange shortages.

Farmers who are not under pressure of debt burdens tend to release the bulk of rice for sale around Christmas time, or early in the new year. The indebted repay loans, or sell rice to service other commitments, at the peak of the harvest (i.e. October/November) when prices are at rock bottom. It is worth noting that **lɔna**, the standard rice loan of two bushels repaid for every one bushel given out, matches the price swing from a pre-harvest maximum of Le 18.00–20.00 to immediate post-harvest low of Le 9.00–10.00.

In a random sample of 30 heads of household interviewed in August about rice sales from the previous year's harvest, just over half (16) reported average sales of 7.6 bushels per household (or 4.1 bu/household averaged over the sample as a whole). In addition, 21 heads of household had remitted rice to kin outside Mogbuama (typically to support young people in towns) at the rate of three bushels per household (or 2.1 bu/household averaged over the sample as a whole). Multiplying these figures by the number of farm households in Mogbuama, sales and remittances from household farms would amount to about 600 bushels, i.e. about 12–15% of all rice produced on farms in this category. Account should then be taken of an additional 960 bushels of rice produced on private swamp farms, the bulk of which (say 700–800 bushels) would normally be sold. Altogether then, total rice sales and remittances might amount to 1300–1400 bushels, i.e. about 21–22% of the harvest. This figure agrees well with the rough estimate of subsistence surplus in Mogbuama

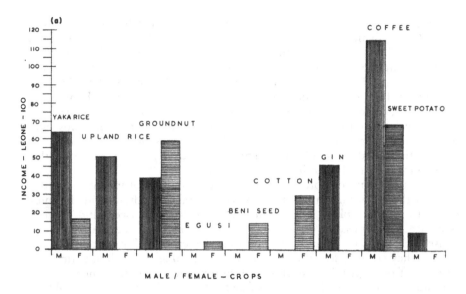

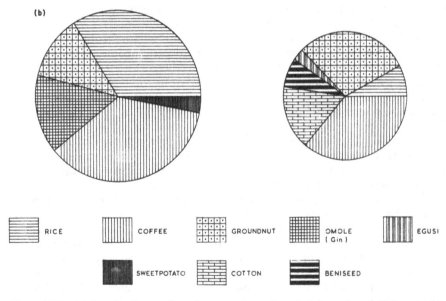

Figure 6.2 (a) Income from sales of crops and produce (total output of all farms). (b) Income from nine cash crops (Left-hand pie, male income = Le 32,760; RH pie, female income = Le 19,240).

computed above. It seems unlikely that the problem of injudicious sales of household foodstocks, as described by Hill (1982) in northern Nigeria, is general in Mogbuama.

Weighting the figures just cited by average prices for the early, main and late-season crop, rice sales in Mogbuama in 1983 were worth approximately Le 13 000.00 (equivalent to Le 133.00 per household, or Le 37.00 per adult). Although Mogbuama, like other villages in the northern half of Kamajei chiefdom, supplies surpluses of rice to the national market, the great importance of cash income from other agricultural produce should also be taken into account. In fact, given major improvements in the Marketing Board price during 1983, coffee may now outstrip rice as a cash earner. The general picture of income derived from the eight most widely distributed crops (i.e. those with more than 20 persons reporting sales in 1982) is presented in Figure 6.2. In constructing this diagram I have used prices reported by informants rather than prices quoted by traders or in official sources.

The main feature of note relates to women's sources of income. The data confirm the economic importance to women of groundnuts and the inter-crops from the upland rice farm (egusi melon, beniseed and cotton). Non-rice intercrops are as valuable in cash terms as rice sales from the household rice farm. Since the non-rice intercrops belong exclusively to women they stand to lose most as a consequence of any switch in agricultural emphasis from upland to swamp rice cultivation. Total cash income from rice and other crops is of the order of Le 52 000 (Le 530.00 per household), of which women claim 37% directly. As already noted, the data underestimate women's share of the swamp rice crop (17%, but in reality probably closer to 40%). If an adjustment is made on these grounds then women (57% of adults in farm households) control about 40% of all cash income from Mogbuama crops. Gender inequality in respect of agricultural income, although not negligible, is perhaps not as high as might have been expected. The question of individual inequalities in access to income from these crops is addressed later.

A further point worth noting in relation to Figure 6.2 is the income derived from sales of ɔmɔle (local gin distilled from palm wine).

This work is particularly associated with the late dry season, and many farmers use it as a strategy for converting surplus labour during the dry season into a durable resource which they can then encash to pay for agricultural labour, especially ploughing labour, later in the year. Previously, it was estimated that ploughing the rice crop in Mogbuama in 1983 required a labour input of 3400 worker-days, at least 75% (2550) of which was group or hired labour. Straight hiring of a labour group may require the farmer to spend Le 3.00–3.50 per man per day. Even for members, group labour requires the recipient to find food worth about Le 2.00 per worker per day (of which the meat or fish, oil, and also rice if the barn is exhausted, must be purchased with ready cash). The total cash requirement, therefore, for group labour during 1983 would have amounted to about Le 5100, a sum roughly equivalent to the total income (Le 4732) reported as deriving from gin distillation during the previous dry season.

Gin is more than simply a source of ready cash. One woman farmer cultivating a large upland rice on her own account in Mogbuama, and an even larger one in a nearby village, was well known for using liberal supplies of home-brew to sustain her labour-recruitment drives. The phrase 'work party' was singularly appropriate when applied to work on her farm.

Agricultural savings in Mogbuama

Studies of agrarian inequality in northern Nigeria by Hill (1972, 1977, 1982) stress inequalities of land ownership and in access to land as determinants of rural poverty. In Mogbuama, where land is in relative abundance, these are factors of lesser significance, and I shall argue instead that agrarian inequality needs to be interpreted more from the standpoint of the way in which 'accidents of nature' interact with, and are mediated by, the politics of clientelism at village level. This is a topic explored at length in Chapter 7. Here, however, it is appropriate to provide some basic data on local means for accumulating wealth.

Two of the most important savings and investments in Mogbuama – not counting the complex question of investments in patronage networks – are livestock and tree crops. As befits their 'banking' role, neither livestock-rearing nor tree-crop production occupies much time or prominence. This does not mean they are of negligible magnitude, however.

There is a small community cattle pen (**wɔlɔ**) managed by a Fula migrant and his household in an area of grassland surrounding a large 'whaleback' in the granite zone three kilometres east of Mogbuama (cf. Fig. 4.2). Between 50 and 100 ndama cattle are raised here. Most of the cattle belong to leading Kamajei merchants and political patrons. Several Mogbuama citizens have cattle here and also at a much larger **wɔlɔ** at Boabu to the east. In December 1983, a two-year-old bull was worth between Le 300.00 and Le 400.00. Prices for cows were higher by about 25%. Cattle are slaughtered when a prominent figure needs to hold a major celebration. An animal might be sold if a political patron runs into urgent difficulties requiring a large cash sum.

Ownership of sheep and goats is more common than cattle ownership, and chickens are ubiquitous. Goats, important as gifts and sacrifices in secret society business, are each worth about Le 50.00 (for a mature female). The equivalent price for a ewe would be about Le 80.00. In a random sample, seven out of 25 heads of households said they owned goats. Two household heads also owned sheep. Only seven household heads claimed to have no livestock of any sort. Theft of small livestock is a regular hazard of village life. One man had six goats stolen during 1982. Women often prefer to carry their chickens to the farm hut each day rather than leave them in town where they may be stolen or donated to important visitors.

Most Mogbuama citizens, if they have the resources, will try and plant a few tree crops. Coffee is the most common choice, followed by plantain, kola, citrus and oil palms. One or two people have experimented with cocoa, but Mogbuama is well outside the zone where cocoa can be grown on an extensive scale (Gwynne-Jones et al. 1978). Tree crops occupy a belt of a half a kilometre or so immediately around the town. In 1982 (the season for which I have data) 21 people sold coffee, 18 plantain, and 11 kola. In addition, four farmers sold ginger, once a major cash crop in this part of central Sierra Leone. Through pledging (Ch. 7), much of the income from these crops is now controlled by a handful of wealthier farmers engaging in money lending. This is apparent from data relating to the coffee harvest. Four out of 21 farmers selling coffee in 1982–83 accounted for 60 per cent of sales (Fig. 6.3).

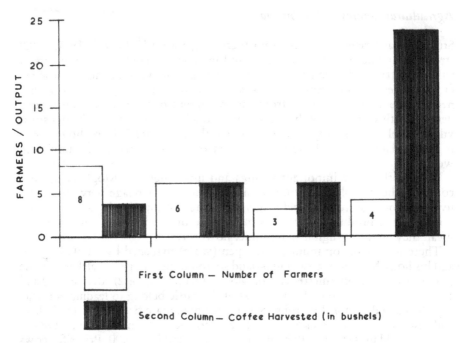

Figure 6.3 The 1982 coffee harvest.

Rice farm yields

Of 32 farms for which I have rice yield data, 17 were located in the river-terrace zone, and 15 in the granite zone. The sample was not random. It depended on who was free and willing to talk to me at a time when the village was preoccupied with **Pɔɔ** initiation. My data appear to be biased towards the smaller farms (averaging 2.7 bushels of rice planted per household compared with an average of 3.12 bushels per household for Mogbuama as a whole).

Total output from this group of 32 farms was 1514 bushels, a return of 17.43 bushels per bushel of rice planted (about 1200 kg/ha). Farmers reported yields for a large range of varieties, but only three varieties were common enough to make it worthwhile calculating averages: **jewulo** and **bɔngɔ**, quick-ripening rices commonly planted on **bati** farms or on the lower slopes of upland farms, and **gbɛŋgbɛŋ**, a medium-duration rice equally at home on **tumu** and **kɔtu** soils, and thought to be especially hardy (Fig. 6.4a, cf. Fig. 8.3). **Gbɛŋgbɛŋ** is grown by the majority of farmers in Mogbuama. Yields were reported for seven cases each of **bɔngɔ** and **jewulo**, for eight cases of **gbɛŋgbɛŋ** on **tumu** soils and nine cases of **gbɛŋgbɛŋ** on **kɔtu** soils. Gbɛŋgbɛŋ on **tumu** soils out-yielded **gbɛŋgbɛŋ** on **kɔtu** soils by a small amount (averaging 17 bushels in the first and 15 bushels in the second case). The quick rices **bɔngɔ** and **jewulo** both appeared to do better than **gbɛŋgbɛŋ** (averaging 25 and 26 bushels, per bushel of seed planted, respectively). Firm conclusions are precluded by the small size of the samples, however.

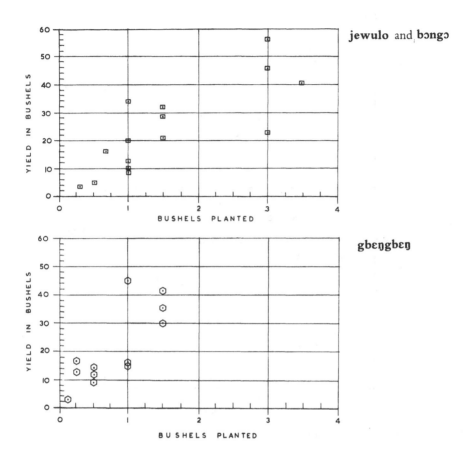

Figure 6.4(a) A comparison between yields of early-ripening rices (**jewulo** and **bɔngɔ**) and a medium-duration rice (**gbɛŋgbɛŋ**).

More definite conclusions are possible when rice-yields are considered on a farm-by-farm basis. On 17 **tumu** farms rice yields averaged 22.5 bushels per bushel planted (standard deviation, 9.02), whereas on **kɔtu** farms the average was only 15.0 bushels (standard deviation, 4.84). These results (Fig. 6.4) confirm farmers' claims that yields on **tumu** soils would tend to be higher, but more variable, than on **kɔtu** soils (standard error of 40% in the first case, and only 32% in the second).

IADP programmes in Sierra Leone have set themselves targets (cf. Karimu & Richards 1981) of increasing average upland rice yields by 10–20 per cent through the 'input package' approach (supply of credit, improved rice seed and fertiliser). It is important to note, therefore, that in the results discussed above, and graphed in Figure 6.4b, the five best farms on **tumu** soils produced 88% more rice per bushel of seed planted than the poorest five (weighted averages 29.5 and 15.7 bushels respectively) and the five best farms on **kɔtu** soils

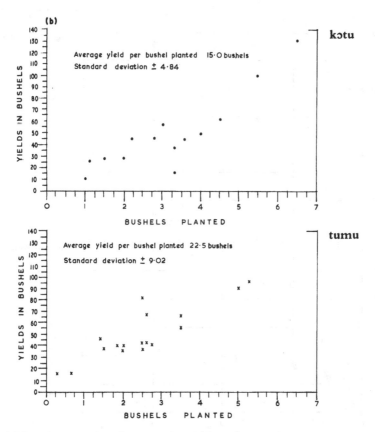

Figure 6.4(b)   A comparison between rice yields on **kɔtu** and **tumu** soils.

produced 95% more rice than the poorest five farms (weighted averages 19.7 and 10.1 bushels repectively). The argument for a shift in R&D emphasis away from technology transfer approaches towards greater support for indigenous initiatives hinges on the claim (supported by these figures) that there is considerable scope for a policy directed at bringing the less effective farmers up to the level of the best results attainable from local practices.

But to explore this possibility it is vital to ask how the variations between better and less good results have arisen. How have the best results been achieved? How much depends on luck and how much on skilful and inventive use of local resources? Could the relevant conditions and methods be replicated on the majority of farms? What, by contrast causes farms to fail? Could R&D resources be directed to solving some of these problems *in situ*, rather than as at present asking farmers to, in effect, start again with alien techniques and new inputs (farmers already in difficulty are not in good shape to take new inputs on board). These questions are central to the agenda of issues addressed in the remaining three chapters. It is appropriate to lead into a discussion of these issues by looking first at farmers' own explanations for their success and failure.

Failure and success

Failures

Bad results were explained in one of two ways: either the household was, to borrow Polly Hill's graphic phrase, 'too poor to farm' (Hill 1982), or the farmer had 'guessed wrong' in relation to ecological hazards.

A number of farmers had insufficient reserves of cash and food to organise labour for timely ploughing and weeding. Some were grappling with chronic indebtedness – still recovering from the effects of early rain in 1981, for example. Others had acute and unprecedented cash and labour crises to contend with. One man's wife had walked out on him, and after the exertions of ploughing he was too tired to weed more than a fraction of the farm by himself. In another case both husband and wife fell sick during June and did not complete the fencing of the farm, with the result that much of the rice was eaten by cane rats. A third man spent all the money saved up to hire labour for ploughing on hospital treatment for a sick relative. In a fourth case the farmer lost an expensive court case. To pay the fines he needed to take casual labouring work to the detriment of his farm. In all these instances and others like them there was never any doubt in farmers' minds about the link between their poverty, the consequent neglect of their farms, and the poor results achieved.

Some farmers accounted for poor results in terms of errors of judgement or bad advice received. Although 1983 was not a difficult year in terms of early rain, one or two farmers reported that their farms burnt badly, either from sheer bad luck (the wind changing direction at the wrong moment, for example) or because they fired the farm too soon (fearing early rain). Some farmers blamed poor harvest on errors in broadcasting their rice – too thick in some cases, too thin in others, and on occasion the wrong variety for the soil in question (sometimes due to lack of experience, sometimes because it was the only variety the farmer had available).

Two farmers working **kɔtu** land along the track to Yeisa had problems because they planted too late. The 1983 rains were surprisingly light in the latter half of the year, and in consequence, so the farm owners believed, their rice failed to reach a normal height before flowering. Neither had farmed this particular area before, and noting that the soils were transitional from **kɔtu** to **tumu** had sought the advice of previous occupants of the site. Both were advised, independently, not to plant too early, but now regretted heeding such advice. In one case the household's problems were compounded by problems of labour and food shortages at weeding time.

Two other farmers in this same area also reported problems. In the first case, a trader, not perhaps as familiar with the details of rice farming as others in the village, complained of a poor harvest and much 'black' rice due to the stony, droughty, character of **kɔtu** soils (more probably the blackened rice resulted from infection by a smut fungus, however). Another farmer, familiar with the site, having cultivated it once previously, nevertheless confessed he had made insufficient allowance for the desiccating impact of **kandi** in the farm, and had planted too early.

Reasons given to explain failures among intercrops were similar to those advanced to account for failures among the rice crop. Sometimes it was bad luck, e.g. ground squirrels had carried off the seeds of egusi melon (**koja**) before they had germinated. In other cases crop failures stemmed from lack of attention, e.g. guinea corn or beniseed raided by birds because no one thought it worthwhile scaring birds after the main rice harvest. Other intercrop failures were consequences of more fundamental problems over labour supply. Some intercrops, e.g. egusi, maize, cassava, okra, and cucumber, are planted as soon as clearing is complete. When there is a subsequent delay in rice planting and the farm becomes choked by weeds it is difficult for the workers to avoid hoeing out the egusi (a creeper) along with the weeds. Other cases reflect bad judgement. The moist **tumu** soils are not well suited to cotton, for example, and the failure rate is high.

A number of errors of judgement (and lessons of experience) were reported in relation to crop mixtures. In one case guinea corn left to ripen in the upland farm after the main rice harvest served to attract the attention of birds to the **yaka** rice in the swamp at the foot of the farm. (Normally **yaka** rice is left unattended since it is reckoned that birds are sated after the main harvest, and are unlikely to attack the long-duration varieties.) Another farmer planted a lot of guinea corn as hedge against problems the following season. His aim was to feed it to the household during brushing in order to conserve rice stocks for the ploughing season. Ploughing groups refuse to work unless fed rice. One 'tomato cup' of seed mixed with a bushel of rice is said to yield, if all goes well, 4 bushels of guinea corn without significantly reducing rice yields, but much depends on how well it is ploughed in and how badly it is attacked by birds. The trouble with this strategy is that guinea corn, if planted too thickly, shades the rice, and lowers yields. Beniseed is another crop that can have a deleterious effect on rice yields if it grows better than expected.

In one or two cases farmers growing rice varieties as mixtures reported problems of a similar nature. L is a stranger in Mogbuama who cultivated a **bati** farm in 1983. At home, on similar land, he commonly mixes a medium–quick variety (**nduliwa**) with a very long duration **yaka** rice, **manɔwa**. He did not have access to these two varieties in Mogbuama, so planted **bɔngɔ** as the quick variety and mixed with it an apparently suitable Mogbuama **yaka** rice **kpaamonyaye**. The **kpaamonyaye** proved to be a shorter duration **yaka** rice than **manɔwa** with the result that it and the **bɔngɔ** got in each other's way. The results were not bad. One bushel of **bɔngɔ** mixed with a quarter bushel of **kpaamonyaye** gave 14 bushels of the quick rice and 17 bushels of the **yaka** rice. Even so, L reckons, from seeing the way the rices competed in the farm, that results might have been better had he chosen another pair of varieties.

Successes
Naturally enough, the factors cited above reappeared in positive form when farmers were asked about their successes. Timing was the factor stressed most frequently. In most cases the key to good timing was having the resources to complete the work at an opportune moment. Some farmers saw this in terms of their ability to sustain, by social skills and management of domestic economy, a large household workforce, and to mobilise extra labour by participating in group labour.

Others, however, stressed the fact that timing is a question of skill as well as capacity. Knowing when to commit resources is as important as having those resources to hand. B insisted that his **tumu** farm had been a success because he had started to plough between 20 and 25 April. Had he begun the work two weeks earlier, like others around him, 'the rice would have grown too high'. Mogbuama farmers are quite concerned by this problem, which they correlate with low yields. I once came across a swamp where the farmer was happy to leave **semenje** (?) to compete for several weeks with his **yaka** rice, on the grounds that to delay weeding would hold back the growth of the rice, which in turn would lead to a more abundant harvest.

My post-harvest interviews contained a number of surprises. Two or three noticeably impoverished and heavily indebted farmers, including a man who by his own account subsisted mainly on bush yams throughout June and July, had excellent results from their farms, suggesting that although poverty and debt makes farm households more vulnerable to failure, failure is by no means predetermined in such conditions. Conversely, a number of farmers I had thought would have had especially good results seemed, in the end, not to have done as well as I (or they) had expected (and this I can report with some confidence in two cases because they were farms where I had kept detailed records throughout the year).

A number of farmers who befriended me initially were among those most actively engaged in village politics. They presented themselves, since I was interested in farming, as expert farmers, and indeed several were. But it was noticeable that as soon as the early harvest was safe and initial worries over rice supplies began to recede their interest in farming began to wane. From July onwards much more of their time began to be directed to a range of activities including court business, trade, chiefdom (and national) politics, craft activities (such as weaving), and the search for employment in the 'state' sector. While it was apparent that many of these activities were in themselves important and worthwhile, it was also apparent that pursuing them took the edge off the agricultural management skills displayed earlier in the year when farming was an all-absorbing preoccupation.

In sharp contrast, two other farmers, who proved to be among the most outstandingly successful in the whole of Mogbuama in 1983, were only names on my survey forms until very late on in my period of residence in the village. This last fact is a not insignificant clue to their success. Throughout the farming season they were rarely to be seen in the village, preferring to 'face their farms' rather than waste time on village-centred social and political activities. Certainly they had little time for courting the attention of a visiting researcher. One of these farmers, F, had built sleeping accommodation in the farm and came to town only rarely between ploughing and harvest. He had a separate **bulu** (early farm rice) which yielded over 30 bushels, more rice than some main farms. He was not able to tell me the final output from the main farm because it produced so much rice that he needed to hire labourers to help tie it (so does not yet know how many bunches went into the barn) but he doubted it could be less than 80–100 bushels (for 5 bushels of rice planted).

Conclusion

This chapter has looked at the results achieved on Mogbuama rice farms in 1983 and at reasons for success and failure. The gap between the best and average results is large enough to suggest that there is considerable scope for increased food output within the context of existing farming technologies. Does failure to get the best out of existing technologies depend on bad luck, inept judgement, or technical and socio-economic constraints? How might the less successful farmer more reliably and regularly attain the best results possible? What help could R&D offer in closing the gap between best and average local results? These questions are to be addressed via an analysis of the phenomenon of the hungry season, and an exploration of the ways in which farmers in Mogbuama experiment with seeds and planting strategies.

7 The hungry season

When a harvest is poor the farm household is liable to run out of rice before the next year's harvest is due. The problem of pre-harvest hunger is at its most intense in July and August. During the months prior to the harvest in 1983 quite a few Mogbuama households had to borrow rice both for planting purposes and for consumption. Much time was spent on hunting and gathering (with the rather bitter-tasting wild yam assuming prominence in diets) and a number of people I knew well lost weight, though apparently remaining fit. Apologies for lack of anything to offer visitors were frequent, and in one or two cases poor people were reduced to stealing because they had no food left. Pre-harvest hunger in 1983 was said to be mild. The 1982 hungry season, by contrast, had been much more severe and general in its impact because early rain had hampered the burning of many farms in 1981.

The purpose of this chapter is to answer the questions how, when, and who does pre-harvest hunger strike, and what can the victims do about it. Most farmers in Mogbuama are vulnerable to the hazards that lead to pre-harvest hunger but there are few years in which these hazards affect all farmers simultaneously. Households short of rice expect to be able to borrow from households with a surplus. Borrowing rice for repayment in kind after the next harvest (**lɔna**) is the main safety net against farm failure. Farmers in a position to make rice loans are often more concerned to use such loans to build up or strengthen their networks of patron–client relations than to make a profit in straight financial terms. This is why so much rice fails to reach the open market even when prices are relatively high. Clientelist political culture in rural Sierra Leone derives much of its legitimacy from the fact that food entitlements are based on hungry season rice loans rather than market exchanges (cf. Sen 1981). I once heard the story of a man who died of starvation. It was emphasised, however, that this man was a stranger without a patron. The story was told not to emphasise the severity of the hungry season phenomenon but to underline the point that, in adversity, the route to survival lay through patronage.

This point is relevant to the dilemmas of the Green Revolution initiative in Sierra Leone. Credit is a central component in the input package supplied by IADPs. The argument for placing the emphasis on credit is that resources in traditional agriculture tend to be allocated inefficiently due to the 'stickiness' of existing credit arrangements (e.g. unsurious interest rates). Ordinary farmers are supposedly in the grip of a narrowly exploitative 'class' of village money lenders (Karimu & Richards 1981). Cheap and efficient credit programmes organised by IADPs are intended to effect a crucial breakthrough by offering an alternative to the local money lender, thus freeing farmers to respond more effectively to 'market signals'.

There are several problems with this scenario (cf. Johnny 1985). Local credit arrangements are as much political as economic transactions. The 'money lenders' of IADP appraisal documents are in fact patrons in a clientelist political system. Clientelist politics retains widespread support and legitimacy in rural Sierra Leone because it addresses crucial local concerns, the most significant of which is the problem of pre-harvest hunger. Rice loans to ward off pre-harvest hunger are not necessarily seen by those who take them as unduly 'exploitative'. This is for two reasons. First, creditors are far from invulnerable to misfortune themselves. The creditor–debtor roles may be reversed on a future occasion. Secondly, Mogbuama farmers remain optimistic in the face of misfortune, due to a well grounded understanding of the moods and quirks of a complex agricultural environment. Local planting strategies offer a range of possibilities for subsequent risk-spreading adjustment. Farmers are given both to gambling and to experiment. If a chosen strategy mix fails many take the view that they can get it right next time. The answer meanwhile is to take a loan from a relative or patron who has had better luck.

The anatomy of pre-harvest hunger in Mogbuama

Causes

Hunger is a direct outcome of the failure of the 'household' rice farm. The most common causes of farm failure are early rainfall, sickness (including accidents) and miscalculations of an interpersonal or micro-political character.

The consequences of early rainfall have been analysed in Chapter 5, and it is unnecessary to repeat the details here. In a random sample of 30 heads of Mogbuama households, 21 reported pre-harvest hunger in 1982, most citing difficulties with early rain in 1981 as the cause. By contrast, only 11 households claimed to have suffered pre-harvest food shortages in 1983 (rainfall in 1982 was normal).

Everyone recognises the crucial importance of staying fit for work if hunger is to be kept at bay. The widespread dislike for swamp work, thought by many farmers in Sierra Leone to be an especially injury- and disease-prone activity, reflects this concern. Older farmers are especially vulnerable to sickness and physical breakdown due to the excessive demands of farm work during the labour bottleneck periods of ploughing and weeding. Brushing is a bad time for injuries affecting old and young alike. Septic wounds to the feet are especially problematic.

Accidents occur at any time. During August G carried a 50 kg sack of cement from the roadhead and spent the next week on his bed, crippled by a severely swollen hip joint. E had set aside a little money to hire labour to complete the ploughing of an especially weedy farm, but her husband developed a severe stomach complaint. A smooth-talking patent medicine seller, claiming to have recently returned from China as a doctor and somewhat incongruously demonstrating his portable stereo sound system as proof, diagnosed the husband as dying and relieved her, in her distress, of Le 30.00 to pay for 'necessary injections'.

A number of older heads of household handicapped by poor eyesight were especially prone to farm failure and consequent hunger. River blindness (onchocerciasis) is endemic in Mogbuama. The village is located between two sets of rapids where the Tibai and Mogboe rivers cross the geological boundary between Basement Complex granites and Rokel River Series rocks. These are potential breeding sites for the disease vector (*Simulium* spp.). Although only a small proportion of those infected eventually go blind, it is possible neverthe-less that onchocerciasis is a serious problem in Mogbuama. Surveys in a nearby community (Baiima) have shown infection rates of up to 50–60% of the total population.

Prospects for mobilising non-household labour at crucial moments in the farming cycle can be seriously affected by interpersonal miscalculations. The chief danger is that funds set aside for labour recruitment will be eaten up by gambling debts or in litigation.

Gambling has a significant part to play in local political culture (cf. Balandier 1970, Burnham 1980). The Mende admire a degree of controlled recklessness as much as they admire open-handed generosity. Some of those who attract attention to themselves in these ways have definite political aims in mind. Their extrovert style is part of the stock-in-trade of the upstart needing to build up a following 'from scratch'. (By contrast, established patrons place their emphasis on a 'quietist' style, giving away verbally as little as possible, thereby cultivat-ing an aura of profundity and mystery.)

Some litigation seems to be pursued with similar aims in view, i.e. to enhance the repute or notoriety of the parties to a dispute (cf. Finnegan 1963). Not all court cases carry such political overtones. Many poor farmers find themselves in court unwillingly, as defendants in debt or adultery cases, or arraigned for breaking local bye-laws. (Offences against the rules of secret societies have similar consequences, but the cases are tried by the society concerned in camera.) Court fines are often heavy. A man who refused to turn out for a day of community labour because he was worried about controlling cane rats on his rice farm was fined Le 30.00. Inability to pay a fine may be the start of a cycle of indebtedness and hunger.

Victims

Who is most likely to suffer from pre-harvest hunger? Two groups seem to be at greatest risk: those who live in smaller than average households (especially where the individuals concerned are old and/or handicapped or chronically sick) and those who become embroiled in litigation (especially where this results from interpersonal rivalry and over-reaching political ambitions).

Among the same sample of 30 household heads interviewed about hunger, nine cases deserve especially close attention. These were the cases in which pre-harvest food shortages were reported for both 1982 and 1983. Set against the average for Mogbuama these nine households had 17% fewer adults, 38% fewer children, and farm size 46% below average. Smaller than average household size is an important factor in continued vulnerability to hunger, because lack of 'in-house' labour restricts scope for recovery from 'random' shocks such as illness or adverse weather conditions. A smaller than average household size is also, in some measure, a symptom of previous failure. A sequence of inept production decisions may cause or increase tension between husband and wife or provoke young people to seek a new patron. A woman with sufficient financial resources to repay bridewealth and pay the court fees is free to sue for divorce. In poorer households women are not even necessarily constrained by finance since the marriage may have contracted on an informal basis (Little 1967).

Such problems are often compounded by a heavy burden of sickness and debt. One elderly couple handicapped by sickness gained a return of only four bushels of rice for every bushel planted (compared with an average input–output ratio of 1:18 to 1:20). Another handicapped man had an even more dramatic failure, harvesting nothing at all from a farm on which he had invested three bushels of rice and a great deal of hired labour. In a third case the head of the household struggled against chronic sickness to complete a farm, was diagnosed in Bo as suffering from stomach cancer, and died shortly before the harvest. A farmer beset with debts from litigation and gambling spent much of his time labouring on the farms of other people to the detriment of his own.

The old and poor are not the only ones to suffer farm failure, however. Aspiring patrons are at times also vulnerable, but more by miscalculation than mischance. Personal prestige is an essential ingredient of clientelist politics. Rising 'big men' not uncommonly become embroiled in a range of competitive activities (hospitality, vigorous personal feuding, heavy gambling, and dramatic litigation) intended to enhance their repute and political 'visibility' at a rival's expense. Court cases sometimes constitute a decisive trial of strength. Village politics is greatly enlivened by such competitions, but the possibilities for miscalculation are great. Boldness may carry the day, but the over-adventurous sometimes go 'over the top' to self-destruction. An opportunist seduced into a series of ill-calculated moves of this sort may find it difficult to complete a farm either because of lack of time or of funds for labour, or both. In litigation where the loser has miscalculated the costs and fines required, the court may sometimes distrain upon the standing crop. Part of A's rice farm was claimed in lieu of an unpaid fine and ever since he has refused to plant **ndeagbo**, the variety concerned.

Coping with hunger in Mogbuama

Self-help strategies on the farm

Mogbuama farm households pursue a number of agronomic strategies for fending off hunger, of which intercropping (especially production of cotton) and planting early rice are among the most important.

INTERCROPPING

The upland rice farm is never planted solely to rice. Cassava, egusi, cucumber, maize and some other vegetables are planted immediately after clearing and well before the rice is ploughed. Maize, especially, is a valuable hunger breaker, since it is ready for harvest from June onwards on farms in the river-terrace zone. Guinea corn, bulrush millet, and cassava from the previous year's farm are also important supplements to rice in the hungry months. Households anticipating difficulties may decide to increase the amount of guinea corn and cassava planted, though not without some risk to the rice harvest (as described in Ch. 6).

The intercrops belong to the women of the household. Those grown mostly for subsistence, e.g. maize and cassava, will be shared freely among members of the household, and indeed among friends and relatives (in July and August my room overflowed with cucumbers). Intercrops such as egusi and beniseed, grown partly or largely for cash, are a different matter however, and subject to some dispute. I have heard men say, jokingly (?), that if the prices of beniseed and egusi continue to rise as they did in 1983 their ownership is a matter that may have to be renegotiated. Some women are pretty reticent, perhaps understandably, to use money from the sales of such crops to bail out their husbands except in all but the direst of circumstances. Part of the attraction of a separate groundnut or swamp rice farm is that it is more clearly a private domain than the upland intercrops. I once gave a friend a small amount of money to help with her swamp farm. She immediately called her mother to take charge of it lest her husband should find out. Although he was not a poor man she had previously seen her savings absorbed into the 'household' kitty at moments of domestic crisis.

Whenever possible household members will cultivate separate plots of **yaka** rice, groundnuts, and sweet potatoes. Sweet potatoes are often grown, along with some cassava, in swamps during the dry season. Groundnut farms are frequently intercropped with cassava, or with a mixture of cassava and maize. In all cases the results belong to the individual not the household. To that extent they buffer the individual against the failure of the household farm. Whereas in extremity the money or produce may be used to help the head of household out of a dilemma, this is far from a foregone conclusion.

It would be wrong to assume that 'subsistence' production is based necessarily on an ethic of sharing. Women, and young men not yet farming independently, have a distinct perception that their interests are opposed to those of husbands or heads of households. At times there may be more 'community spirit' among young women from different households than there is a spirit of co-operation between man and wife. Much depends on the circumstances. A head of household who has been generous in the past may elicit loyal support from his farm household in times of difficulty. If on the other hand the cause of the difficulty is something for which junior members of the household have little sympathy – politically inspired litigation or ill-judged gambling, for example – their co-operation may be given much more grudgingly.

COTTON AND COUNTRY CLOTH

Of the crops belonging to women cotton seems to be something of an exception to the above strictures about the use of 'private' crops in an emergency. Cotton is primarily a 'cash' crop, in that most of it is produced explicitly for exchange (though some of these exchanges are of ritual rather than commercial significance). 'Country cloth' made from local cotton is important as a gift at weddings and funerals. Because of its importance in ritual exchanges country cloth maintains its value as a convertible asset despite imports of European manufactured cloth. It is a medium of exchange through which some of life's major crises are negotiated. If a funeral requires country cloth it is also the source to which a woman turns when a member of her family falls seriously sick and money is needed for hospital expenses. Difficulties over paying for

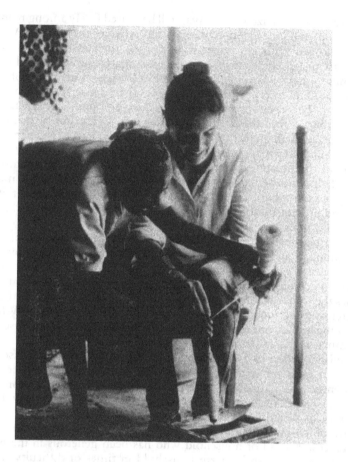

Figure 7.1 Drop-spindle spinning of local cotton.

hired labour to plough a badly delayed farm might be similarly solved by
judicious sale of country cloth. The role of country cloth in solving such crises is
of major significance, therefore, as a currency of social reproduction (cf.
Abraham & Fyle 1976, Little 1967).

About half of all households in Mogbuama (52%) either produced country
cloth in 1982 or planned to do so in 1983 (i.e. cotton had been planted in the
current farm). In 1982, 28 households produced enough thread for 82 country
cloths (an average of about three cloths per household). In 1983 a single
medium-sized cloth was notionally worth about Le 20.00, but the actual price
depends on the urgency of the need to make a sale. In an emergency the price
received might be very much less than the notional value, especially if cash is
tight in the village at the time (e.g. during the hungry season). Not every
household produces cloth every year. This will depend on the farm, on the
amount of cloth already held, and on time available for spinning. Some women

steadily try and equip each member of their immediate family with a stock of cloth, maybe giving one to the husband this year, one to a child next year, and keeping one for herself in the year following.

Cotton is spun by the drop-spindle method (Fig. 7.1). This is a very labour-intensive activity, but one which can be tackled by even the very frail and elderly, and at slack moments, especially during the dry season. Weaving, using the tripod-framed double-heddle loom, is a male speciality. The woman owning the thread will make arrangements to hire a weaver on a daily-wage basis (in 1983 typically Le 2.00 per day plus food). Five or ten men in Mogbuama undertake weaving as a part-time activity. It is mainly work for the dry season, and weather permitting, for the period just prior to harvesting. Every aspect of the technology – spindle, dyes, loom – is based on local materials, with one exception. Women rely on imported steel carding combs, the price of which has recently become prohibitive (in mid-1983 a pair of combs sold for Le 40.00 in Bo).

EARLY RICE

The importance of early varieties grown in **bati** farms or on the lower slopes of catenary farms in the granite zone has already been discussed in earlier chapters. A sizeable **bati** farm is a difficult undertaking without adequate supplies of capital and labour because the first crop must be well enough advanced to cope with periodic floods from June onwards. The early rices grown on **bati** farms are not flood-tolerant varieties. Since **bati** farms may at times be under a metre or more of standing water any delay in ploughing prejudices the whole operation. But the rewards are great. **Bati** farms typically yield about 30 bushels or more per bushel of rice planted and the owner of a two-bushel farm would probably be in a position, after deducting his subsistence requirements, to sell or lend between two thirds and three quarters of the total output, each bushel fetching twice the price of rice later in the year. Although one of the most successful **bati** farms in 1983 was made by a stranger a full-size farm of this sort is not normally a business for the impoverished because of the risks involved.

Most farmers, however, are able to plant a small amount of early rice on **bati** land or on the moist soils of the lowest part of the catenary profile in the granite zone, provided they do not outstep the limitations of available household labour supply. The harvest from these plots is enough to bring a rapid end to the hungry season in late August/early September, and in a few cases to leave a small surplus for sale while prices remain high. Planting up the topographic sequence has the additional advantage of spreading the labour requirement both for ploughing and for all subsequent farm activities.

Three early rices in Mogbuama are noted as being relatively high-yielding (approximately 20–25 bushels per bushel planted): **jewulo**, **bɔngɔ** and **jɛtɛ**. Each ripens within 100 to 110 days, though **jewulo** is generally reckoned to be the quickest, by a week or so. These varieties predominate on the lower slopes and in **bati** farms. Special note should be taken, however, of the *glaberrima* variety, **pende**, which is the quickest of all rices grown in Mogbuama, ripening in 85–90 days (cf. Table 8.2). **Pende** is grown both in **bati** farms and on **kɔtu**

Figure 7.2 Preparing bees' wax.

uplands. Because it tillers abundantly (cf. Fig. 9.1) it is broadcast much more thinly than other rices. This characteristic taken in conjunction with its speed in ripening makes it a useful hedge against the hungry season for farmers short of seed.

Fifty Mogbuama households (51% of the total) each planted an average of 0.94 bushels of early rice in 1983. Poorer farmers appear to be as likely to plant early rice as anyone else. Nine of the 11 farmers reporting a hungry season as a result of a poor harvest in 1982 had planted early rice, averaging 0.77 bushels each, in 1983. It seems reasonable to conclude that early varieties and a knowledge of catenary planting techniques are among the more important and widely accessible agronomic strategies for solving the problems posed by periodic hunger-inducing hazards such as early rainfall.

Off-farm self-help strategies

HUNTING AND GATHERING ACTIVITIES

The Mogbuama farm bush and adjacent forest and grasslands provide a wide range of foodstuffs and other useful products more or less freely to anyone with the knowledge, interest and time to collect them. The wild yam, **ngawu** (*Dioscorea minutiflora*), is one of the more important of these, in terms of hungry-season survival. It is common enough in cleared farms to serve as a short-term staple where all the rice has been eaten. **Sɔgbɛ** (*Urena lobata*), a major weed in unploughed upland farms, has a secondary significance as a source of fibre for making twine used, for example, for hammocks and hunting nets. In addition to a variety of plant materials used in village medicine, some farmers collect and sell the Calabar bean (**kio**: *Physostigma venenosum*), for which there is a pharmaceutical demand overseas. Honey and beeswax are other gathered commodities which generate a small cash income (Fig. 7.2).

There are insufficient oil palms in Mogbuama to meet local demands for oil. As frequently happens in areas where the palm is not numerous its primary use is as a source of palm wine. This is simple economics. When used for wine, oil palms generate more, and more regular, income than when harvested for oil. Many farmers, including the poorest, tap palm wine on a regular basis for their own consumption. Sales are most common at holiday and festival times. During the hungry season palm wine is a not unimportant nutritional supplement, but perhaps its main significance in minimising hunger lies in the fact that it is one of the major raw materials (the other being sugar) in the distillation of gin. The preparation of gin during the late dry season provides a means to convert 'slack season' labour into a readily marketable commodity, the sale of which can be used later to finance ploughing. Over the 1982/83 dry season a third of all households (32 out of 98) prepared gin, at an average value of Le 52.7 per 'jug'. The typical household produced between one and three jugs, but five households produced five or more jugs each. Maximum production by one household was 16 jugs, worth Le 704.00 in all (each jug having been sold for Le 44.00).

Hitherto, older farmers without dependents – one of the groups most likely to experience seasonal hunger – sometimes used gin distillation as a way of financing a farm. One of the farmers worst affected by failure in 1982 was nevertheless able to proceed with his 1983 farm because he had two jugs of gin to sell. Recent trends, however, make it increasingly unlikely that the poor will be able to continue to use this strategy. Because of the deepening foreign exchange crisis, and consequent petrol shortage, the price of second-hand oil drums (two of which are needed for distillation) doubled during 1983. (Drums previously worth about Le 10.00 were selling in January 1983 at Le 22.00 each, but their price subsequently went much higher.) A newcomer to distillation will now find it expensive to acquire the basic equipment. An even more serious obstacle was the threefold increase in the price of sugar during 1983, following the cessation of imports. Distillation of one jug of gin needs about half a bag of sugar, costing about Le 20.00 at the beginning of the year and Le 60.00 by August. Even farmers with adequate capital reserves then concluded that distillation was too expensive to continue.

Fish and game are abundant in the area around Mogbuama. Women regularly fish dry-season pools and men trap rodents in the course of pest control work in upland rice farms. In addition there are a number of richer if less predictable prizes. Giant cat fish (weighing up to 10–12 kg) sometimes invade **bati** lands on the rising flood in July and August. Two brothers sharing adjacent **bati** farms caught as many as five in 1983, each being worth about Le 40.00. Many farmers build special bridge traps to catch monkeys where they cross streams. Monkey meat is valued in many households, though Muslims refuse to eat it. Professional monkey hunters from Liberia, looking mostly for bigger species such as the red colobus, operated in Kamajei chiefdom duing 1983, and provided a certain amount of incidental employment for labourers willing to carry the smoked meat down to the road head where they were met by a regular lorry from Monrovia. Monkey hunting by Liberians has recently been proscribed by the Government. Finally, a number of farmers hunt bigger game with guns. There are about half a dozen shot guns in Mogbuama, and one local blacksmith makes flintlocks, including a heavy type used to hunt 'bush cow' (the African Buffalo, *Syncerus caffer*). Bush cow and warthog are abundant in the boli grassland west of Mogbuama, though not every owner of a gun has the courage or knowledge to hunt them. Taking bush cow requires a special 'double strength' charge made from two shot-gun cartridges, and a wounded animal is quite notoriously aggressive and especially dangerous. One hunter described the process thus: 'After the shot is fired, you fall down, the gun falls down, the bush cow falls down, and it is then a question of who gets up first'. From time to time hunters from Mogbuama have been gored to death by wounded animals.

The rewards from this kind of hunting are high if infrequent. To my knowledge, only one bush cow was killed during 1983. The meat was valued at Le 500–600. Good fortune might at one blow thus favour the hunter with a return equivalent in value to the rice produced by an entire year's farming effort. One way to regard bush cow hunting is to see it as a form of 'gambling', upon which a number of Mogbuama 'big men' have founded their success. Gun hunting in Mogbuama is threatened by the high and rising cost of cartridges. A single cartridge, costing Le 2.00 in 1982, was Le 3.50 by August 1983. It is not an activity for the poor. Expert hunters among the poor hunt large game in the boli grasslands using either pit trapping techniques or their patron's gun and cartridges. It is worth adding that when the poor say they are suffering from a 'hungry season' they mean they are short of the staple, rice, and perhaps cooking oil. It is only very rarely that they are entirely short of vegetable produce or local fish and 'bush meat', except for cases where anything caught or trapped is immediately sold to pay for urgent farm work such as ploughing.

LABOURING, GAMBLING, AND THEFT

Some farmers attempt to solve the hungry-season problem by labouring for cash. Men may join a ploughing group or women a weeding group with this partly in mind. Some groups work some extra turns which they aim from the outset to sell for cash to non-members. As already described the poorer members of such a group may also end up selling their own regular turns for cash to the detriment of their farms, thus escaping hunger one year only to meet it again in the year following. Regular work for a labour group also serves to conserve household food stocks, since the farmer receiving the group is responsible for all feeding. Food shortage may be a factor in a labour company member's decision to sell his turn.

Poor farmers also sometimes take casual work head-loading, especially during the latter half of the year when the road to Fala is closed to vehicles. The major streams cutting the track south of Mogbuama cannot be forded by vehicles until January. Mogbuama traders begin to ship out large quantities of produce – mainly rice, groundnuts and beniseed – in November. The pre-Christmas rush in 1983 provided an abundance of head-loading work of this kind, much of it done in the small hours of the morning. Some carriers would make the 10 km round trip to the road head two or three times a night at Le 1.00 per trip.

There are ten or 15 regular gamblers in Mogbuama. All-night sessions of cards and a game called 'top' take place in one quarter of the town, and it is said that sizeable sums can be won and lost – up to Le 40.00 in a night. One man is rumoured to have benefited his fellow gamblers to the tune of an entire IADP seasonal loan (about Le 90.00). Gambling may be more than entertainment or an element in a 'culture of poverty'. As already argued it can also be a way in which younger men attract notoriety and thus advance minor political ambitions.

Desperate circumstances sometimes provoke desperate remedies. One night during early August the town crier toured the town to report a theft of some tobacco. The thief was soon identified because she had sold the tobacco immediately to buy rice. The woman and her household had not eaten for two days because they had nothing left in the farm. Thus far she had resisted borrowing money, but accused of the theft and threatened with the punishment of being made to 'dance' in shame and ridicule around the town she was forced into a loan agreement in order to restore the tobacco, pay a fine and buy rice.

On 3 September, R reported the theft the previous night of some early rice (**jewulo**). Suspicion fell on J who had been seen earlier in the day arranging the sale of a quantity of **jewulo**, a rice he was thought not to have planted on his farm. The town crier names no names but provides unmistakeable clues to the identity of the person suspected. Despite this prompting, no witnesses came forward. If J has stolen the rice there is little chance of proving it provided he does not lose his nerve and confess. R decides to step up the pressure by threatening J with a 'swear', in which both parties would be required to testify in court over a 'medicine' deemed to have power to harm the guilty or untruthful. The plaintiff will seize on any circumstantial evidence that a 'swear' works – e.g. three suspected thieves in a neighbouring village recently struck by lightning – but this may not be enough to shake a cool, or desperate, customer. The dangers of crop thieving at this time of year are as great as the sanctions against it are ineffective. Solid pragmatists refuse to rely on mystical sanctions alone. They sleep in their farms.

Help from others

When all prospects for self-help have been exhausted a hungry household must turn to others for assistance. This help takes three main forms: informal assistance among kin, pledging, and formal borrowing on interest.

HELP FROM KIN

This is clearly a very important category of help in time of trouble but because it is in the nature of things 'informal' firm data are hard to come by. Among the kinds of help I noted were numerous cases where uncles and nephews and mothers and daughters might help each other on the farm or share food. A man recruiting labour might expect his kinsfolk to work for a slightly lower rate of pay, in return, perhaps, for some small token of recognition at harvest time. Much collaboration of this sort appeared to be free and easy. On the other hand I was told that sometimes close relatives only agreed to provide assistance, e.g. a loan of seed rice at ploughing time, at usual rates of interest. I know of one case where a mother is said to have refused to lend to her own sons and was thought by some to be quite justified in doing so.

PLEDGING

The owner of tree crops – coffee, kola, citrus, and (in a few cases) oil palms – can borrow money against the security of the trees. Pledging is relevant only to wealthier citizen farmers. The chronically poor lack the capital to invest in plantations and strangers lack land rights to plant tree crops. Trees are sometimes pledged when the owner plans to migrate to town. The money is valuable in financing the costs of the move and a successful migrant should be able to redeem the plantation easily enough upon returning. Pledging is also a way of defending a political ambition threatened by sudden misfortune. The following case seems typical.

A few years ago, Z, a farmer in an outlying village, needed Le 80.00 to cover the costs of a court case. He was described to me as a man who worked very hard in the farming season, but who during the dry season could not resist trying to appear a 'big man'. The way he attempted to do this was to commit himself, recklessly, to court cases and quarrels. His style, when boosted by drink, was to threaten litigation regardless of the financial consequences, with the result that accumulated legal expenses and court fines drove him deeply into debt. He pledged his coffee plantation to S in order to borrow enough money to cope with these debts. S has the use of the plantation, in lieu of interest, for as long as the debt remains unpaid.

So far as I can tell the severity of the current recession has meant that pledging is now more of a one-way process. Without access to his coffee, and unless his political gambles succeed, Z has little chance of repaying the original loan. But meanwhile S gains the windfall profits of high producer prices. He sold the coffee harvest for Le 42.00 in 1981, for Le 67.00 in 1982, and with young bushes beginning to bear for the first time and a near-doubling of Marketing Board coffee prices announced in the budget in July expected to be able to realise more than Le 200.00 in 1983. Meanwhile, any further development of the plantation is at a standstill since it is not up to S to manage it.

INDEBTEDNESS

I found it impossible to collect 'data' (in any formal sense) on indebtedness. Debt relations stand at the core of the local political system and to talk of such things freely is tantamount to social suicide. Nevertheless I was able to acquire some sort of general picture of who was and who was not most heavily in debt, and why, by getting to know some of the principal lenders and borrowers and by observing a number of transactions directly. By the end of my stay I knew of perhaps 20 or 25 people who fairly regularly lent money and rice. The greater part of their business was in loans of rice (**lɔna**). Four lenders who took me into their confidence (three younger men and an old woman) had between them loaned over 110 bushels of rice (some to households outside Mogbuama) by the end of August 1983. If these figures are typical and if my estimate of the number of lenders is reasonably accurate then something like 10–20% of the total Mogbuama rice crop is used as capital for credit operations. This is the same order of magnitude as my estimate for the proportion of the total rice harvest that reaches the market.

Borrowing is the last resort when all other resources are exhausted. In a typical year perhaps as many as a quarter or a third of Mogbuama heads of household are forced to borrow (**lɔnɛi hou**) in order to cope with pre-harvest hunger, to hire labour for farming and to meet sudden emergencies such as court fines or sickness. My estimate for the number of individuals able and willing to lend is somewhere between 30 and 50, depending on the year and season. There are about ten produce traders and five or ten current or past holders of political office who appear to be in a position to offer loans in both cash and kind at most times of the year. There are perhaps another ten or 15 regular lenders who deal largely or solely in rice. Others lend only rice and only on an occasional basis, depending on how good their harvest was or whether they were able to produce early rice from **bati** farms.

Among the group of regular lenders there are a number of older women, divorced or widowed, who make their living (sometimes independently of any farm household) from lending rice and sometimes money as well. The rice they use as capital has either been inherited or built up through trade. Lending activities and produce trading provide ways for older women to become independent of household and husband. It is clear that a number of women aspire to such independence. It is important to note, however, that these women are far from the conventional stereotype of the 'village money-lender'. In fact in terms of vulnerability they could be classed as belonging to the poorer sections of village society. Without their lending activities some would be destitute.

The lack of hostility to lenders as a group (provided they were of 'local' origin) is perhaps surprising. Far from being the subject of scandalous comment, **lɔna** seemed to be thought of as helpful, even meritorious, and rates of interest unremarkable. The standard rate of two bushels repaid in November for one loaned in July – a rate reported in the 1920s by Mackie et al. (1927) – matched closely the inter-seasonal price differential (Le 18.00–20.00 in July and Le 8.00–10.00 in November) on national and regional markets. It could be argued, therefore, that local interest rates on rice loans are no higher than is necessary to prevent rice leaving the village during the 'hungry season'.

Preventing rice from leaving Mogbuama in the period prior to the main rice harvest is something that both borrowers and lenders see as desirable. When the hungry season is severe the village and chiefdom authorities enact bye-laws to forbid the sale of rice to external traders. Local traders are allowed to buy, because their stores are in Mogbuama, and should hunger become widespread the rice is on hand to be loaned rather than exported. Local traders are willing to loan rice rather than sell it because they have a stake in village politics. Gaining clients through loaning rice is as valuable to them as cash in hand from sales to the national market. In fact, in times of high inflation and great market uncertainties an investment in the local political system may well have more enduring results than a quick cash return.

Borrowers appear to acquiesce in, even support, the system because in the first place it solves their immediate and most pressing problem, lack of rice. There may be more to it than this, however. The local view would appear to be that, although 'the poor ye have with you alway', in relation to environmental hazards in Mogbuama it is not always the same people twice. Lucky breaks – success at hunting, a good early farm, an undiscovered theft – allow some to set out on the road which in time might allow them to become a successful patron. Conversely, I came across other cases where established patrons were deep in difficulty, looking to raise loans to pursue a court case or to finish a farm. Thus a high level of inherent uncertainty in rice cultivation in Mogbuama appears to translate into an expectation that social fortunes might easily be reversed. Each year enough individuals, by fair means or foul, get off the hook of hunger, and enough established patrons get into difficulties, for the deeply indebted to continue to believe that one day their luck will turn.

Patronage and entitlement

Rice loans and money lending today substitute for older forms of political patronage, e.g. the protection provided by a warrior. A patron uses these resources to sustain a group not unlike an 'extended family' which provides in return domestic, political, and economic support. For example, in elections, chieftancy disputes, and court cases clients may be expected to offer testimony, votes and help in canvassing. In more mundane economic projects a patron will expect to be able to make prior claims on clients' time when hiring labour for ploughing a farm, carrying loads, and work on various 'community' tasks assigned to the patron in question.

Although patronage is by no means an ideal welfare system, it does have certain points in its favour. The most important, in relation to the hungry season, is that it is not in a patron's interest to allow a client to 'go broke'. Able bodies are at a premium in a 'labour shortage' rural economy such as Mogbuama, where rival settlements may be happy to accommodate the disaffected. In circumstances of intense competition to recruit followings patrons can no more allow clients to starve, even when they default on loan repayments, than countries in debt to the IMF can be allowed to go bankrupt.

At present the system of food entitlements grounded in patron–client relationships seems to be both buoyant and durable. The system has adapted to 'monetisation' of many aspects of economic and social life in the 20th century. In this respect it might be well to be cautious before concluding that the spread of modern currencies into rural areas during the colonial period necessarily signified a process of 'capitalist penetration'. From the late 1930s until recently the external economy of Sierra Leone was dominated by mining (van der Laan 1965, Saylor 1967) which operated as an enclave, requiring relatively little in the way of re-organisation of the agrarian sector along capitalist lines. When the 'normal surplus' was inadequate to feed the labour force drawn into mining, the foreign exchange generated by mining allowed governments to import rice. Under these conditions much of the wealth from mining flowing back into rural areas – both from migrant labourers and from 'bucket-and-spade' diamond miners, many of whom worked illicitly and only seasonally in the diamond fields – appears to have equipped old political formations with renewed energy and resources to pursue non-capitalist lines of development.

The future for the Sierra Leonian brand of clientelist politics is at present especially unclear because in the 1980s two rather different sets of factors – decline in the mineral economy due to exhaustion of the best diamond deposits and the impact of the world trade recession – have become fused. It seems probable, however, that while the recession remains severe and agricultural export commodity prices low, local clientelist politics will remain buoyant. In Mogbuama in 1983 people with rice to spare seemed to think first in terms of meeting local demands for loans and only second about rice sales. Although there is potentially a large demand for local rice, to replace the amounts hitherto imported, it is doubtful, given the reduced levels of economic activity within the urban and mining sectors, whether the price would be high enough to divert rice presently within local loan circuits on to the open market. The danger of a serious breakdown in existing patronage-based food entitlements will become an issue only if the lifting of recession conditions is followed by an intense period of capitalist agrarian re-organisation.

Conclusion

It has sometimes been argued that the hungry season in West Africa is evidence of population pressure (Miracle 1961). There is little if any evidence for declining output consequent on reduced fallow intervals on rice farms in this part of central Sierra Leone. The evidence reviewed in this chapter suggests that 'hunger' is most likely to be experienced by households short of labour. The farmers who experience hunger do so not because they are short of land but because they have lost control of their dependents and cannot find the resources to mobilise non-household work groups. The clearest evidence that hunger in Mogbuama is not malthusian in origin, is the failure by some farmers to complete the ploughing of cleared farms because of labour difficulties. It is hard to imagine that a reduction in population density would help solve such difficulties.

Capitalist penetration arguments (cf. Franke & Chasin 1980, Watts 1983) seem equally inadequate to account for the persistence of seasonal hunger or the durability and inventiveness of local entitlement systems in rural Sierra Leone. In Mogbuama 'hunger' and 'indebtedness' are issues in the politics of patron–client relations. It is insufficient to see these relations simply as 'outmoded' survivors of pre-colonial politics. Rather they represent a further working out of possibilities inherent in pre-colonial politics but drawing on modern 'technical' resources of a 'cash economy'. Present recession conditions are likely to prolong rather than shorten the life of monetised but non-capitalist food entitlement systems of this kind.

Are these indigenous entitlement arrangements as bad as they are sometimes painted? Current IADP policy in Sierra Leone aims to offer farmer credit at a 'fair' rate in order to break the grip of an exploitative 'class' of money lenders. The data in this chapter suggest a rather different picture. Local credit arrangements are seen as an essential corollary to the normal ups and downs of an uncertain environment. Patronage relations in Mogbuama are very fluid, reflecting a high level of intrinsic riskiness in productive activities. There is a good case for seeing local credit arrangements as a safety net above which farmers are in some measure free to experiment and innovate in a complex and changeable landscape.

8 Rice varieties and farmer experiments

In 1942 an officer of the Department of Agriculture, F. A. Squire, made a collection of Mende rice varieties from farms in Kenema, Kailahun and Kono Districts. In a short report introducing this collection (Squire 1943) he wrote:

> One might be tempted to imagine that primitive farmers would be blind to the importance or even the existence of varieties. Nothing could be further from the truth. There are at least fourteen and probably as many as twenty varieties well known to farmers who can recognise them at once and unerringly when shown samples. Moreover, every precaution is taken to keep the varieties pure. Seed rice is reaped from the centre of fields while the borderline between fields of different varieties is eschewed. During the drying process the *padi* is carefully rogued before the seed is put away for the next planting. Almost everybody in the native village appears to be well acquainted with the varieties and the rogueing is generally done by women and even children ... All the listed varieties are well liked and widely grown and each farmer may have several fancies. Some are reputedly quick, others heavy yielders; still others most suitable for certain types of 'bush' according to individual experience ... Yet the subject has received but little attention judging by the absence of records and collections.

Table 8.1 Rices planted by Mogbuama farmers in 1983.

Variety (times planted)	Grain size*		Awns (mm)	Husk	Bran
	Length (mm)	Breadth (mm)			
(a) early varieties					
bányálɔ́jɔ̀pòíhùn (9)	8.06	3.31	<2.00	yellow	white
bɔ́ngɔ́ (16)	8.10	3.18	<3.00	pale straw	red
'jɛnɛti'† (1)	7.72	2.95	—	yellow	red
'jɛtɛ' (3)	8.49	2.97	—	pale straw	red
jéwúló (24)	9.03	3.65	—	coffee	red
jéwúló gówè (?)	8.7	3.11	—	straw	red
péndé† (3)	7.92	2.86	—	olive/yellow	red

Table 8.1(*Cont.*)

| Variety (times planted) | Grain size* | | Awns (mm) | Husk | Bran |
	Length (mm)	Breadth (mm)			
'plakongo' (2)	8.52	3.08	—	olive/gold	red
(b) Medium-duration varieties					
bàìkɔ̀ (5)	8.86	3.41	—	yellow/gold	white
'baikɔpei' (?)	8.98	3.33	—	yellow/gold	white
'bògùtì' (10)	8.17	2.89	—	pale straw	red
gbòndòbà (?)	8.18	3.5	—	brown	red
fɛ̀lɛ́gbàkò (1)	8.4	3.35	—	golden	white
fìlíwà (4)	8.38	3.13	59.5	golden	white
gbɛ̀ŋgbɛ̀ŋ (52)	7.62	3.69	—	rust/straw (mottled)	red
gbɛ̀ŋgbɛ̀ŋ (awned) (1)	8.23	3.28	35.0	rust/straw (mottled)	red
gbɛ̀ŋgbɛ̀ŋ gòwè (1)	7.38	3.47	—	straw/rust (mottled)	red
gbɛ̀ŋgbɛ̀ŋtéé (1)	8.26	3.67	—	pale straw	red
'gboekondo' (5)	7.61	3.94	—	straw	red
gètɛ̀ (?)	7.61	4.4	8.32	straw	pink
góbé (12)	8.33	3.09	—	straw	orange
hélékpó (1)	7.64	3.57	—	straw	red
jùmùkù (6)	7.58	4.06	—	straw	red
kákàtáà (4)	8.9	3.31	<2.00	straw/yellow	white
'kátàtáà' (1)	8.44	2.97	—	yellow/brown	red
kɔ̀kɔ́ (5)	8.85	3.51	<15.0	straw	red
kɔ̀kúmbà (3)	8.09	2.76	7.5	orange/brown	red
'mbeimbeihun' (1)	8.71	3.33	<3.00	pale straw	white
ndɔ̀gbɔ́lùkpé (4)	8.34	3.01	—	dark straw	red
ngíyémá yàká (2)	10.11	2.94	—	straw	white

Table 8.1 (*Cont.*)

Variety (times planted)	Grain size* Length (mm)	Breadth (mm)	Awns (mm)	Husk	Bran
ngòló yómbò (2)	7.99	3.06	45.4	mottled brown (purple awns)	red
'puusawe' (1)	8.40	3.34	—	coffee	red
shàkí (?)	9.37	3.26	—	rust/straw (mottled)	white
tɔ́kpɔ́éhuǹ (2)	9.93	2.83	—	straw	red
'wadi' (1)	8.38	3.23	—	gold/brown	red
wóndé yákà (8)	8.88	3.11	<25.0	yellow	white
'yɔni' (11)	8.44	3.08	—	straw	red
(c) **Yaka** rices **kálɛ́mbááma** (8)	9.15	3.42	—	olive/yellow	red
kàvúnjí (1)	8.00	4.06	—	olive	red
kɔ̀kɔ̀yê (8)	7.95	2.62	—	rust+straw	white
kpààmɔ́nyáyé (4)	8.79	3.14	—	yellow	white
'soganji' (2)	8.00	2.83	—	straw+brown	white
'wɔɔgowe' (1)	7.67	3.07	—	straw	white
(d) Miscellaneous **'kɛbili'** (1)	7.98	2.97	—	olive/yellow	red
'mabaji' (1)	8.17	3.20	—	red/brown	red
sángányáá† (widespread weed, sometimes cultivated)	7.58	2.98	—	yellow	red
unnamed variety (1)	9.28	3.18	—	yellow	red

(e) Varieties also cultivated in Mogbuama in 1983 but for which specimens were not collected
'jomoi' (1), **'kailahun'** (3) (Long-duration **yàká** rice), **kónú** (1) (= **góbé** ?), **'lokope'** (1) (= **'puusawe'** = **'wadi'** ?), **màígà** (13), **'piema'** (1), **'plajoe'** (2).

---

*Average of ten randomly selected grains per variety.
†*Oryza glaberrima*, all others *O. sativa*.
Orthography based on Innes (1969) except for varieties within inverted commas.

Table 8.2 Planting to flowering intervals for eight Mogbuama rice varieties.

Variety	Planted	Flowered	Duration (months)*
pende	26/5	28/7	3
tɔkpɔehun	26/5	24/8	4
wonde yakai	17/5	28/8	4.5
jumuku	17/5	3/9	4.5
kakataa	17/5	3/9	4.5
banyalojɔpoihun	17/5	3/9	4.5
gboekondo	17/5	18/9	5
ngiyema yaka	17/5	25/9	5

*Median flowering date for 20 plants. Interval from flowering to harvest typically 25–30 days.

Mogbuama farmers differentiate between 70 rices by name of which 49 were planted by 98 farm households active in 1983. A collection representing each of these varieties was made during the harvest season (Table 8.1). About 20 varieties were also sampled at planting time, and eight were grown out in small trial plots to establish basic growth characteristics, e.g. interval between germination and flowering (Table 8.2). Much if not all of this material has been collected in recent years by plant exploration teams working in conjunction with IITA and Rokupr. So far as I know, however, little attention has been paid to how farmers themselves select and use local planting materials, apart from the comments by Squire quoted above. Yet the theme is an important one because, as this chapter will endeavour to show, it provides both insights into the way local farming systems operate and information on farmers' priorities for plant improvement programmes.

Rice classification in Mogbuama

Farmers in Mogbuama recognise three main groups of cultivated rice and two non-cultivated types. The first group of cultivated rices embraces the 'quick' varieties planted early in **bati** farms and on moisture-retentive soils. They ripen, on average, within 90–120 days. Yields are often quite low, but it is difficult to judge how much this is an intrinsic feature of the rices in question and how much is due to bird damage and theft (birds, like humans, suffer from a 'hungry season').

Jewulo and **bɔngɔ**, planted by 18 and 14 farmers respectively, were the two most common rices in this category in 1983, a position occupied in the past by **pende** and **jɛtɛ. Pende** is a *glaberrima* rice. According to Phillips (1964) **jɛtɛ** was once a recommended variety in western Nigeria (an interesting example of 'sideways extension' in the colonial period). With a quick-growing rice in a low-lying farm there is time and sufficient moisture for the stubble to regenerate, thus providing a second, rattoon, crop. Farmers referred to this as **jɔngɔ** (note, however, that Innes, [1969] glosses **jɔngɔ** as 'rice that grows from ears that have fallen to the ground during harvest').

The second group of cultivated rices is made up of medium-duration higher-yielding types. These are the archetypical 'upland' varieties, planted in May/June and harvested in October/November (ripening in about 120–150 days). The most common of all these varieties in 1983 was **gbɛŋgbɛŋ**, planted by 45 farmers. No other variety approached it in popularity. The next most frequently cultivated varieties were **maiga** and **yɔni**, each planted by ten farmers, and **boguti** and **wonde yaka**, each planted by eight farmers (the last named is a **yaka** rice which also grows satisfactorily in upland conditions).

Some farmers subdivide the medium-duration upland group into those which take about the same length of time to ripen as **gbɛŋgbɛŋ** and those which are a week or two quicker. According to one informant, **nduliwa, helekpo, gbondoba, baikɔ, kakataa, filiwa, maiga, jumuku** and **ngiyema yaka** are among those, like **gbɛŋgbɛŋ**, that ripen within four-and-a-half months (about 130–140 days). **Boguti, ndɔgbɔlukpe, yɔni, banyalojɔpoihun, gboekondo** and **gobe** are a week or two quicker. Of eight medium-duration varieties I cultivated for myself in 1983 the earliest to flower were **tɔkpɔehun** and **wonde yaka**, followed about a week to ten days later by **kakataa, jumuku, banyalojɔpoihun** and **yɔni**, and two to three weeks later by **gboekondo** and **ngiyema yaka**. These results are not always consistent with what I was told by farmers. It should be noted, however, that duration from planting to ripening is subject to a considerable range of statistical variation, depending on factors such as soil type, soil moisture at planting and consequent speed of germination, and subsequent climatic conditions. Disagreement among farmers about the length of time each variety takes is not surprising, therefore. On the other hand the matter is always of great local interest. 'How long does it take to ripen?' is one of the first two questions asked about any new variety. The other is 'Where does it grow best?'.

Among the medium-duration rices some varieties, e.g. **kɛbili**, are reputed to be better than average in 'weak' (i.e. short-fallow) bush. Although Mogbuama farmers are not short of land, varieties which do well on poor soils are useful for occasions on which a farmer finds not enough bush has been cleared and a patch of short-fallow land has to be taken in to make up the farm to size. Other rices, e.g. **ndɔgbɔlukpe** ('drives bush', cf. **lukpeya**, 'stand aside, make way for' [Innes 1969]), are thought to be especially suitable for long-fallow or otherwise especially fertile farms. The great appeal of **gbɛŋgbɛŋ** is that it is seen as a hardy, reliable rice which does well in a variety of conditions.

The third group of cultivated rices comprises the long-duration flood-tolerant or 'floating' rices; varieties which can be planted, in spare moments, in inland valley swamps and water ways and left to fend for themselves (cf. Fig. 4.1) due to their ability to withstand temporary submergence or match their growth to the depth of flood. (File 202/8/4 of 22 November 1931 in the Njala herbarium includes a specimen, **yakei** or **yaka guwi**, to which is appended the note 'Cultivated rice in inland marsh – this is the original Mende swamp rice as planted by the Mendes not introduced by the Agriculture Department'.) Typically, **yaka** varieties take between 150 and 180 days to ripen, and are generally heavy yielders. The ten or so varieties in this category planted by Mogbuama farmers are a very useful income supplement when grown on private plots. The supplementary as opposed to central role of these rices is apparent in the fact that although varieties are known by specific names few farmers ever call them anything other than **yaka** rice, unless specifically pressed. The taste of **yaka** rice is considered inferior and most of the crop is sold.

Some of the advantage of the typical high yield of **yaka** varieties is diminished by the fact that they are harvested in December when there is a glut of rice on the market and prices are at rock bottom. Agricultural development agencies have failed to comprehend this point when pressing the merits of the case for increased emphasis on swamp rice cultivation in Sierra Leone. To the Mogbuama farmer the idea of 'swamp cultivation' carries with it the cultural associations of **yaka** rice. When IADP bunded swamps are under discussion and farmers are shown the recommended 'improved' varieties (e.g. CP 4) they often remark that these are **yaka** rices, good for those with spare time and money, but inappropriate for the household farm. The fact that many of these improved rices ripen much more quickly than familiar swamp varieties (cf. Jordan 1951) is not necessarily seen as an advantage, since in places like Mogbuama this would mean that the swamp and upland harvest would coincide, exacerbating an already difficult labour supply problem.

Mogbuama farmers recognise two categories of non-cultivated rice. **Sanganyaa** is a term applied to a self-sown rice sometimes found as a weed in upland rice farms. The specimens I collected have the characteristic pear-shaped grains and short ligules of O. *glaberrima*. Farmers recognise that **sanganyaa** is closely related to **pende**, once the pre-eminent early rice and now one of only two upland *glaberrima* rices still cultivated regularly in Mogbuama. The main difference between **pende** and **sanganyaa** is that the latter takes longer to ripen. Generally, **sanganyaa** is separated from all other rices because it is more difficult to husk. Some people reckon that it is sweet to eat, and it is said to be cultivated from time to time. K told me he would plant **sanganyaa** if he was short of seed and still had some cleared land to plough. An old man, N, recalled that it was a variety commonly planted in **bati** farms in his youth.

Wild rice is termed **ngewɔ-bɛi** (literally, 'God's rice'). The annual species O. *barthii* (O. *breviligulata*) and the perennial species O. *longistaminata* are both indigenous to Sierra Leone. I collected several specimens of a wild rice with short ligules and no rhizomes (O. *barthii*?) from uncultivated grassy swamps in the granite zone north and east of Mogbuama. These were described to me by one informant as **yaka sanganyaa ngew ɔ-bɛi**, i.e. 'wild sanganya-like swamp rice'. None of my specimens had yet flowered, but I was told that some people gather this type of rice by shaking the grains into a calabash when it ripens in December (it shatters too easily for the panicles to be cut with a knife).

The categories so far covered reflect the major concern of Mogbuama cultivators to spread out labour inputs and secure a 'balanced' farm – some early rice to stave off hunger, a major medium-duration upland variety to meet household needs and some **yaka** rice to provide private income for individuals. In addition to locating any rice within this general scheme, farmers also consider each of their varieties in relation to a lengthy check-list of secondary characteristics.

In relation to the growing plant, features upon which farmers most commonly comment are height (and therefore ability to withstand variable flood

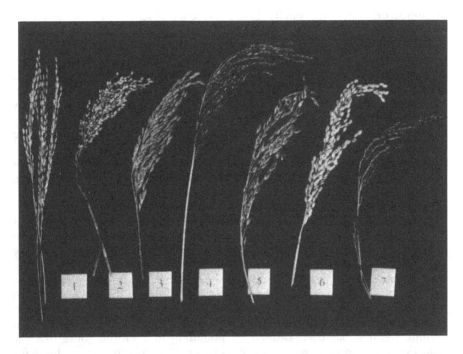

Figure 8.1 Seven Mogbuama rices: 1, **sanganyaa**; 2, **kpengee**; 3, **jewulo**; 4, **gbɛŋgbɛŋ**; 5, **kalɛmbaama**; 6, **gètè**; 7, **ngolo-yombo**.

conditions), tillering, length of panicle, and resistance to lodging and shatter-ing. For example, **pende** is noted for its dense tillering, and the **yaka** rice **kɔkɔyɛ** is noted for the extent to which the grain shatters during harvest. An 'improved' rice, LAC 23, distributed to Mogbuama farmers during 1983, was greatly admired because of the length of its panicles.

Among grain characteristics, lengthy awns (**fili**) and pronounced outer glumes (**kalɛ**) are considered important because birds find varieties with these features less palatable. Varieties with long awns (50 mm or more) are often referred to under the more or less general designation **fili-wa**. The equivalent general name for long-glumed varieties (i.e. those where the outer glumes run the full length of the grain) is **kalɛmbaama**. One such variety is a **yaka** rice known as Madam Yebu (Fig. 8.1).

The colour of the husk (**ka**) and bran (**gima**) is also of interest. Some farmers are attracted to grains with unusual colours. For example, **ngolo-yombo** ('chimpanzee hair') is admired for its deep reddish husk and long red-black awns (Fig. 8.1). A number of **yaka** rices introduced in the colonial period (e.g. **pladisi**, ex-Temne **pa** D.C., Demerara Creole, introduced from British Guiana in about 1914) have white bran, a preferred characteristic on the world market (Grist 1975). Mende farmers view matters in an opposite light. Upland varieties with white bran are sometimes treated with suspicion for fear that they will be grouped by local buyers and borrowers with the little-favoured **yaka** rices. Conversely, a **yaka** rice with red bran is at an advantage by comparison with others in its class, because it is able, by appearance at least, to pass as a 'proper' rice (cf. Table 8.1).

Some rices are easier to husk than others. Some take longer to cook than others, and take up more water in the process. Some keep better than others after cooking. Women are careful to classify varieties according to such criteria because these are matters which vitally affect their workloads. How long will it take to husk rice needed for family consumption? Which types may be safely mixed in the barn and which at all costs must be kept separate because they require different cooking times? Which varieties become sticky in cooking and unpleasant when served up cold? This last factor is important in the context of seasonal labour shortages. A good firm rice, which remains palatable after it has gone cold, may be served on a second occasion and saves valuable time when women are busy on the farm.

A final set of characteristics of some concern to Mogbuama farmers concerns the relationship between grain 'on the stalk', in husk, and milled ready for consumption or sale. Due to the widespread use of more or less standard volumetric measures – the 'butter cup', the 'threepence pan', the 'one party pan', the four-gallon kerosine drum (a half bushel measure) and the oblong wooden bushel box – most people are quite well aware of the relativities involved. It is generally reckoned that in order to fill one bushel it is necessary to thrash (or rather, to tread out, because this is how the women do the work) 15 ordinary sized bunches of grain, and that a bushel of paddy reduces to half that volume when it has been cleaned by pounding in a mortar (note that the reduction is not so great when measured in weight terms, because volume for volume clean rice is about 33% heavier than husk rice). It is widely recognised that these conversion rates can vary with rice variety. Some apparently heavy panicles give relatively little paddy, some apparently fat grains give relatively little clean rice because they have unusually thick husks. For this reason, a number of rices (including some 'improved' varieties) look better in the field than they turn out on the plate, and farmers are rarely slow to spot such differences.

Development of indigenous rice varieties: selection and experiment

Experience teaches that any harvest will contain types the farmer was not aware of planting. Such occurrences are sometimes put down to the accidental mechanical mixing of two seed types or to the work of birds and animals. One recent find of this kind (tɔkpɔeihun, 'on the palm tree') was multiplied from a single shoot found germinated on the crown of a palm tree, where it was presumed to have been dropped by a bird. Farmers believe, however, that it is also in the nature of rice to change from time to time. I never found anyone who was prepared to venture beyond 'God has made it so' if pushed for further explanation of this point. No one in Mogbuama admitted to any knowledge of cross pollination, though Squire (1943), quoted above, reported that farmers in eastern Sierra Leone kept well clear of field boundaries and boundaries between different stands when harvesting seed rice (arguably evidence of an intuitive understanding of natural crossing).

Figure 8.2   A farmer experiment (**hungɔɔ**) – swamp rice trial.

Although the source of change in planting material may be a mystery to Mogbuama farmers there is little hesitation in reacting to such changes after they have taken place. This reaction takes two forms: the roguing of unwanted material and the conservation of interesting material for experimentation and further use.

A farmer's first concern with unfamiliar material is whether or not it ripens at the same time as the variety with which it is growing. If it is slower to ripen its separation is ensured because it is left on one side by the harvesters (this is an advantage of the panicle by panicle harvesting techniques over the sickle harvesting undertaken in some parts of northern Sierra Leone). An early ripening variety will already have attracted the attention of the farm household, who may have taken the chance to harvest it ahead of the main crop for their own consumption. An unwanted variety drying with the main crop (rejected because it is more difficult to husk than the main variety, for example) will be carefully rogued as the bunches are made up, or before the women tread the rice. Particular care is taken to separate out **sanganyaa** in this way.

Sanganyaa is an interesting case. It is much more common in some fields than others, and my questions about this were several times met with the answer 'Who can tell! If only a few grains fall into the seed rice then it will be abundant in next year's farm', until one day it was pointed out to me that **sanganyaa** was often a problem on the farms of clients, strangers and people heavily in debt. It seems that some regular lenders of rice simply failed to bother to rogue **sanganyaa** from rice destined for credit. Where a lender suspects borrowed rice might be used for seed not for consumption it is a courtesy to warn the borrower that it is unrogued but this does not always happen.

The evidence so far suggests that most farmers have the knowledge, and provided they stay clear of debt (and this is an important proviso) also the opportunity, to maintain varieties by careful selection of planting material. And yet, apart from the case of **sanganyaa**, there appears to be greater interest in roguing as a source of new and curious planting materials than as a technique for maintaining 'pure' or 'stable' seed stock. Any new material thus identified is separated out and tried on its own to determine its useful properties. Such trial plots are known as **hungɔɔ** or **saini** (Fig. 8.2).

Innes (1969) glosses the phrase **ti mbɛi sainiilɔ** as 'they tried out the rice (e.g. in a seed bed to determine whether it would grow, before full-scale sowing)'. A trial of this sort is the recognised way to assess any new planting material, including unfamiliar varieties obtained from relatives, friends and visitors. During 1983, I distributed 50 packets of half a kilogramme or so of three 'improved' rices – a short-straw Asian swamp variety, CCA, a medium-long duration upland variety (ripening in 140–150 days) from Liberia, LAC 23, and ROK 4, a swamp variety developed at Rokupr – in order to monitor how farmers set about evaluating new varieties. I provided only a minimum of information and advice about where to grow them, namely, whether the vareity was a swamp or upland type and the approximate duration from planting to harvest. As far as I was able to determine, all the seed I distributed was planted out (some of it reached outlying villages, where I was not able to check plots at first hand). About half the trials were outright failures due to misfortune or neglect.

Initially, there was much interest in ROK 4, because it grew strongly, with dense tillering. The eventual results were poor because the water levels in swamps and **bati** farms in this escarpment region are so unpredictable. Some farmers tried ROK 4 in **bati** farms where, because it was slower than varieties such as **jewulo**, it was drowned by floods in June and July. The variety CCA, released as a 'quick rice' suitable for double cropping in swamps, was too slow, and generally too short in the stem, to succeed without water control. V made a useful discovery, however. Late with his work, the water had already risen in his **bati** when he came to plant the CCA, so instead he decided to try it on the lower part of his **tumu** farm in the river-terrace zone where it did very well. He harvested over one bushel (all of which was kept as seed for next year's farm) from five 'butter cups' (approximately 1.0 kg) of seed. At 180 'butter cups' to one bushel this amounts to an input–output ratio of better than 1 : 35. It is quite common for farmers to take careful note, using their own system of volumetric measurements, of input–output ratios when they lay out trials of this sort (Johnny 1979).

LAC 23 was the most successful of these varieties. On a short visit to Mogbuama in June 1985 I was told that several farmers had carefully multiplied enough LAC 23 to make it one of their main upland varieties.

Mogbuama farmers test any rice with which they are unfamiliar in the way that they checked out the three varieties of rice I brought with me to Mogbuama. If in the first instance the results of these trials are not good most farmers will reckon to try a different location, moving a rice from swamp into

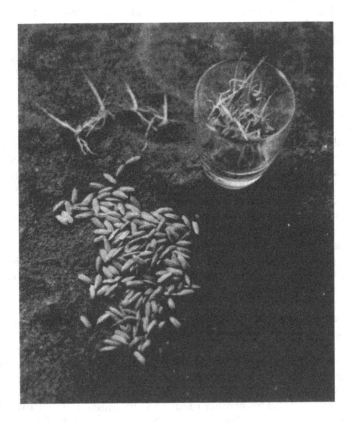

Figure 8.3 A farmer experiment – a germination trial.

bati or from a dry stony soil on to **tumu** land, for example. With an unfamiliar variety, and little or no advice on where to plant it, most farmers would look for a fertile, moisture-retentive patch of soil sufficiently near the farm hut to discourage attack by pests and allow progress to be monitored easily. Inter-zones between soil types (e.g. the junction between **kɔtu** and **ɔanya** soils in a catenary farm) are often favoured as sites for such trials, as are the specially fertile spots where sticks were piled for burning during the clearing of the farm. Soils around termite hills and palm trees are sometimes favoured because they are said to be unusually moisture retentive (cf. Miedema & van Vuure 1977). In deciding where to try out an unfamiliar variety, some farmers are guided by the appearance of the grains. Upland varieties with white bran (such as **katataa**) are thought to be best suited to **tumu** soils and **bati** farms, for example.

On occasion, farmers will also test the germination potential of a batch of seed (especially if this has been borrowed and is of uncertain provenance). One way to do this is take a hundred or so seeds mixed in a little mud and to wrap them in a suitable leaf. The large moisture-conserving leaves of a swamp tree (**mbowanda**) are a popular choice because they can keep for up to a month without cracking. The parcel is unwrapped after four or five days and the contents inspected to assess the proportion of seeds which have germinated (**mba mijingɔ**). If the ungerminated seeds are numerous the batch will be rejected for planting. The same test is sometimes carried out by dropping a handful of seed in a cup and soaking it in water for a few days (Fig. 8.3). A germination test, like a rice trial, will be referred to as **hungɔɔ**.

When, after some seasons, a farmer notices that a given type of rice has become very variable in appearance a decision may be taken to sort out the planting material for next year's farm into its component parts. One farmer said this was a decision he would take in consultation with the women of the farm household who would then supervise the harvest to ensure the sorting was well done. The variants thus isolated are sometimes recognised as, or assimilated to, an established category. In other cases the material may be unfamiliar. P has noticed, for example, that over the last year or two his **jewulo** has begun to include a type with lengthy awns. He is interested in the possibility of being able to separate this out eventually, because of its potential resistance to bird attack. Thus far all the long-awned rices with which he is familiar are medium-duration types. A long-awned quick rice would be especially useful.

I was unable to make any estimate of how frequently Mogbuama farmers succeed in isolating a new variety with useful properties – this might occur two or three times a generation. The search takes place at all times, however. Four or five 'finds' of potentially interesting material were made during the 1983 harvest season, and I came across two current experiments in which earlier selections were being 'field tested' and multiplied for full-scale cultivation. In one of these cases W and his brother rogued an unfamiliar variety from a field of **gbɛngbɛŋ** in 1981. In 1982 they planted a handful around the farm hut, from which they harvested over a bushel which W is multiplying in his current farm. So far, they refer to it as **'kakataa'** because it is similar to **kakataa** in external appearance. Unlike true **kakataa**, however, it has a red bran, so W thought it might need a specific name of its own in future. The other experiment along these lines also relates to material found in a field of **gbɛngbɛŋ**. The rice in question is like **gbɛngbɛŋ** except that it has long awns (cf. Fig. 8.1).

Mogbuama farmers have three main sources of planting materials for rice farms, therefore. Some rices are introductions – begged or bought from visitors, neighbouring villages, and returning migrants, for example. Others are adventitious arrivals – varieties found mixed in with other types of seed or spread by birds or passers-by. (The name of the upland variety **kɔ́kɔ́** translates literally as 'find'.) Thirdly, some varieties are farmers' own selections or spontaneous crosses (cf. Chandraratna 1964). In farmers' eyes all three processes are significant sources of useful planting materials.

Mogbuama farmers have considerable confidence in local procedures for selecting and testing planting materials. Several informants drew attention to the case of **gbɛngbɛŋ**, currently grown on one in two farms in Mogbuama and generally considered to be the most reliable of the medium-duration upland rices. **Gbɛŋgbɛŋ** is believed to be the result of the selective development of **nduliwa**, a rice not cultivated in Mogbuama in 1983 but well remembered by older residents, who frequently cited it as one of the most important upland rices during their youth. B recalls first seeing **gbɛŋgbɛŋ** in Mano in 1935, and claims to have introduced it to Mogbuama in 1945 after being given half a bushel of seed by his mother-in-law. Some Mogbuama farmers speculate that **gbɛŋgbɛŋ** was originally selected by farmers in Bumpe, a town on the old road between Njala and Bo and a noted centre for indigenous experimentation.

Whether it would be appropriate to re-think conventional approaches to seed multiplication and distribution given the evident success of a number of local selections of this sort is a question taken up in the conclusion to this chapter.

Adoption and abandonment of rice varieties

After making a complete inventory of rice varieties planted in Mogbuama during 1983 I undertook a further survey of a random sample of 30 farm households to enquire about their sources of rice planting materials. Heads of farm household were asked when they had first started to grow their current rice varieties, where and how they had obtained the seed, whether their current varieties had replaced any which they did not now cultivate, and why these changes or substitutions had been made.

The 30 respondents provided details relating to 73 cases involving 26 different rices. Four quick rices were cited 17 times, 17 medium-duration upland rices were cited 50 times, and five **yaka** types were mentioned six times. In 44 cases the variety in question had been obtained by loan or purchase, and in 27 cases by gift or exchange. Most varieties had been acquired within Mogbuama (53 cases) or in surrounding settlements in Kamajei chiefdom (14 cases). The balance comprised varieties brought in by migrants or acquired by villagers when on their travels. The majority of current varieties (49 out of 73) were replacements for varieties previously cultivated. These substitutions stretched back over a period of 25 years, but the bulk were recent (38 in the last ten years and 24 within the last five years). Of the remaining cases, there were 21 instances where a rice had been grown without interruption, two instances of a variety being dropped without replacement, and one where a new variety had been added to, not substituted in, the farmer's range of rices.

Looked at farmer by farmer, only four farm households (three of which were newly or recently formed as independent units) reported no changes at all. Of the remaining 26 households, 11 farmers reported a sequence of substitutions, e.g. trying out two or three varieties in succession. No one reported reverting to a variety tried previously. It is clear, then, that in relation to planting materials the experience of change and experiment is normal rather than unusual.

Some of these changes are forced by circumstances. Where hunger, debt and the ill-fortune cause a 'stranger' farmer to leave home and seek a better future elsewhere almost certainly it will be the case that the seed rice is finished also. Of 46 reasons given to account for substitutions among varieties, farm failure, hunger, indebtedness, theft, and migration were cited 24 times. In the majority of cases I was told simply that the variety had 'failed'. Some respondents were more explicit: seed stock for the variety in question was 'lost' paying debts or fines, left behind when migrating to Mogbuama, or eaten by relatives or members of the household in an unguarded moment. Explaining why he no longer grew a variety he quite liked, H observed, somewhat tersely, that 'all was consumed by relatives and animals'. Another informant had become disenchanted with early rices because of the importunings of his kinsfolk.

Where personal difficulties are directly attributable to a farm failure it is understandable that those seeking to borrow rice will be unlikely to ask for the varieties most closely associated with their present plight. Despite the wide support for **gbeŋgbeŋ** as the most reliable of indigenous varieties, five of the 15 farmers in the sample who had tried it had changed to something else subsequent to a major farm failure. Changing variety is part of the process of making a new start, and happens irrespective of the 'objective' merits (widely admitted in the case of **gbeŋgbeŋ**) of the variety in question. This is an important factor in Mogbuama farmers' evident desire to maintain as large a range of varietal choice as possible: 25 medium-duration upland varieties planted in 1983, for example, not one of which, apart from **gbeŋgbeŋ**, was grown on more than one farm in ten.

Some varieties were said to have been substituted for ecological reasons. Two farmers changed varieties considered best suited to **tumu** soils when they moved to farm **kɔtu** soils. Three cases were reported where a batch of seed was abandoned because it had become infested with **sanganyaa** or hopelessly mixed in the barn. Four farmers abandoned their current variety because they had become bored with it or because they thought it looked 'tired'. One informant complained that **nduliwa** 'looked like an old rice even when it was new'.

In over a third of all cases farmers claimed they took on a new rice because they liked the look of it and wanted to see what it could do. Some of the comments offered suggested that the farmer in question had been impressed by a friend's or neighbour's success, but others equally clearly asserted an attitude of curiosity for curiosity's sake: e.g. 'I thought it was attractive to look at', or 'It has interesting features', or 'I wanted to see what happens when planted alongside my other rices'. An upland rice (**kpengee**) with unusually small round grains (Fig. 8.1), grown in Kowa chiefdom, attracted great interest when I took a handful of seeds to Mogbuama. People stopped me on the street with requests to display 'the dwarf'.

During numerous discussions on rice and its infinite variety – a subject likely to elicit a more lively interest than almost any other topic on the fieldworker's check-list – I was to discover that no one ever saw anything odd in responding to the question 'Why did you plant this type of rice?' with the simple answer 'For experiment'. 'Peasant conservatism' is simply not a relevant concept in this context. Playing with rice is the national sport of rural Sierra Leone.

Conclusion

This chapter has illustrated the extent to which despite (or perhaps because of) their poverty Mogbuama farmers are prepared to probe and attack agricultural problems with a marked sense of inventiveness and flair for experimentation. This suggests that efforts to surmount the agricultural crisis now facing resource-poor farmers in Africa might be more effective if local inventiveness of the sort illustrated in the present chapter could be linked to formal-sector R&D initiatives. It is appropriate, therefore, to draw attention to three specific questions raised by the way in which Mogbuama farmers experiment with planting materials.

(a) *Do farmers and formal-sector agencies experiment with the same ends in mind?* From the point of view of formal-sector agencies the range of indigenous planting material available in a village like Mogbuama is unnecessarily large, and a valid objective of agricultural development is to replace a profusion of uncertain and unstable variants of local land races with a much smaller range of fixed and reliable seed types. This view is not necessarily shared by villagers. My evidence is that Mogbuama farmers are as keenly interested in 'variability' as in 'varietal stability'. The belief that it is in the nature of rice planting materials to change over time is both widely held and deeply engrained in social as well as ecological practices. Rices are rogued as much to provide interesting new materials – materials with which to make a new start after misfortune or to gamble one's way to a useful measure of social notoriety, for example – as to maintain a planting stock with fixed characters. Few Mogbuama farmers would be willing to cut down on the variety available to them while they believe that there are still useful and productive discoveries to be made through matching new or interesting varieties to local ecological niches. And who is to say that they are wrong? In these circumstances hyper-variability among rices is invested with a rich cultural significance. If rice is a 'currency' in which many social relations – relations of patronage and clientship – are computed, then rice varieties have assumed something of the significance of gambling chips in a game of social mobility. Proposing a reduction the number of varieties available might well be greeted with as much enthusiasm as a plan to abolish football pools.

(b) *Might science have something to learn from attempts by peasant farmers to resist 'the modern trend to narrow [the] genetic diversity in rice by concentrating on only one or two types of rice culture . . . (Buddenhagen 1978)?*
Central to formal sector rice research in Sierra Leone in the last half century has been the idea of developing high-yielding varieties with specific agro-ecological regions in mind. Thus, varieties have been selected for suitability, for example, to iron-rich soils of the boliland region, to the special soil conditions and flood regimes of the riverine grasslands of the lower Sewa and the tidal mangrove swamps of the Scarcies Estuaries, and to inland valley swamp environments. But as is now apparent from the case study, resource-poor farmers are unlikely to find the concept of 'agro-ecological regions' of much help. Even within the compass of a single household the key to survival is found in the cultivation of a diversity of land types. Since most farming enterprises involve the combination of 'upland' cultivation with two types of swamp cultivation – quick varieties planted on the rising flood and long duration floating varieties planted in inland valley swamps – farmers are less interested in piecemeal improvements to one

or other of these areas than they are in how the elements of the system work in combination. The lesson for rice research agencies of the way in which Mogbuama farmers handle their own rice planting material is that the 'single variety' approach is of less relevance than an approach based on a suite of improved rices selected to operate as an integrated package.

(c) *Might development projects make use of farmer skills in the area of plant selection?*

In Sierra Leone currently, bulk supplies of improved varieties are produced by a centralised seed rice multiplication project and then distributed through Ministry of Agriculture regional offices and IADPs. Typically, farmers apply for credit to finance seed purchases, register their requirements with the project in the dry season, and receive seed a few weeks prior to planting. The procedure is an epitome of top-down development and its problems. Due both to production and transport problems the seed multiplication project often has difficulty in meeting IADP bulk orders. Few farmers need more than a bushel or two at a time, and IADPs incur heavy administrative overheads organising delivery of a large number of small orders (especially if credit is also involved). These overheads are out of proportion to the often rather modest yield increases from use of improved varieties in preference to the best local varieties (typically of the order of 10 per cent for upland rices). The system is not only wasteful of scarce development capital but also alienates farmers whenever there is a hiccup or breakdown in the supply chain. Improved seeds delivered late are worse than useless because someone still has to pay for them. Village-based seed multiplication programmes would cut out problems of this sort at a stroke. The data presented above suggest that decentralised seed multiplication is well within the bounds of feasibility from the point of view of farmer skills. The main priority for development agencies should be the regular local dissemination of small amounts of pedigree seed (on a 'gift packet' basis). My experience in Mogbuama suggests that farmers have the knowledge to maintain favoured rice varieties through mass-selection techniques (roguing each generation of planting material for off-types) and are capable of supplying all local needs through informal channels within two or three years of the date of release of the pedigree material.

It is not irrelevant to end by recounting the story of how I myself acquired improved seed for trials with farmers in Mogbuama in 1983. Several trips to Ministry offices in Bo had proved fruitless. In the end, the Agricultural Officer, anxious to help but harassed by the non-arrival of expected supplies due to transport difficulties, arranged for his extension staff to purchase seed privately on my behalf. They fulfilled the order in no time at all by going to a village some kilometres away and buying several bushels of good quality seed stock from peasant farmers known to have the varieties in which I was interested.

9 Rice R&D in Sierra Leone: a farmer-first-and-last scenario

Lessons of the case study

Few would quarrel with the argument that Sierra Leone wetland environments are well-suited to further expansion of rice production. It has been recognised for some time, however, that small-scale producers (as in many parts of West Africa) are quite tightly constrained by labour shortages, especially seasonal labour bottlenecks. The case study has shown not only that seasonal labour shortages are serious constraints on production but, even more significantly, that vicious cycles of debt and hunger are often first triggered by labour-supply difficulties. In these circumstances it is not surprising to find that many farmers are sceptical about labour-intensive methods of wetland rice cultivation.

The basic principle underlying the range of rice cultivation practices in Mogbuama is that of combining the use of different soil types (often in catenary sequences) in order to spread risks. By planting a mixture of early rices on moisture-retentive soils, medium-duration rices on upland farms, and long-duration flood-tolerant (**yaka**) rices in inland valley swamps and water courses, most households are able both to spread their labour requirements in a manageable way and to lengthen the harvest period. Various strategy mixes are possible within this broad framework, the major choice being between planting in the river-terrace zone, where the rice harvest is early but sometimes badly affected by unseasonal rainfall, and planting in the granite zone where the harvest is longer delayed but more secure. Because the early and medium-duration rices are crucial for household consumption they take priority over the swamp (**yaka**) rices. Early and medium-duration rices are cultivated on a household basis. **Yaka** rice plots in inland valley swamps and water courses are planted by individual members of the household on a private basis. Little if any **yaka** rice is used for consumption (swamp varieties are disliked because it is said they taste poor and cook badly). Sales of **yaka** rice are an important source of cash income for wives and junior members of the household, e.g. young males farming jointly with an older man.

Yaka rice is cultivated without any attempt at water control. The main management skill is to select a variety suitable to the water regime in the swamp in question (i.e. to choose flood-tolerant or floating varieties for deep-flooding swamps or swamps with very variable water levels). Once the original swamp vegetation has been cleared labour demands are minimal. It could hardly be otherwise, since work on the household farm takes precedence over any private work. **Yaka** plots have to be cultivated at odd moments during the main period of labour shortage (June–August). Most **yaka** rices are long-duration varieties, taking about five to six months to ripen. They suffer relatively little from bird damage and are effectively left to their own devices until the main rice harvest on the household farm is complete.

The nub of the problem with the Green Revolution strategy in Sierra Leone is the extent to which the emphasis has been placed on labour-intensive methods of water control for the expansion of rice cultivation in swamps. Unlike local methods of swamp cultivation the packages of water-controlled methods proffered by IADPs cannot be incorporated readily into the larger picture of inter-dependent land-use types and household and private farming ventures described in the case study, because the increased labour requirement associated with the 'improved' method would undermine the delicately equilibriated labour economy of the typical 'catenary' farm.

As a general rule resource-poor farmers have little if any scope for anything other than phased integration of new methods. Mogbuama farmers are unlikely to abandon the flexibility of the catenary farming system (with its range of crops, harvest dates, and labour spreading possibilities) for an untried alternative producing only rice. The best chance for new methods of swamp cultivation would be to try them on an experimental basis as replacements for components in the existing system. It is in this respect that IADP swamp packages fall down badly. Their natural 'point of entry' into the existing system would be as replacements for existing methods of cultivating **yaka** rice, but they are ill-adapted for this purpose because farmers most interested in this form of cultivation (women and young males especially) rarely meet IADP credit-worthiness criteria, and have insufficient time to spare for a cultivation system almost certain to clash with more pressing duties on the household farm.

It seems clear, then, that wetland developments, and improvements to rice farming systems more generally, for small-scale farmers in Sierra Leone require a new approach. Potentially fruitful R&D agenda are already apparent in indigenous practices, experiments and innovations associated with the kinds of catenary farming systems described in the case study. Some of the issues are outlined in the following discussion. What is needed, it is suggested, is a balanced and integrated approach to the cultivation of upland, swamp and intermediate land. Each of these aspects is discussed in turn, starting with the all-important boundary zone between swamp and upland.

Early rice

The case study has focused attention on land transitional between true upland and swamp: colluvial footslopes, river terraces, riverine flood plains. Although the target of much indigenous initiative and experimental ingenuity this inter-mediate zone has been neglected by formal-sector R&D agencies.

What are farmers' own R&D priorities for this zone? From the case study it is clear that the performance of early rices is one of these priorities. The main 'improved' upland rices currently available in Sierra Leone (e.g. ROK 3, LAC 23) are unsuitable for the intermediate zone because they are medium-duration varieties (ripening in 130–150 days). To be of significant use as hunger breakers or to catch the market when prices peak in July and August rices for planting in the intermediate zone need to ripen within 90–120 days.

Figure 9.1 Dense-tillering early-ripening *glaberrima* rice (**pende**).

One of the quickest of local varieties grown on moisture-retentive soils in Mogbuama – the *glaberrima* rice **pende** – was the subject of one of Douglas Scotland's rice trials in the first season of experimental work at Njala in 1912. It is characteristic of the conceptual 'gap' between farmers' priorities and the priorities of researchers in the formal sector that work on **pende** was abandoned because yields were low compared with other upland varieties (four trials gave average yields between 11.6 and 12.7 bu/acre). Even so it was recognised in this early work that **pende** was interesting both because it ripened so quickly and because it tillered so profusely that only half the normal amount of seed was needed (average yields from **pende** planted at 0.5 bu/acre were as high as when planted at 1.0 bu/acre). The single plant illustrated in Figure 9.1, collected from a Mogbuama **bati** farm in July 1983, had 51 tillers and gave 91 grammes of husk rice. Until recently the potential of the *glaberrima* rices has been neglected in international rice research programmes. The survival of varieties such as **pende** with quick-ripening properties suggests that this neglect ought to be repaired.

Mogbuama farmers stress the problem of bird damage to early rices (again, this was a point noted by Scotland in 1912). Local preference is to try and select varieties with long awns and long outer glumes, both properties said to minimise bird damage (even if awned varieties are less easy to thresh with bare feet). The Rokupr improved variety ROK 16 is popular in some parts of Sierra Leone because it combines long purple awns (similar to **ngolo-yombo**) with high yields. It is unsuitable for use in the intermediate zone, however, because it takes 130–145 days to ripen. Discussion with Mogbuama farmers suggests that

Figure 9.2 Intercropping early and long-duration rices on a bati farm (**jewulo** being harvested, **kalɛmbaama** at panicle-initiation stage).

the ideal intermediate-zone rice would ripen in less than 120 days, tiller strongly (thus minimising the amount of seed rice needed per farm), have long awns and be able to withstand early-season rainfall irregularities. Given that rice prices in July and August are double those prevailing after the main harvest, high yield is less important a characteristic than the ability to perform reliably despite early-season climatic uncertainties. From the case study it will be apparent that a degree of drought tolerance together with the ability to perform reliably even in poorly burnt bush would be more important than high yields in optimum conditions.

One of the most interesting local experimental initiatives in the intermediate zone is the attempt to double-crop **bati** farms by interplanting an early-ripening variety with a long-duration flood-tolerant type (Fig. 9.2). The key issues Mogbuama farmers address when searching for effective combinations are, first, to ensure that the early-ripening variety is quick and tall enough to avoid being caught by the rising flood in July–August, secondly, to ensure that in the early stages of growth the long-duration variety does not compete so strongly that it depresses the yield from the early variety, and third, to select a long-duration variety that tillers sufficiently to 'fill up the farm' after the first harvest. Formal-sector research agencies might consider picking up these issues and trying to take them further.

There are a number of other ways in which farmers in Mogbuama attempt to double-crop in the intermediate zone. Maize and cowpeas are sometimes planted to make use of residual moisture in **bati** farms and on **tumu** soils. (Cowpea cultivation after the rice harvest is very important around Tabe in neighbouring Kowa chiefdom.) Alternatively, where harvested early enough, rice will sometimes regenerate and yield a second (rattoon) crop. Although this regrowth rarely yields more than 100–200 kg/ha no additional labour input is required except to harvest it. Rattooning is only a feasible option for early-planted quick-ripening varieties (e.g. **pende** in **bati** farms). Mogbuama farmers will welcome the fact that WARDA researchers are currently running a programme to test the rattooning properties of a range of rice varieties on colluvial footslopes at Rokupr.

Mogbuama farmers face two major land-management hazards in the intermediate zone – accelerated soil erosion (Millington 1985b) and excessive weed growth on moisture-retentive soils in the weeks prior to ploughing. While it is probable that local initiatives are adequate to deal with the first of these hazards, the weed problem on moisture-retentive soils stands out as an area where formal-sector R&D initiatives might pay especial dividends.

Farmers recognise that gravel-free moisture-retentive soils ideal for early rice cultivation are highly vulnerable to erosion, especially where there are marked 'steps' between river terrace levels. In 1983 K cleared nine-year bush for a catenary farm encompassing three soil types: kɔtu at the top, ŋanya in the middle section and waterlogged soils along the stream. The soft sandy ŋanya soils sloped quite steeply towards the stream, and gulleys began to develop with the first rains. When these first appeared K was still busy clearing the farm. He decided to try and arrest the gulley erosion before losing too much soil from a site where he hoped to cultivate the bulk of his early rice. To achieve this he built a sequence of simple stick bunds, at about 1.0–1.5 m apart, down each of the three main gulleys, pegging in cleared branches, and backing them up with stones where necessary. This stabilised the gulleys and the area produced a successful rice crop. The technique is quite widespread among small-scale farmers in Sierra Leone, and its effectiveness has been endorsed by an expert in soil conservation (Millington 1982).

The case study has made clear the particular significance of pre-planting weed emergence on moisture-retentive soils in the intermediate zone, especially when aggravated by early rainfall, in the genesis of cycles of labour supply difficulties, debt, and hunger. Historical evidence suggests that the problem is both long-established and widespread throughout Sierra Leone. Previous work on the weed ecology of upland rice in Sierra Leone (Nyoka 1980) has focused on post-planting weed problems. Equal attention is now needed to weed ecology on rice farms in the period between burning and 'ploughing', especially where moisture-retentive soils are concerned. Since these soils are, in economic terms, among the most productive for rice cultivation the possibility of herbicide treatments should not be ruled out of the experimental design (Nyoka's study suggests that herbicide treatments are unlikely to be economically viable on ordinary upland farms).

Upland farms

Mogbuama is typical of much of Sierra Leone in that farmers still produce much of their rice from uplands. Upland cultivation systems have proven much more durable and adaptable than was at one time expected. Much of this durability appears to derive from complex ecological complementarities associated with intercropping (e.g. the capacity of appropriate crop mixtures to suppress weeds and pests and speed fertility restoration in fallow periods). In part, however, the durability of upland intercropping derives from its economic benefits, e.g. the ability to make the most effective use of scarce household labour and to satisfy a wide range of both subsistence and cash needs for both men and women. When asked about intercropping farmers say they are equally keen both to spread risks and ensure subsistence targets on the one hand and to exploit new market opportunities on the other. R&D initiatives directed to the improvement of upland farming systems should take these twin aims fully into account.

A first priority in this kind of work must be to select rice varieties well suited to the kind of complex intercropping systems identified in the case study. The second priority should be work on 'subsistence' intercrops. Over much of Sierra Leone the most important of these are cotton and sorghum/millet. Lack of commercial success with cotton cultivation in Sierra Leone should not be allowed to obscure its significance for village social security. Women in Mogbuama say they would be interested to try out any improved or exotic types of cotton, provided that they are adapted to intercropping on upland rice farms (though perhaps an even greater priority should attach to developing a local substitute for expensive imported carding combs, the only item of non-local technology common in village cloth production). Sorghum and millet are important because they are direct substitutes for rice in the months before the harvest. Some farmers use sorghum for family consumption in order to reserve rice for work parties. It is recognised that if too much sorghum and millet is planted in a rice farm, rice yields are adversely affected. New varieties of sorghum and millet adapted to intercropping and high rainfall conditions, and optimal planting strategies for rice/sorghum/millet mixtures are both, therefore, issues of considerable local interest. Beniseed and egusi are two of the more important cash crops produced by women on the upland farm. Again, any 'improved' varieties must be selected with intercropping in mind.

Although fallow periods are not yet subject to undue shortening, Mogbuama farmers are interested, nevertheless, in the wide range of factors affecting farm performance on uplands. Rotational bush fallowing is a fine school for studies in dynamic ecology, and farmers are not slow to learn from comparing their current upland farm with the results achieved when the same plot was last cultivated. The intricate detailed ecological interdependencies between fallow period, soil type, climatic hazards thus revealed raise doubts about 'standard' fertiliser recommendations emanating from IADPs. My own experience of giving out small packets of 20–20–0 fertiliser in the course of fieldwork suggests that there is considerable scope to organise a 'participatory research' programme in which farmers are encouraged to develop more specific fertiliser recommendations for local upland soils on the basis of their own experiments. Local knowledge of fallow dynamics (as seen for example in farmers' concern to foster rapid bush regrowth and awareness of the fertility-enhancing properties of exotic weeds such as *Pueraria phaseoloides* and *Calapogonium mucunoides* first introduced to Sierra Leone in the 1930s as nitrogen-fixing cover crops) suggests that experiments with 'planted fallows' would be well received (cf. the alley-intercropping methods developed recently at IITA, based on the idea, long familiar to farmers in high-population districts of eastern Nigeria, of incorporating nitrogen-fixing shrubs into upland intercropping schedules to speed up subsequent fallow regeneration).

Another important way in which Mogbuama farmers have attempted to increase the productivity of upland farms has been to experiment with a range of 'pseudo-rotations'. The technique involves planting part of the previous year's rice farm to groundnuts, cassava, maize, or a mixture of these crops. This is a practice which is said to have expanded a good deal in recent years. Formerly these three crops were mainly grown in the rice farm as intercrops. Separate groundnut farms have become a common feature during the past 10–15 years. Much of this work has been pioneered by women. Labour shortage is the main current limitation on further use of old rice farms in this way. Maize, cassava, and groundnut varieties selected with this land-use trend in mind will be different from varieties grown intercropped with rice. The latter are for subsistence (thus, for example, it is important to consider only 'sweet' cassavas with leaves suitable for use as a vegetable) whereas in the former case the harvest is mainly for sale (with the possibility that farmers will be interested in, say, feedstock maizes and bitter cassavas).

In all, then, it can be seen that upland farming in Sierra Leone is far from static or 'traditional'. Research programmes need to be designed to support and further encourage current indigenous development trends on upland farms. Recent interest in the international agencies and at Rokupr in upland rice and intercropping systems is a welcome trend (Rice Research Station 1983). As Grist 1975, p. 189) notes, 'there is no doubt that had the same amount of [research] attention been given to dryland varieties [as to wetland types] the results would have placed this method of cultivation in a more favourable position than it at present occupies.'

Swamp rice

Greenland (1984), referring to possible new directions in rice research at the International Rice Research Institute, notes that the most improved varieties have been developed for water-controlled environments, but that only 30% of all rice hectarage in the tropics is 'irrigated land' in this strict sense. In areal terms 20% of rice land in the tropical zone is rain-fed upland and 50% is naturally flooded land. In this 70% of rice land 'subject to drought or flood or a combination of both' farmers are 'largely restricted to use of varieties able to yield little better than 1 t ha^{-1}.' According to Greenland, research addressed to the problems of rice cultivation in these less advantaged areas ought now to be a major priority at IRRI and other international agricultural research centres.

This significant change of emphasis is apparently based on an acceptance of the fact that many small-scale rice farmers in the tropics are in the position of those described in the case study, of being unable or unwilling to develop water-control procedures due to conflicting demands on time and limited resources. In such circumstances more and better use of swamp land will depend on improvements which make few additional labour demands and which integrate well with other agricultural and household activities. In cases where women do much of the swamp cultivation rice research programmes will need to be redesigned around a thorough understanding of female activity patterns in typical resource-poor peasant households (cf. Dey 1981). In the Sierra Leone case, labour-intensive innovations (water control through bunding and ditching, and transplanting) are especially problematic for women farmers and young dependents because they require large amounts of extra labour at a time of the year when agricultural labour is in short supply generally.

The Sierra Leonian case suggests two themes, therefore, upon which swamp rice research for resource-poor farmers might now be focused: 'floating' rices and dry-season use of wetland environments.

The first detailed evidence that 'improved' wetland management practices might not be economically advantageous under West African conditions came from a study of swamp farming practices in Liberia in the 1950s (Buchanan et al. 1956). They argued that the way to proceed with further swamp development was to cut down water control to a minimum and abandon transplanting, 'since transplanting under the conditions attempted so far in Liberia has not demonstrated the advantage it was supposed to have – the elimination or at least reduction of the weed control problem'. In effect, they endorse indigenous swamp cultivation practices based on broadcasting of rice varieties adapted to variable flood conditions. The present study has confirmed that such practices minimise labour constraints and secure a rice harvest from land that might otherwise not be brought into cultivation. It follows that a programme to support indigenous initiatives ought to focus attention on 'floating' and flood-tolerant rices. The *glaberrima* floating rices, largely neglected by R&D agencies hitherto, might merit special attention (O'Reilly 1983).

Glanville, in the 1930s, pointed out that one of the factors encouraging farmers to clear inland valley swamp land for farming purposes was the possibility of dry-season cultivation. Typically, this dry-season cultivation focuses on crops such as sweet potato, cassava, and groundnuts grown on heaps and makes use of residual moisture in swamp soils (Glanville 1938). Inland valley swamp soils in Sierra Leone sometimes experience a sharp drop in fertility after they have been farmed for a season or two. Heaping and digging in of rice straw residues is a useful antidote to this problem. Another advantage of dry-season cultivation of swamps would appear to be that women find their labour under less pressure in the early dry-season than at any other time of the year. Cultivation on the falling flood is perhaps the most important 'space' for the expansion of women's agricultural activities in rural Sierra Leone. As far as resource-poor farmers in Sierra Leone are concerned, therefore, research support for further dry-season use of swamps is probably a greater priority than wet-season double cropping.

Conclusion

This chapter has outlined a scenario for rice R&D suggested by the interests and priorities of small-scale farmers in central Sierra Leone. Practical implementation would require a vigorous programme of with-farmer research and on-farm trials (cf. Rhoades & Booth 1982, Ngambeki & Wilson 1983, Kirkby 1984). For any such programme to be truly 'adaptive' both logic and logistics require that as much of the work as possible be in the hands of local interest groups. The case study has demonstrated that small-scale rice farmers in Sierra Leone are not without an experimental turn of mind. The question now is how to support and further stimulate local experimental initiatives. Young men's labour groups and women's organisations might be the appropriate focus for any initiatives in relation to swamps and the **yaka** rices. Initiatives in relation to upland rices and 'intermediate zone' developments would need to be directed towards heads of households. There may be some scope for integrating with-farmer, on-farm research with community-based adult education initiatives. Peasant groups in Sierra Leone have a long history of self-help literacy learning. An indigenous system for writing Mende was invented in the 1920s by a tailor from Potoru, Kisimi Kamara (Dalby 1967). **Kikaku** script is still used in some parts of Mende-land to keep records of loans, bridewealth and funeral transactions, dreams and personal histories. I have even seen farm experiments documented in this way. A number of voluntary agencies in Sierra Leone have been involved in community-focused self-help literacy learning programmes, influenced in some cases by the ideas of Paolo Freire (Freire 1972, 1978, Street 1984). Freire's central idea is that rural people should 'capture' literacy to express their own ideas and needs. The motivation to master reading and writing 'takes off', as it were, from peasant attempts to define and develop a critical analysis of their current situation. Karimu (pers communication) has recently initiated a participatory research programme for rice farmers in central Sierra Leone in which literacy learning is linked to attempts to provide sharper definition of farming problems and priorities. The rich Mende vocabulary for land intermediate between swamp and upland might prove an appropriate starting point for work of this kind. This would be a first step towards delimiting a conceptual 'space' within which to foster alternatives to the upland-swamp dichotomy that has bedevilled rice farming system developments in Sierra Leone for 50 years or more.

Conclusion

Why have agricultural development initiatives in Africa so often missed the mark as far as poor, hazard-prone farmers have been concerned?

Recent attempts to answer this question have concentrated in particular on perceptual and institutional barriers to communication and understanding between researchers and resource-poor farmers. Chambers (1983) argues that agricultural development policies are unduly affected by urban, road-side, dry-season, male-biased perceptions of rural life and its problems. Biggs and Clay (1983) suggest that professional and institutional factors, e.g. peer-group rivalries and concern for career advancement, are deeply implicated when agricultural research programmes move off in directions inappropriate to farmers' needs and concerns (cf. Biggs 1984, Maxwell 1984, Heinemann & Biggs 1985). Problems of this sort are further complicated by lack of attention to feed-back at the stage of project implementation. Most IADPs now have monitoring and evaluation units, but this work is dominated by accountancy criteria – rates of return and cost–benefit ratios – to the exclusion of formal mechanisms for reporting farmers' needs, responses to new technologies, and ideas about possible modifications (Biggs 1984). Feedback surveys ought to be a regular part of the duties of agricultural extension services (Barker *et al.* 1977) but training of extension workers is still largely focused on 'top-down' communications skills (e.g. the 'Training and Visit' system widely adopted by World Bank funded projects in Africa).

The particular contribution of the present study to this debate has been to suggest that underpinning these institutional and perceptual difficulties there lies a major conceptual problem. Formal-sector research agencies look at land and land resources from an analytical perspective. The landscape is broken up into component parts. Each component is assessed in terms of its optimum usage. Recommendations are then based on the theoretical 'best use' of each box in an ecological mosaic. This kind of approach is responsible for the notion that 'swamp' and 'upland' are distinct, substitutable, production environments. By contrast, farmers view the landscape in synthetic terms. The landscape is habitat. It is a living form. The tendency to carry out agricultural research in distinct ecological 'boxes' makes little sense to those whose survival depends on their skill in integrating land use across 'the complete landscape form'.

This fundamental distinction is manifested in the way in which land use categories are defined and used. Last (1981) points out that indigenous medical practitioners and their patients in northern Nigeria often resist being pinned down to all-embracing terminological schemata and systems of explanation. Rigidly defined terms may block off options unnecessarily and inhibit flexible adjustment and experimentation. Mogbuama farmers are equally free-and-easy in the way they employ land-use categorisations. This unwillingness to be pinned down to precise use of terms is crucial to understanding the conceptual gap separating farmers and scientific researchers. The issue for farmers in Mogbuama is not whether this or that piece of farmland can be subdivided into distinct soil or land-use types (analogous to soil series or land systems) but that it contains a transition from one state, vaguely defined perhaps, to another, equally vaguely defined, but *different*. This enthusiasm for the 'fuzzy logic' of ecotonal transitions and boundary dynamics is manifest in the number of farm experiments carried out in boundary zones between 'upland' and 'wetland' or up and down a section of the soil catena. 'If it fails, we know in which direction to move' was the way farmers sometimes explained their own experimental methodology. To Governor Wilkinson the junction between 'upland' and 'wetland' was an historically momentous boundary. To step across it marked the beginnings of the journey from primitive to progressive agriculture. Mogbuama farmers decisively reject this interpretation. To them, the upland-wetland ecotone is not so much a boundary (far less one of historical significance) as a zone where a number of important opportunities for improving and expanding farming operations converge and come into focus.

I once asked an old farmer whether he thought the greatest local priority was for a farm access road, an improved water supply or a school. He thought for a moment, and then said he would answer the question by asking me one in turn. If he offered to build me a house, would I prefer it to have walls or a roof? The point of the present study has been to suggest that rice farming systems in central Sierra Leone are, from the cultivator's point of view, rather like the old man's house. What matters is that the walls are as good and strong as the roof, and that the two fit and stay together. This is an insight with far reaching consequences for farming systems research in African conditions. Researchers cannot continue to operate by remote control. At whatever discomfort and logistical inconvenience to themselves, they must become fully absorbed in the landscapes for which their innovations are intended. In the development of improved agricultural technologies for resource-poor farmers there is no alternative to a long-term participatory approach and situation-specific design.

Postscript

My most poignant memories of fieldwork in Mogbuama are of the times when having been cut a stint at ploughing I would struggle to complete my portion long after every one else had finished. Panting in the wake of even the youngest member of the group I would be quite literally speechless (by virtue of being breathless) with amazement at the Mende farmer's capacity for endurance. A book about West African agriculture published at the height of the world recession in the 1930s was prefaced with the remark that 'since the chief lines of this book were planned, the world-wide economic crisis has arrived and has clearly shown up one of the strong points of peasant farming . . . that is its great resistance to adverse conditions' (Jones 1936). The present study has tried to show that in matters of landscape management this capacity for resistance is more than an ability to hold the line. The most impressive characteristic of farming in Mogbuama in 1983 was a capacity for integrative experimentation in the face of adversity. To cope with hunger in Africa today governments and planning agencies can ill afford to ignore this obstinate tradition of peasant ecological inventiveness.

References*

Abraham, A. 1978. *Mende government and politics under colonial rule: a historical study of political change in Sierra Leone 1890–1937.* Freetown: Sierra Leone University Press.

Abraham, A. and C. Magbaily Fyle 1976. The country cloth culture. In *Topics in Sierra Leone history: a counter-colonial interpretation*, A. Abraham (ed.), pp. 42–7. Freetown: Leone Publishers.

Ahn, P. M. 1970. *West African soils.* Oxford: Oxford University Press.

Airey, A., J. A. Binns and P. K. Mitchell 1979. To integrate or ...? Agricultural development in Sierra Leone. *Inst. Dev. Studies Bull.* **10** (4), 20–7.

Balandier, G. 1970. *The sociology of Black Africa: social dynamics in Central Africa* (Trans. D. Garman). London: André Deutsch.

Baldwin, K. D. S. 1957. *The Niger Agricultural Project: an experiment in African development.* Oxford: Oxford University Press.

Barker, D., J. S. Oguntoyinbo and P. Richards 1977. *The utility of the Nigerian peasant farmer's knowledge in the monitoring of agricultural resources.* General Report Series, no. 4, Monitoring and Assessment Research Centre, Chelsea College.

Biggs, S. D. 1984. Awkward but common themes in agricultural policy. In *Room for manoeuvre: an exploration of public policy planning in agriculture and rural development*, E. J. Clay and B. B. Schaffer (eds), pp. 59–74. London: Heinemann.

Biggs, S. D. and E. J. Clay 1981. Sources of innovation in agricultural technology. *World Development* **9**, 321–36.

Biggs, S. D. and E. J. Clay 1983. *Generation and diffusion of agricultural technology: a review of theories and experiences.* ILO World Employment Programme Research Working Paper, no. 122.

Binswanger, H. P. and V. W. Ruttan 1978. *Induced innovation: technology, institutions and development.* Baltimore: Johns Hopkins University Press.

Bledsoe, C. 1984. The political use of Sande ideology and symbolism. *Am. Ethnol.* **11**, 455–72.

Bloch, M. 1973. The long term and the short term: the economic and political significance of the morality of kinship. In *The character of kinship*, J. Goody (ed.), pp. 75–87. Cambridge: Cambridge University Press.

Buchanan, T. S., H. Prejean, L. V. Girardot and M. F. Harris 1956. *Studies to determine the most economical system of rice production for Liberia.* Special Report no. 1, Central Agricultural Experiment Station, Suakoko, Liberia.

Buddenhagen, I. W. 1978. Rice ecosystems in Africa. In *Rice in Africa*, I. W. Buddenhagen and G. J. Persley (eds), 11–27. London: Academic Press.

Burnham, P. 1980. *Opportunity and constraint in a savanna society: the Gbaya of Meiganga, Cameroon.* London: Academic Press.

Byerlee, D. and M. P. Collinson 1980. *Planning technologies appropriate to farmers – concepts and procedures.* CIMMYT, Mexico.

Byerlee, D., L. Harrington and D. L. Winkelmann 1982. Farming systems research: issues in research strategy and technology design. *Am. J. Agric. Econ.* **64**, 897–904.

Carloni, A. 1983. *Technical report on socio-economic constraints to land and water development for inland valley swamps in Sierra Leone*, mimeo.

*Unless otherwise stated, unpublished material cited in this list of references is to be found in the Sierra Leone Collection of the Library of Njala University College.

Carpenter, A. J. 1978. The history of rice in Africa. In *Rice in Africa*, I. W. Buddenhagen and G. J. Persley (eds), pp. 3–10. London: Academic Press.

Cartwright, J. R. 1978. *Political leadership in Sierra Leone*. London: Croom Helm.

Chambers, R. 1983. *Rural development: putting the last first*. Harlow: Longman.

Chambers, R. and B. P. Ghildyal 1985. *Agricultural research for resource-poor farmers: the farmer-first-and-last model*. Discussion Papers, Institute of Development Studies, Sussex, no. 203.

Chandraratna, M. F. 1964. *The genetics and breeding of rice*. London: Longman.

Churchill, W. 1922. *Churchill to Maxwell (SL 151 of 24/4/22). Correspondence and report on irrigation for and cultivation of rice in Sierra Leone*. Freetown: Government Printer.

Cole, N. H. A. 1968. *The vegetation of Sierra Leone*. Njala: Njala University College.

Collier, R. 1974. *The Plague of the Spanish Lady: the influenza pandemic of 1918–1919*. London: Macmillan.

Dalby, D. 1967. A survey of the indigenous scripts of Liberia and Sierra Leone: Vai, Mende, Loma, Kpelle and Bassa. *Afr. Lang. Studs* **8**, 1–51.

Dawe, M. T. 1924. *Comments in Despatches on the subject of rice cultivation in Sierra Leone, Sessional Paper no. 8 of 1924*. Freetown: Government Printer.

Deighton, F. C. 1957. *Vernacular botanical vocabulary for Sierra Leone*. London: Crown Agents.

Department of Agriculture 1923, *Annual report*. Freetown: Government Printer.

Department of Agriculture 1929, *Annual report*. Freetown: Government Printer.

Department of Agriculture 1931, *Annual report*. Freetown: Government Printer.

Department of Agriculture 1936, *Annual report*. Freetown: Government Printer.

Department of Agriculture 1949, *Annual report*. Freetown: Government Printer.

Department of Agriculture 1959, *Annual report*. Freetown: Government Printer.

Dey, J. 1981. Gambian women: unequal partners in rice development projects. *J. Development Studies* **17**, 109–22.

Farm Demonstration Team, 1964. *Interim report of the Farming Demonstration Team from the Republic of China in Sierra Leone (May 14th to November 15th)*. Ministry of Agriculture and Natural Resources, mimeo.

Farmer, B. H. 1981. The 'Green Revolution' in South Asia. *Geography* **66**, 202–7.

Finnegan, R. 1963. The traditional concept of chiefship among the Limba. *Sierra Leone Studs* (New Series) **17**, 241–53.

Fortes, M. 1949. *The web of kinship among the Tallensi*. London: Oxford University Press.

Franke, R. W. and B. H. Chasin 1980. *Seeds of famine: ecological destruction and the development dilemma in the West African Sahel*. Montclair, NJ: Allenheld Osmun.

Freire, P. 1972. *The pedagogy of the oppressed* (trans. M. B. Ramos). Harmondsworth: Penguin.

Freire, P. 1978. *Pedagogy in process: letters to Guinea-Bissau*. London: Readers' and Writers' Co-operative.

Furley, J. T. 1924. *Despatches on the subject of rice cultivation in Sierra Leone, Sessional Paper no. 8 of 1924*. Freetown: Government Printer.

Garvie, R. S. 1957. Memorandum on land drainage and irrigation in Sierra Leone. Appendix to *Report on water control and swamp development in Sierra Leone*. G. Lacey. Department of Agriculture, mimeo.

Gellner, E. 1977. Patrons and clients. In *Patrons and clients in Mediterranean societies*, E. Gellner and J. Waterbury (eds). London: Duckworth.

Glanville, R. R. 1933. *Sierra Leone: rice cultivation. Report on a visit to Ceylon and South India with proposals for Sierra Leone*. Freetown: Government Printer.

Glanville, R. R. 1938. *Rice production on swamps*. Sierra Leone Agricultural Notes no. 7, mimeo.

Gleave, M. B. 1977. *Mechanisation of peasant farming: experience in Sierra Leone*. Discussion Papers in Geography, no. 3, Department of Geography, University of Salford.

Goody, J. 1958. The fission of domestic groups among the LoDagaba. In *The developmental cycle in domestic groups*, J. Goody (ed.), pp. 53–91. Cambridge: Cambridge University Press.

Goody, J. 1971. *Technology, tradition and the state in Africa*. London: International African Institute.

Greenland, D. J. 1984. Rice. *Biologist* **31**, 219–25.

Griffin, K. 1979. *The political economy of agrarian change: an essay on the green revolution*, 2nd edn. London: Macmillan.

Grist, D. H. 1975. *Rice*, 5th edn. London: Longman.

Gwynne-Jones, D. R. G., P. K. Mitchell, M. E. Harvey and K. Swindell 1978. *A new geography of Sierra Leone*. London: Longman.

Haas, A. W. 1974. *Diffusion of innovations in Sierra Leone, West Africa*. Leiden: Institute of Cultural and Social Studies (mimeo).

Harriss, J. (ed.) 1982. *Rural development: theories of peasant economy and agrarian change*. London: Hutchinson.

Hart, K. 1982. *The political economy of West African agriculture*. Cambridge: Cambridge University Press.

Heinemann, E. and S. D. Biggs 1985. Farming systems research: an evolutionary approach to implementation. *J. Agric. Econ.* **36**, 59–65.

Hill, P. 1972. *Rural Hausa: a village and a setting*. Cambridge: Cambridge University Press.

Hill, P. 1977. *Population, prosperity and poverty: rural Kano 1900 and 1970*. Cambridge: Cambridge University Press.

Hill, P. 1982. *Dry grain farming families: Hausaland (Nigeria) and Karanataka (India) compared*. Cambridge: Cambridge University Press.

Hobsbawm, E. J. and T. Ranger (eds) 1983. *The invention of tradition*. Cambridge: Cambridge University Press.

Innes, G. 1969. *A Mende–English dictionary*. Cambridge: Cambridge University Press.

Isaac, B. L. 1982. Economic development and subsistence farming: the case of the Mende of Upper Bambara Chiefdom, Sierra Leone. *Central Issues Anthropol.* **4**, 1–20.

Jedrej, M. C. 1980. Structural aspects of a West African secret society. *Ethnol. Zeit.* **1**, 133–42.

Jedrej, M. C. 1983. The growth and decline of a mechanical agriculture scheme in West Africa. *Afr. Affairs* **82**, 541–58.

Johnny, M. M. P. 1979. *Traditional farmers' perceptions of farming and farming problems in the Moyamba area*, MA thesis: University of Sierra Leone.

Johnny, M. M. P. 1985. *Informal credit for integrated rural development in Sierra Leone*. PhD thesis: University of Giessen.

Jones, A. 1983. *From slaves to palm kernels: a history of the Galinhas country (West Africa) 1730–1890*. Wiesbaden: Steiner Verlag.

Jones, G. H. 1936. *The earth goddess: a study of native farming on the West African coast*. London: Longman, Green.

Jordan, H. D. 1951. *Some notes on inland valley swamps and upland rice cultivation in Sierra Leone*. Rokupr Rice Research Station, typescript.

Jordan, H. D. 1966. Rice in the economy of Sierra Leone. *Annual Report for 1964–5*, West African Rice Research Station, Rokupr.

Jordan, H. D. n.d. *Development of mangrove swamp areas in Sierra Leone*, mimeo.

Karimu, J. 1981. *Strategies for peasant farmer development: an evaluation of a rural development project in northern Sierra Leone*. PhD Thesis, University of London.
Karimu, J. A. and P. Richards 1981. *The Northern Area Integrated Agricultural Development Project: social and economic impact of planning for rural change in northern Sierra Leone*. Occasional Papers (New Series) no. 3, Department of Geography, School of Oriental & African Studies.
Kirkby, R. A. (ed.) 1984. *Crop improvement in eastern and southern Africa: research objectives and on-farm testing*. Ottawa: International Development Research Centre.

Laan, H. L. van der 1965. *The Sierra Leone diamonds: an economic study covering the years 1952–1961*. London: Oxford University Press.
Lacey, G. 1957. *Report on water control and swamp development in Sierra Leone*. Department of Agriculture, mimeo.
Land Resources Survey 1979. *Land in Sierra Leone: a reconnaissance survey and evaluation for agriculture*. Freetown: UNDP/FAO.
Lappia, J. N. L. 1980. *The economics of swamp rice cultivation in the Integrated Agricultural Development Project, Eastern Region, Sierra Leone*. Dept. of Agricultural Economics & Extension, Njala University College.
Last, M. 1981. the importance of knowing about not knowing. *Soc. Sci. Med.* **15** B, 387–92.
Lee, K. E. and T. G. Wood 1971. *Termites and soils*. London: Academic Press.
Levi, J. (ed.) 1976. *African agriculture: economic action and reaction in Sierra Leone*. Farnham Royal: Commonwealth Agricultural Bureaux.
Levi, J. and M. Havinden 1982. *Economics of African agriculture*. London: Longman.
Lipton, M. and R. Longhurst 1985. *Modern varieties, international agricultural research, and the poor*. Working Paper no. 2; CGIAR Impact Study, World Bank, Washington DC.
Little, K. 1948a. The Mende farming household. *Sociol. Rev.* **40**, 37–55.
Little, K. 1948b. Land and labour among the Mende. *Afr. Affairs* **47**, 23–31.
Little, K. 1951. The Mende rice farm and its cost. *Zaire* **5**, 227–73, 371–80.
Little, K. 1967. *The Mende of Sierra Leone*, 2nd edn. London: Routledge and Kegan Paul.
Littlefield, D. C. 1981. *Rice and slaves: ethnicity and the slave trade in colonial South Carolina*. Baton Rouge: Louisiana State University Press.

Mackie, R. B., M. T. Dawe and C. F. Loxley 1927. *Report of the Rice Commission on its enquiry into the position of the rice industry. Sessional Paper no. 7 of 1927*. Freetown: Government Printer.
Maxwell, S. 1984. *Farming systems research: hitting a moving target*. Discussion Paper No. 99, Institute of Development Studies, University of Sussex.
Miedema, R. and W. van Vuure 1977. The morphological, physical and chemical properties of two mounds of *Macrotermes bellicosus* (Smeathman) compared with surrounding soils in Sierra Leone. *J. Soil Sci.* **28**, 112–24.
Millington, A. C. 1982. Soil conservation techniques for the humid tropics. *Approp. technol.* **9**(2), 17–18.
Millington, A. C. 1985a. *Environmental degradation, soil conservation and agricultural policies in Sierra Leone, 1895–1984* (mimeo).
Millington, A. C. 1985b. *Soil erosion and agricultural land use in Sierra Leone*, D.Phil. thesis, University of Sussex.
Miracle, M. P. 1961. seasonal hunger: a vague concept and an unexplored problem. *Bull. IFAN* **22**, 373–83.
Moorman, F. R. and N. van Breemen 1978. *Rice: soil, water, land*. Los Banos: International Rice Research Institute.

Moorman, F. R. and W. J. Veldkamp 1978. Land and rice in Africa: constraints and potentials. In *Rice in Africa*, I. W. Buddenhagen and G. W. Persley (eds), pp. 29–43. London: Academic Press.

Murphy, W. P. 1980. Secret knowledge as property and power in Kpelle society: elders versus youth. *Africa* **50**, 193–207.

Murphy, W. P. 1981. The rhetorical management of dangerous knowledge in Kpelle brokerage. *Am. Ethnol.* **8**, 667–85.

Ngambeki, D. S. and G. F. Wilson 1983. Moving research to farmers' fields. *IITA Research Briefs* **4**(4), 1, 7–8.

Njoku, A. O. 1979. The economics of Mende upland rice farming. In *Essays on the economic anthropology of Liberia and Sierra Leone*, V. Dorjahn and B. Isaac (eds), pp. 103–20. Philadelphia: Institute of Liberian Studies.

Njoku, A. O. and G. L. Karr 1973. Labour and upland rice production. *J. Agric. Econ.* **24**, 289–99.

Nyoka, G. C. 1980. *Studies on the germination, growth and control of weeds in upland rice fields under different fallow periods in Sierra Leone*. PhD Thesis: University of Sierra Leone.

Okali, C., D. Oben and T. Ojo-Atere 1980. *The management and use of hydromorphic toposequences in the Ogun River basin: the case of traditional farmers in the Ofada area of Ogun State*. Discussion Paper 5/80. International Institute of Tropical Agriculture (Agricultural Economics Section).

O'Reilly, F. 1983. *Wet rice farming with fluctuating water resources: a case study of the Sokoto valley, Northwestern Nigeria*. Paper presented to the Institute of British Geographers' Annual Conference, Edinburgh, January, 1983.

Pain, A. 1983. *Agricultural research in Sri Lanka: an historical account*. School of Development Studies, University of East Anglia (mimeo).

Patterson, K. D. 1981. The demographic impact of the 1918–19 influenza pandemic in sub-Saharan Africa: a preliminary assessment. In *African historical demography*, vol. 2, pp. 401–32. Edinburgh: Centre for African Studies, 1981.

Pearse, A. 1980. *Seeds of plenty, seeds of want: social and economic implications of the Green Revolution*. Oxford: Clarendon Press.

Pearson, S. R., J. D. Stryker and C. P. Humphreys 1981. *Rice in West Africa: policy and economics*. Stanford: Stanford University Press.

Peel, J. D. Y. 1968. *Aladura*. London: Oxford University Press.

Pelissier, P. 1966. *Les Paysans du Senegal: Les Civilizations agraires du Cayor a la Casamance*. St.-Yrieux: Imprimerie Fabrègue.

Phillips, T. A. 1964. *An agricultural notebook*. London: Longman.

Piggott, C. J. 1954. The use of phosphate fertilisers in Sierra Leone. *Proceedings of the 2nd Inter-African Soils Conference, Leopoldville*.

Pillai, A. C. 1921. Report of Senior Agricultural Instructor to Director of Agriculture, Njala, for half year ending December, 1921. *Correspondence and report on irrigation for and cultivation of rice in Sierra Leone*. Freetown: Government Printer.

Pitty, A. F. 1979. *Geography and soil properties*. London: Methuen.

Rhoades, R. E. and R. H. Booth 1982. Farmer-back-to-farmer: a model for generating acceptable agricultural technology. *Agric. Admin.* **11**, 127–37.

Rice Research Station 1983. *Annual Report of the Rice Research Station, Rokupr for 1982–3*, mimeo.

Richards, P. 1983 Farming systems research and agrarian change in West Africa. *Prog. Human Geog.* **7**, 1–39.

Richards, P. 1985. *Indigenous agricultural revolution: ecology and food production in West Africa*. London: Hutchinson.

Ruthenberg, H. 1980. *Farming systems in the tropics*, 2nd edn. London: Oxford University Press.

Sahlins, M. 1974. *Stone-age economics*. London: Tavistock.
Saylor, R. G. 1967. *The economic system of Sierra Leone*. Durham, NC: Duke University Press.
Scotland, D. 1918. *Department of Agriculture Annual Report for 1918*. Typescript, Njala University College Library.
Scott, J. 1977. Patronage or exploitation? In *Patrons and clients in Mediterranean societies*, E. Gellner and J. Waterbury (eds), pp. 21–39. London: Duckworth.
Seibel, H. D. and A. Massing 1974. *Traditional organizations and economic development: studies of indigenous co-operatives in Liberia*. New York: Praeger.
Sen, A. 1981. *Poverty and famines: an essay on entitlement and deprivation*. Oxford: Clarendon Press.
Sharpe, B. 1982. *Group formation and economic interrelations amongst some communities of Kauru District: Hausa, Kaivi, Rishuwa, Ruruma*. PhD thesis, University of London.
Spencer, D. S. C. 1975. *The economics of rice production in Sierra Leone. i. Upland rice*. Njala: Department of Agricultural Economics and Extension, Njala University College.
Spencer, D. S. C. and D. Byerlee 1976. Technical change, labor use, and small farmer development: evidence from Sierra Leone. *Am. J. Agric. Econ.* **58**, 874–80.
Spitzer, L. 1975. *The Creoles of Sierra Leone: responses to colonialism, 1870–1945*. Ile-Ife: University of Ife Press.
Squire, F. A. 1943. *Notes on Mende rice varieties*. Sierra Leone Agricultural Notes no. 10 (mimeo).
Starkey, P. H. 1981. *Farming with work-oxen in Sierra Leone*. Freetown: Government Printer.
Steiner, K. G. 1982. *Intercropping in tropical smallholder agriculture with special reference to West Africa*. Deutsche Gesellschaft für Technische Zusammenarbeit: Eschborn.
Stobbs, A. R. 1963. *The soils and geography of the Boliland region of Sierra Leone*. Freetown: Government Printer.
Stockdale, F. A. 1936. *Report by Mr F. A. Stockdale CMG, CBE, Agricultural Adviser to the Secretary of State for the Colonies on his visit to Sierra Leone in Janaury, 1936. Sessional Paper no. 2 of 1936*. Freetown: Government Printer.
Street, B. V. 1934. *Literacy in theory and practice*. Cambridge: Cambridge University Press.
Strong, T. H. 1970. *Sierra Leone: possible agricultural development projects for financing in Sierra Leone*. UNDP (SF)/FAO Project IDAS, Working Paper.

Vuure, W. van, R. T. Odell and P. M. Stutton 1972. *Soil survey of the Njala area, Sierra Leone*. Njala University College Bulletin, no. 3.
Virmani, S. S., J. O. Olufowote and A. O. Abifarin 1978. Rice improvement in tropical anglophone Africa. In *Rice in Africa*, I. W. Buddenhagen and G. J. Persley (eds), pp. 101–16. London: Academic Press.

Waldock, E. A., E. S. Capstick and A. J. Browning 1951. *Soil conservation and land use in Sierra Leone*. Freetown: Government Printer.
Watts, M. 1983. *Silent violence: Food, famine and peasantry in northern Nigeria*. Berkeley: University of California Press.
Weatherhead, E. K. 1984. *Small-scale swamp development – approaches to swamp development, the role of government, non-government organisations and donors, manpower and training requirements*. Silsoe: Silsoe College, Cranfield Institute of Technology.

Wilkinson, R. J. 1920. *Wilkinson to Viscount Milner (SL No 28 of 21/1/20). Correspondence and report on irrigation for and cultivation of rice in Sierra Leone.* Freetown: Government Printer.

Will, H., G. S. Banya and C. D. Williams 1969. Upland observation collection. In *Experimental Report for 1969*, Rokupr Rice Research Station: Njala University College, mimeo.

Will, H., G. S. Banya, C. D. Williams and S. M. Funnah 1969. Upland comparative field trial. In *Experimental Report for 1969*, Rokupr Rice Research Station: Njala University College, mimeo.

World Bank 1975. *Sector policy paper on rural development.* Washington DC: World Bank.

Glossary

Mende words cited in the text

Orthography and tones are based on Innes (1969) supplemented by Joko Sengova (pers. comm.). Words in inverted commas are provisional transcriptions only. Botanical identifications follow Deighton (1957). For a more complete listing of Mogbuama rice varieties, see Table 8.1.

bàìkɔ̀   Rice variety.
bányálojɔ̀pòíhùn   Rice variety.
bàtì   Seasonally flooded riverine swamp.
bèmbè   Hoeing group working for hire.
bògùtù   Rice variety.
bòndàà   Family.
bɔ̀bɔ̂   Clay.
bɔ̌bɔ̀   *Irvingia gabonensis*.
bɔ́ngɔ́   Early rice variety.
bùlù   Small farm of early rice on moisture-retentive soil.

fáámà   Bare rock outcrops.
fílíwà   Rice variety (lit. 'big awn').
fòní   Grassland with shorter grasses.

gáŋá   Soil with boulders and rocky fragments.
'ganga'   Foreman.
gbèŋgbèŋ   Rice variety (lit. 'big-big').
'gboekondo'   Rice variety.
gbòndòbáì   Rice variety.
gbɔ́ɔ́, gbɔ́lɔ́   Personal farm plot of a dependent.
gbɔ̀tɔ̀   Teenage work group for hoeing.
gìmà   Rice bran.
góbé   Rice variety.

hélékpô   Rice variety (lit. 'elephant dung').
hélèmɔ̀   Town crier.
hèlú   *Sida stipulata*.
hótá   Stranger, guest.
hùngɔ́ɔ̀   Trial, experiment.

'jetɛ'   Early rice variety.
jéwúló   Early rice variety.
jɔ̀bɔ́   Rice variety.
jɔ̀ngɔ̂   Rattoon rice crop.
jùmùkù   Rice variety.

kǎ, mbà gá,à   Rice chaff, husk.
kákàtáà   Rice variety.
kálɛ́   Bone.

kálémbáámá Rice variety.
káli Hoe.
kándí *Anisophyllea laurina.*
kélé Slit drum.
kényà Mother's brother.
'kɛbili' Rice variety.
kíkàkú Mende syllabic script.
kíò *Physostigma venenosum.*
kóbá *Sterculia tragancantha.*
kòjâ Egusi melon.
'kokaa' ?*Uncaria africana.*
kɔ́kɔ́ Soil eating termites.
kɔ̀kɔ̂ Rice variety (lit. 'a find').
kɔ̀kɔ̀yê Swamp rice variety (lit. 'bush fowl').
kɔ́mbì Co-operative work group.
kɔ̀tú Stony soil.
kɔ̀tú-ndúmú Mixed stony-silty soil.
kɔ́wù The Mende bushel box.
kpáá má lùwá Pre-planting weeds in rice farms.
kpàà wâ Main rice farm.
'kpaamonyaye' Rice variety.
kpàkò Important person.
kpéngéé Rice variety (lit. 'very small').
kpété Swamp.
kpòkpò Small farm on short-fallow land.
kpòwá Farm hut.

lóbá Land cleared but not planted, e.g. due to a poor burn.
lɔ̀nà Rice loan
lùkpéyà 'Stand aside', 'make way for'.

màígà Rice variety.
'mákàyíà' Town messenger.
mákéló Apprentice, foster child.
mámbó *Dialium guineense.*
màmɔ̀ Landlord, person in charge.
mánɔ́wâ Rice variety.
màwéé Household.
màwú Portion covered by a work group in one session.
mbǎ màgbémá Bird scaring platform (= **mbɛi tɛ**).
mbǎ mijìngɔ̀ Germinated rice.
mbáá Side of the jaw.
mbélà Father-in-law.
'mbele' Rice harvesting work group.
mbélí *Harungana madagascariensis.*
'mbowanda' Large-leaved swamp tree.

'ndeagbo' Rice variety.
ndéhú Lineage.
ndéwé *Macaranga* spp.
'ndodanguli' ?*Paullinia pinnata.*
ndóká Farm felled but not yet cleared.
ndǒndókɔ̀ Various convolvulaceous weeds.

ndɔ̀gbɔ́ Bush, forest.
ndɔ̀gbɔ́lùkpé Rice (lit. 'bush stand aside').
ndùlìwâ Rice variety (lit. 'smokey').
ngàlá Grassland with taller grasses.
nglánglá Gathering up sticks (lit. 'one by one').
ngàwú 'Bush yam' (*Dioscorea minutiflora*).
Ngèwɔ́-bà Wild rice (lit. 'God's rice').
ngíyémá yàkà Rice variety.
ngòlò-yómbò Rice variety (lit. 'chimpanzee hair').
ngɔ̀ngɔ́yɔ̀ Gravelly soil.
njèwɔ̀ ?*Guarea leonensis*.
númúwâ Important person.
'nyɛbu' *Anthostema senegalense*.

ŋànyá Sandy soil.

ɔ̀mɔ̀lé Gin distilled from palm wine.

péndé Short duration *glaberrima* rice variety.
'pladisi' Rice variety (Demerara Creole).
Pɔ́ɔ́ Man's secret society.
'pɔɔvɔ' Work group 'sergeant'.
pɔ̀tɔ̀pɔ́tɔ̀ Mud, muddy place.
pú to 'plough' (plant) upland rice.

sáìnì Trial, experiment.
Sàndè Women's secret society.
sángányáá Adventitious rice (*O. glaberrima*).
'semenje' Weed in swamp farms.
sɔ̀gbé *Urena lobata*.

tà yéngè Town work.
tǎlì Citizen.
téê, tè'è té'è 'By turns' work group (lit. 'to go from place to place').
tìjò *Phyllanthus discoideus*.
tɔ́kpɔ́éhùn Rice variety (lit. 'in the palm tree').
túgbéɛ̀ Various sedges.
túmú Silty soil (lit. 'dust' or 'powder').

wóndé yákà Rice variety.
Wúndé Kpa Mende political society.
wɔ̀lɔ́ Cattle pen.

yàká Swamp rice (especially flood-tolerant and floating types).
yàká gúwù Mende floating rice.
yéngɛ́ gbété Deep swamp.

Common, botanical and Mende names for crops referred to in the text

Common name	Botanical name	Mende name
banana	*Musa sapientum*	sélé
beniseed	*Sesamum indicum*	màndè
bush yam	*Dioscorea minutiflora*	ngàwú
cassava	*Manihot utilissima*	tàngá
cocoyam	Colocasia esculenta	kpójì
	Xanthosoma sagittifolium	kòkó
coffee	*Coffea robusta*	kɔfì
cotton	*Gossypium barbadense*	fàndé wâ
	ditto var. Brown lint	ndùlù vándè
	G. hirsutum	kwande
cow peas	*Vigna unguiculata*	hɔ́ndɔ̀
cucumber	*Cucumis sativus*	kɔkúmbà
egg plant	*Solanum melongena*	kɔbɔkɔ́bɔ́
egusi (melon seed)	*Colocynthis citrullus*	kòjâ
	Cucumeropsis edulis	
groundnut	*Arachis hypogaea*	nìkílì
jakato	*Solanum melongena* var.	kòjô
kola	*Cola nitida*	tòólò
krinkrin	*Corchorus olitorius*	ngèngéé
lima beans	*Phaseolus lunatus*	tɔ̀wɔ̀
maize	*Zea mays*	nyɔ̌
millet	*Pennisetum leonis*	kpélé nyɔ̂
oil palm	*Elaeis quineensis*	tɔ́kpɔ́
okra	*Hibiscus esculentus*	bɔndɔ́
orange	*Citrus sinensis*	sálò/lùmbélè
pawpaw	*Carica papaya*	fàkálì
pepper	*Capsicum* spp.	pùjè
plantain	*Musa paradisiaca*	mǎnà
pumpkin	*Cucurbita pepo*	tówá
raffia palm	*Raphia vinifera*	ndúvú
rice	*Oryza sativa*	mbǎ
	O. glaberrima	
sweet potato	*Ipomoea batatas*	njòwó
sorghum (Guinea corn)	*Sorghum* spp.	kèté
sour-sour	*Hibiscus sabdariffa*	sàtò
spinach	*Amaranthus* spp.	hɔndî
yam	*Dioscorea* spp.	mbòlé, nyámísì

Index

References to Figures are in italic.

Abidjan 57
accidents 28, 91, 93, 116
adaptive research 16, 17, 25
African Development Bank 48, 55
Aladura Christians 55
Alikalia 22
alley intercropping 153
alluvium, alluvial soils 33
Anisophyllea Iaurina 76
Anthostema senegalense 77
apprentices (*see also* **makɛlo**) 54

Baga 5
bati 15, 38–40, *3.5, 3.6, 3.7*
　(*see also* farm types)
beeswax 123, *7.2*
beniseed (sesame) 10, 106, 112, 119, 152
'big persons' *see* patrons
Bintimani 31
birds, bird-damage to crops 86, 88, 96, 112,
　134, 142–3, 148, 149
bird-scaring 68, 86, 96–7, 112
　after ploughing 96
　before harvest 96–7
　bird scaring platforms 96
　see also labour and pest control
blacksmithing 77
block farming 96
Bo 56, 57, 146
bolilands, boli grasslands 15, 31, 60, 64, 124,
　145
bondaa 52, 61
bobo (*Irvingia gabonensis*) 76
bride service 73
bridewealth 51, 53, 117
bridges 48, 55
British Empire Exhibition 10
broadcasting 11, 86, 89, 154, *5.4*, Table 5.1
　errors 111
　on different soil types 86, 89, Table 5.1
　seed rates 86, 88–9, Table 5.1
　see also rice
brushing (*see also* labour) 68, 76–9, 116
bulu *see* farm types
Bumpe 143
Bumpeh Creek 13, 58
bunding *see* irrigation
burn, bush burning 5, 38, 39, 60, 77, 79–85,
　94, 111, 115
　at night 83

block burning 83–5
　consequences of poor burning 111, 115, 150
　in the afternoon 83
　on river terrace soils 83–4
　timing 82–4
bush cow 124
'bush yams' *see* yams

Calabar bean *see* **kio**
Calopogonium mucunoides 153
Cane rats (*Thryonomys swinderianus*) 96, 111,
　117
Cape Mount (Liberia) 29
capital asets 48, 106–7
CARE (development agency) 46
cash crops (*see also* crop sales and income) 90,
　106, 147, *6.2*
cassava 58, 86, 112, 118–19, 153, 154
catena 5, 28–33, 38–9, 44, 57, 58, 122, 147,
　157, *3.8, 3.9, 3.16*
　as an R&D agenda 148
　catenary farms, farming systems 5, 97,
　121–2, 141, 145, 148
　intermediate zone 148
　interzones 141
　staggered planting across catena 23–5, 28,
　90, 121, 128, 156
　see also rice, toposequence and unit of
　landscape
catfish 124
cation exchange capacity (CEC) 44, Table 3.1
cattle, 48, 64, 107
Chadwick, D. 7
chickens 107
Chiefdom Councillors 48
Churchill, W. 8
citrus 107, 126
clearing 79, 85–6
clientelism *see* patron–client relations
climatic hazards 150, *5.1, 5.2, 5.3*
　drought 38, 40
　early rainfall 5, 38, 40, 79–83, 89–90, 111,
　115, 116, 147, 151
cocoa 107
coffee 58, 106, 107, 126, 6.2, 6.3
colluvial footslopes (*see also* **ŋanya**) 5, 29, 148,
　3.9
colluvium 13
Colonial Welfare and Development Fund 12
commodities, commodity trade 54

Consultative Group on International
     Agricultural Research (CGIAR) 16–17, 25
cooking 68
   for work groups 68, 87
   see also labour
cotton 68, 106, 112, 118, 119–21, 152
   carding 152
   costs and returns 121
   country cloth 119–21
   spinning (drop-spindle) 68, 121, 7.1
   weaving 68, 113, 121
   see also intercropping, labour, women
country cloth see cotton
court, court cases (see also litigation) 49, 52,
     113, 125, 126, 127, 128
cowpeas 59, 151
credit 48, 54, 55, 74, 151, 125, 127–8
   interest rates 127
   money lenders 48, 61, 94, 115, 127
   patrons and traders as money lenders 54, 61,
     115, 126–30
   rice loans (lona) 49, 67, 94, 104, 115, 123,
     127–8, 139
   savings and credit societies 74
   women as creditors 127
   see also debt, indebtedness
crop rotation 6
crop sales (see also gender inequality, income,
     women) 103, 104–6, 6.2
cucumber 112, 118
cultural evolution 7, 27
   stage theories of agricultural development 7
cutlasses 76–7

dance societies 73
Dawe, M. T. 7, 9
debt (see also credit and indebtedness) 53, 54,
     61, 67, 71, 104, 118, 139, 147, 151
Deighton, F. C. 9
descent groups 49, 51, 52–4
   and land tenure 60–4
Dialium guineense 84
diamond boom (1950s) 1, 15, 54
diamond mining 22, 51, 57, 129
Dioscorea minutiflora (see yams)
divorce 53, 98, 117, 127
Dougall, H. W. 13
Doyne, E. C. 9
drought 38, 40
drumming (for work groups) 71–2
   impact on work efficiency 87, Table 5.2
   see also kele

early rainfall see climatic hazards,
     environmental hazards
ecotonal transitions 156
education see schooling
egusi (melon) 106, 112, 118, 152
1898 uprising 47

Ellis, Col. W. N. 7
environmental hazards 111
erosion 44, 48
escarpment, escarpment zone 33, 3.2, 3.4
experimentation (by farmers) (see also
     hungɔɔ) 3, 27, 116, 131–46, 153, 155,
     8.2, 8.3
extension services 156

faama 39
factionalism (in local politics) 53–4
Fala 46, 56, 92
fallow
   bush fallowing 58, 64, 152
   fallow periods 44, 64–5, 76, 94 4.3
   fertility restoration 152
   kpokpo 65
   lobai 65
   long-fallow farms 64, 76, 79, 135
   short-fallow land, 135
famine (1919) 1, 12
farm types 58, 78, 90–1, 92, 93, 94, 97, 103,
     108, 112, 121, 124, 127
   bati farms 58, 78, 90–1, 92, 93, 94, 97, 103,
     108, 112, 121, 124, 127, 134, 136, 140–1,
     149–51, 3.6, 3.7
   bulu 58, 113
   gbɔɔ 58
   groundnut farms 60, 90, 119, 153
   household farms 57–60, 65–8, 136, 147
   joint farms 60
   large farms 67
   private farms (see also women and youths as
     farmers) 59–60, 104, 135–6
   run-off plots 58
   swamp farms 59, 104, 4.1
farm hut see kpowa
farmer-first-and-last-research paradigm 1,
     147–55
farming systems research (FSR) 25, 26
fencing (against rodents) 96
fertiliser 17–19, 48, 55, 109, 153
fines 67
firewood 82, 85
fishing 68, 88
foni 38
food entitlements (see also patron–client
     relations) 115, 128–30
footpaths (upkeep) 48
fostering 61
Freetown 56, 57
   cost of living 57
   food supply 12, 15
funerals 119

gambling 61, 92, 98, 116, 117, 118, 119, 125,
     145
ganga 55
gbɔɔ see farm types

gender inequality (*see also* women) 106, *6.2*
gima (rice bran) 137
gin distillation 106, 123, *6.2*
Glanville, R. R. 9–11, 13, 19
goats 107
Gondama 45–8, 51, 56
granite zone 38–41, 60, 63, 90, 91, 94, 107, 121, 147, *3.8, 3.9, 3.16*
Green Revolution 3, 16–27, 28, 115, 148
Griffin, A. E. 12
groundnuts 49, 57, 58, 90, 98, 106, 119, 153, 154
Guarea leonensis 77
Guinea (Republic of) 47
guinea corn 112, 118, 152
guns (for hunting) 124

Hargreaves, E. 9
Harungana madagascariensis 76
harvest, harvesting, 97–8, 102–14
  causes of success and failure 111–13
  labour bottlenecks 136
  techniques 139
  timing 139
helemɔ 54
helu (*Sida stipulata*) 95, Tables 5.5 and 5.6
hired labour *see* labour
hoes, hoe types 87
honey 123
hota *see* strangers
households 51–2, *4.4*
  farm 49, 51–2, 58, 65–8, 94
  female-headed 51–2, 60
  labour 85, 93
  male-headed 60
  reproduction 67–8
  residential (**mawɛɛ**) 49, 51–2
  size and hunger 117
hungɔɔ (*see also* experimentation) 140, 142, *8.2, 8.3*
hungry season (pre-harvest hunger) 6, 38, 49, 54, 56–7, 58, 70, 91, 96, 115–30, 143, 151
  bye-laws (against hungry-season rice exports) 127–8
  hunger breaker crops 10, 118–19, 122, 136
  hungry season indebtedness 71, 93, 117, 127
  labour during 89, 127
  labour shortages and hunger 129, 147
  see also seasonality
hunting, hunting and gathering (*see also* labour) 68, 88, 96, 115, 123–4, 128
hydromorphic soils 29

imam 53
income 104–7, *6.2*
indebtedness (*see also* credit, debt, hungry season, money lenders, patrons) 9, 38, 96, 102, 111, 113, 117, 126–8, 143
infant mortality 51

influenza pandemic (1919) 6
inland valley swamps 11, 16, 18–27, 136, 145–6, 147, 154
Integrated Agricultural Development Projects (IADPs) 16, 18, 19–22, 25, 109, 115, 130, 136, 146, 156, *2.1*, Table 2.1
  credit programmes 23, 54, 109, 125, 146
  Eastern IADP 19
  monitoring and evaluation 156
  Mayamba Integrated Rural Development Project 48, 55
  Northern IADP 20, 25
intercropping 58, 106, 112, 118–19, 152
  groundnut–maize–cassava intercrops 119, 153
  rice varieties grown as mixtures 112, 149, *3.7, 9.2*
International Agricultural Research Centers 16–17
International Development Association (IDA) 17, 19
International Institute of Tropical Agriculture (IITA) 16, 18, 153
International Rice Research Institute (IRRI) 16, 26, 153
irrigation, 7, 12–27, *2.2*
  acidification in swamps 12, 18, 22
  bunding 12, 18–19, 22, 136, 154
  experience in Liberia 154
  Irrigation and Drainage Unit 12
  labour requirements 22–5, 148, 153–4
  large-scale 7, 12–15, 25
  polder irrigation and drainage 12–15, 29
  small-scale 9, 14, 16–27
  water control 9, 18–20, 28, 148, 153–4
  see also wetland cultivation
Ivory Coast 17

jɔngɔ (*see also* rattoon crop) 134

ka (rice husk/chaff) 137
Kailahun 47
Kamagai Chiefdom 45–8
Kamajei Chiefdom 3, 45–8, 60, 71, 124, *3.17, 3.20*
kandi (*Anisophyllea laurina*) 76, 111
Kangari hills 33
kele 71
kenya (mother's brother) 52, 61
kikaku (script) 155
kio (*Physostigma venenosum*) 123
Kisimi Kamara 155
koba (*Sterculia tragacantha*) 76
Kobai 47
koja *see* egusi
kokaa (? *Uncaria africana*) 77
kola 107, 126
Kono 47
kɔkɔ 38, 44

kɔtu *see* soils
Kowa Chiefdom 144, 151
Kpaa Mende state 46
kpaa wa *(see also* households: farm) 58–61, 77
kpete *(see also* swamp cultivation) 59
kpowa (farm hut) 67, 68, 85, 93, 97

labour
  bembɛ (ploughing group) 70–1, 88, 91
  bottlenecks, seasonal bottlenecks 22–5, 28, 78, 89, 92, 98, 116, 121, 136, 147
  children's labour 68–9, 87–8, 89, 91, 92, 93, 96
  communal, community labour (ta yenge) 48, 52, 54–5, 117
  competition (in work groups) 78
  competition to secure 91
  control by elders and patrons 71, 73
  discipline 72
  food for labourers 73, 89, 106, 112
  for forest clearance *(see also* brushing) 64, 76
  gbɔtɔ 8, 71–2, 88
  gender specialisation 68–9, 87, 92, 93, 98
  harvesting 72–3, 74
  hire rates 72, 73, 88, 90, 91, 106
  hired labour 25, 65, 70, 78, 85, 89, 90, 92, 93, 98, 106, 120, 124–5
  household labour *see* households
  inputs 70, 97
  kɔmbi 73–4, 92
  mawu (stint) 71
  mbele 72–3
  men's 68–9, 88, 92
  non-household 69–74
  old-people's 68, 93–4, 97
  productivity 22–4, 94, 97, Tables 5.2 to 5.4
  shortages 8, 15, 17, 22–5, 29–33, 49, 61, 75, 89, 112, 151, 153
  tee 70, 92
  timeliness 78, 79, 89, 92
  water collection 68, 87
  women's 68–9, 87, 89, 92
  work group rules 72, 73–4, 88
  work groups 69–74, 76, 88–92, 95, 98, 106, 113
  work rates *(see also* labour: productivity) 91, 93, 97, Tables 5.2 to 5.4
Lacey, G. 15, 25
land
  inequalities in access 107
  pledging 107
  shortage 17, 23
  tenure 49, 52, 60–3, 106, *4.2*
  types in Mogbuama 30–44, 58–63, 68–74, *3.3, 3.5, 3.6, 3.7, 3.8, 3.9*
landlords *(see also* mamɔ) 52, 54, 60, 76
leaf litter 76
Lebanese merchants 6, 54
  food riots against 6

Liberia 17, 124, 154
literacy 63
litigation 53, 117–18, 119, 126
  'swears' 53, 125
lobai (land cleared but not farmed) 86, 91
local government 48
Luawa Chiefdom 8
lɔna *see* credit

Macaranga spp. 76
McNamara, R. 17
Madras Department of Agriculture 8
maize 112, 118–19, 151, 153
Maje Chiefdom 46–8, 51
makayia 54
makelo 54, 66
Makump 19
Mali 17
mambo (*Dialium guineense*) 84
mamɔ 51
mangrove swamps *(see also* rice) 8
Mano 46, 143
marriage alliances 53, 63
Martin, F. J. 9, 18
matrilateral kinship 52
mawɛɛ *see* households
mawu (stint) 87
mba magbema 96
mba mijingɔ 142
mbela 73
mbɛli (*Harungana madagascariensis*) 76
mbowanda 142
men *6.2*
  involvement in hunting and trapping 124
  sources of cash income 152, *6.2*
  see also labour
merchants *see* trade
migration 22, 50–1, 54, 56–7, 142, 143
  remittances 57, 104
millet 10, 118
mining *(see also* diamond mining) 49, 51, 129
mixed cropping *see* intercropping
Mobaiwa 71
money lenders *see* credit
monkey meat 124
  exports to Liberia 124
mosque 55
music *(see also* drumming) 73, 96

ndehu 52
ndɛwɛ (*Macaranga spp.*) 76
ndodanguli (? *Paullinia pinnata*) 95, Tables 5.5 and 5.6
ndoka 77
ndɔgbɔ 38
ngala 38
ngawu *see* yam
Ngiyeya 48
nglangla 85

ngɔngɔyɔ *see* soils
Nigeria 153
Njala 6, 7, 10, 38, 44, 56–7, 80–2, 86, 149
njewɔ 77
numuwa 48
nyɛbu 77
ŋanya *see* soils

Ofada (western Nigeria) 29
oil palms 107, 123, 126
okra 112
on-farm trials (*see also* experimentation) 1, 140, 155
ɔmɔle *see* gin distillation

palm oil 92, 123
palm wine 123
Paramount Chief 48
participant observation 3, 28, 157
patron–client relations 30, 48–9, 51, 53–4, 56, 57, 61–3, 65, 69, 98, 107, 115, 118, 126–30, 139, 145
patrons *see* patron–client relations, **numuwa**
Peace Corp 19, 22
Pelewahun 46
pest control (*see also* bird scaring) 86, 96–7, 152
phosphate levels (in soils) 79
Phyllanthus discoideus 76
Physostigma venenosum see **kio**
Pillai, A. C. 8
planting strategies 90
pledging *see* land
ploughing (rice planting) 68, 86–92, 106, 120, 5.4, Tables 5.1 to 5.4
    covering ploughed seed 87
    failure to complete due to misfortune 91
    minimum tillage 88
    significance of weeds 86–8, 5.5 Table 5.4
    timeliness 95, 111
    work rates 91, Tables 5.1 to 5.4
    see also labour and broadcasting
politics (impact on farming) (*see also* patron–client relations) 113, 129
polygymy 69
population density 50–1
Poro (**pɔɔ**) 48, 52–3, 102, 108
poverty 113
Pre-Cambrian Basement Complex 31
pseudo-rotations 153
pu *see* ploughing

rattoon crop (of rice) 134, 151
Red Colobus monkey 124
religious allegiances in Mogbuama 55
Research and Development (R&D) priorities 110, 147–55
Revolving Seed Distribution Scheme 12
Rhizophora racemosa 13

Rice Commission (1927) 9
rice cultivation *2.3*
    double (multiple) cropping 16, 19, 150
    dry rice (*see also* upland cultivation) 7
    in inland valley swamps 135
    in mangrove swamps 8, 13, 145
    intercropping of short and long duration varieties 90, 112, 150, *9.2*
    planting *see* ploughing
    roguing (seed rice) 134, 139, 142, 145, 146
    seed rice (sources and criteria for selection) 138, 143–4, *8.3*
    transplanting 8, 11, 18, 154
    wet rice (*see also* swamp and wetland cultivation) 7–8, 12–13, 16–27, 49, 135
    see also broadcasting, harvest/harvesting
rice imports 15, 54
rice loans *see* credit
rice prices 104
rice varieties and their properties (*see also* intercropping) 5, 10, 197–215, *8.1* Tables 8.1 and 8.2
    African rice (*Oryza glaberrima*) 4, 10, 134, 136, 148–9, 154, *9.1*
    Asian rice (*O. sativa*) 4
    awned varieties 97, 142, 149
    baikɔ 135
    banyalojɔpoihun 135
    bogutu 135
    bɔngɔ 97, 108, 112, 121, 134, *3.7, 6.4*
    CCA 18, 140
    cooking properties 138
    CP4 136
    crossing 138
    Demerara Creole (Pa D. C.) 137
    duration (from planting to harvest) 135
    early-ripening varieties 32–8, 40, 90, 96, 97, 103, 104, 108, 118, 121–2, 128, 136, 147, 148–51
    fili, filiwa 97, 135, 137
    floating varieties 23, 33–8, 90, 135, 145
    flood-tolerant varieties 23, 33–8, 59, 90, 135, 147, 150, 154, *4.1*
    gbɛngbɛn 108, 135, 142–3, 144, *6.4, 8.1*
    gboekondo 135
    gbondobai 97, 135
    germination potential (farmer tests) 141
    gobe 135
    helekpo 135
    high-yielding varieties (HYVs) 14, 16–17, 26
    husking (ease of) 138
    improved varieties 9, 14, 26, 48, 55
    IR8 16
    japonica rices 19
    jewulo 97, 108, 121, 125, 128, 140, 142, *3.7, 6.4, 8.1*
    jɛtɛ 121, 134
    jɔbɔ 10

jumuku 135
kakataa 135, 141–2
kalɛmbaama 97, 137, *8.1*
kɛbili 135
kɔkɔ 142
kɔkɔyɔ 137
kpaamonyaye 77
kpengee 144, *8.1*
LAC23 26, 137, 140, 148
lodging 137
long-duration varieties 59, 104, 136, 147, 149
long-glumed varieties 97, 137, 149
Madam Yebu 97, 137
manɔwa 112
medium duration varieties 32–8, 104, 108, 135, 147
milling out-turn 138
ndeagbo 118
ndɔgbɔlukpe 135
nduliwa 112, 135, 142, 144
Ngewɔ-ba *see* rice varieties: wild annual rice
ngiyema yaka 26, 135
ngolo-yombo 97, 137, 149, *8.1*
pa fodea 10
pa litoma 10
panicle length 137
pende 10, 121, 134, 136–7, 149–51, *9.1*
quick-yielding varieties 18, 91, 121–3, 134, 140
resistance to bird attack 97
ROK3 26, 148
ROK4 140
ROK16, 26, 149
sanganyaa 136, 139–40, 144, *8.1*
shattering 137
short-straw varieties 18
taste factors 136
tillering 10, 137, 140, 149, *9.1*
tɔkpɔehun 135, 138
wonde yaka 135
yaka (swamp) rices 59, 60, 90, 97, 103–4, 106, 112–13, 119, 135–7, 143, 147–8, 155, *4.1*
yaka guwu 135
yɔni 135
wild annual rice (*O. barthii*) 136
wild perennial rice (*O. longistaminata*) 15, 136
yields 108–10, 134, *6.4*
risk avoidance 147, 149, 152
river blindness (onchocerciasis) 116
river terraces 32–40, 57, 148, *3.2, 3.5, 3.6, 3.7*
river-terrace soils (*see also* soils, tumu) 32–8, 44
river-terrace zone 60, 63, 82, 90, 91, 94, 97, 118, 140, 147, *3.3, 3.5, 3.6, 3.7*
riverine grasslands *see* bati

roads, farm-access roads 18, 46
Roddan, G. 12
roguing *see* rice cultivation
Rokel River Series 31–3
Rokupr (rice research station) 10, 11, 26, 140, 149–51, 153
Rosino 12, 13
Rotifunk 13
run-off plot 58

Sande 48, 52–3
savings 107
Scarcies 7, 8, 9, 11–15, 25, 29, 145
Great Scarcies 12, 15
Little Scarcies 12
Scarcies' estuaries 7, 12
schooling 53, 56–7
primary 53, 56
primary school work group 71
secondary 56
Scotland, D. 6, 7, 10, 86, 149
seasonality (*see also* labour and hungry season) 28, 76–99, 115–30, *3.10*
secret societies 52–3, 117
initiation fees 53
legal cases 117
seed multiplication (rice) 146
self-help groups *see* labour
semenje 113
Senegal 17
Senehun 45–8, 51, 55–6
settlement pattern 49–51, *3.20*
Sewa 15
sheep 107
shifting cultivation *see* fallow and upland cultivation
sickness (as a factor in farm management) 93, 111, 116, 118, 127
sideways extension 3, 134
Simulium spp. 117
sleeping platforms 97
soil survey (Njala area) 44
soils, soil types 29–44, *3.3, 3.6, 3.8, 3.9, 3.12, 3.14, 3.15* Tables 3.1 and 3.2
bɔbɔ 38
colour 76
erosion 151
fertility, fertility indicators 44, 64, *3.14, 3.15, 3.16* Table 3.1
free-draining soils (*see also* kɔtu and ŋanya 38–44, 57, 90, 94, 141, 151
gana 39
kɔtu 39–44, 60, 63–5, 76, 78, 83, 86, 88–9, 90, 91, 94, 108–9, 111, 121, 140, 144, 151, *3.12, 3.13, 6.4* Tables 3.1 and 5.3
moisture retentive soils (*see also* tumu) 40–1, 57, 77, 151
ngɔngɔyɔ 39, *3.12, 3.13*, Table 3.1
ŋanya 40, 44, 58, *3.12, 3.13*, Table 3.1

pH, 79, Tables 3.1 & 3.2
pɔtɔ-pɔtɔ 38
tumu 38, 44, 58, 60, 63–5, 77, 83, 86, 88–9,
    91, 93, 94, 108–9, 111–12, 113, 140–1,
    144, 151, *3.12, 3.13, 6.4* Tables 3.1 & 5.3
    (*see also* river terraces, upland
    cultivation
sorghum *see* guinea corn
sɔgbɛ (*Urena lobata*) 95, 123, Tables 5.5 and
    5.6
starvation 115, 128
Sterculia tragacantha 76
stick bunds (against erosion) 151
Stockdale, F. A. 9, 10
strangers 48, 51, 52, 54, 56, 61, 66, 139, 143,
    4.2
    access to land 60–3, 76, *4.2*
    and tree crops 60
    see also **hota**
swamp cultivation 5, 7, 8, 10, 11, 32, 48, 55,
    59, 104–6, 116, 119, 145, 147, 153–5, *3.5,
    3.6, 3.7, 4.1, 9.2*
    associated swamps 13
    dry-season cultivation 11, 59, 154
    flood-recession cultivation 154
    hazards and injuries 116
    riverine flood plains 148
    water levels 140
    see also wetland cultivation, irrigation and
    inland valley swamps
sweet potato 11, 59, 86, 119, 154
Syncerus caffer see bush cow

ta yenge (*see also* labour) 54
Tabe 151
Taiama 46
tali 48
taxation 50
teachers 53, 54, 71
technology transfer 10, 110
    Asian green revolution model 3, 5, 14,
    16–27, *2.2*
    Asian wet-rice cultivation methods 2, 5, 8,
    22, 25, 26
    cultural evolutionist perspectives 7
    from Burma 12
    from Ceylon 9, 19
    from Guyana 12
    from India 9
    from Madras 19
    from Malaya 7
    from South-east Asia 7, 8, 12
    from Taiwan 16, 18
    see also Green Revolution
Temne 45
    migrants 13
Tendihun 71
termites
    soil-eating species *see* kɔkɔ

wood-eating species (*Macrotermes bellicosus*)
    82, 141
theft (of crops) 98, 125, 128, 134, 143
threshing 97
Tibai (river) 38
tijo (*Phyllanthus discoideus*) 76
tobacco 11
toposequence *3.8, 3.9, 3.16,* Table 3.1
    integrated upland and valley land use 13,
    90–1, 145–6, *3.5, 3.8*
    staggered planting across a toposequence
    23–5, 28, 90–1, 121, 156
    valley topographic sequence 13, 28, *3.8, 3.9*
    see also catena
total exchangeable bases (TEB) 45, Tables 3.1
    and 3.2
tractors, tractor mechanisation 13–15
trade, traders 53, 54–5, 56, 58, 113, 127
'Training & Visit' (extension) 156
transplanting *see* rice cultivation
trapping 96
tree crops 48, 60, 107, *6.2, 6.3*
    pledging 125–6
tugbɛɛ 95, Tables 5.5 and 5.6
tumu *see* soils, river terraces, river-terrace
    soils
Turner's Peninsula 15

UMC (Methodist) church 55
Uncaria africana 77
unit of landscape 13, 156
upland cultivation 3, 6, 24, 28, 152–3
    upland shifting cultivation 6
    upland rice varieties 26, 135
urban employment 56
Urena lobata see sɔgbɛ

vegetables 11, 58, 86, 118
Viscount Milner 6–7

Waanje 15
warthogs 124
weaving, weavers *see* cotton
weddings 119
weeds, weeding 79, 87–90, 92–6, 111, 112,
    123, 151–2, 153, *5.5,* Tables 5.4 to 5.6
    chemical control 95, 152
    labour shortages 111, 151
    pre-planting weeds and weeding (kpaa ma
    luwa) 95, 123, 151–2, *5.5,* Table 5.4
    post-planting weeds and weeding 95, 151
West African Examination Council 56
West African Rice Development Association
    (WARDA) 17, 151
West African Rice Zone 4–5
wetland cultivation (*see also* inland valley
    swamp, irrigation, and swamp
    cultivation) 3, 7, 11, 13, 16–27, 28–9
widows 127

Wilkinson (Colonial Governor) 6–8, 12
wɔlɔ (woreh) 107
women
  as agricultural innovators 153
  chiefs 54
  crops belonging to women 68, 90, 106, 118,
    6.2, 7.1
  fishing 88, 124
  heads of households *see* households
  in local politics 53
  independent farmers 58, 84
  involvement in swamp farming 154
  recruitment of female labour 92
  rice variety preferences 138
  role in roguing rice varieties 142
  sources of income 106, 147, 152, *6.2*
  weeding 92
  see also credit and labour

work groups *see* labour
World Bank 17, 19
World War II 12
Wunde 48, 53

xylophones 96

yams (wild) (*see also* **ngawu**) 113, 115,
  123
Yele 46
yenge gbete (*see also* swamp cultivation) 59,
  94, *4.1*
yield data (and input–output ratios) 104–6,
  107–110, *6.4*
  timing as a factor in determining yield
    112–13, 140
  yields on different soil types 108–9, *6.4*
youths as farmers 90, 147